LITERATURE AGAINST CRITICISM

Literature Against Criticism

University English and Contemporary Fiction in Conflict

Martin Paul Eve

OpenBook Publishers

https://www.openbookpublishers.com

© 2016 Martin Paul Eve

This work is licensed under a Creative Commons Attribution 4.0 International license (CC BY 4.0). This license allows you to share, copy, distribute and transmit the text; to adapt the text and to make commercial use of the text providing attribution is made to the author (but not in any way that suggests that he endorses you or your use of the work). Attribution should include the following information:

Martin Paul Eve, *Literature Against Criticism: University English and Contemporary Fiction in Conflict*. Cambridge, UK: Open Book Publishers, 2016. http://dx.doi.org/10.11647/OBP.0102

In order to access detailed and updated information on the license, please visit https://www.openbookpublishers.com/isbn/9781783742738#copyright

Further details about CC BY licenses are available at https://creativecommons.org/licenses/by/4.0/

All external links were active on 3/10/2016 unless otherwise stated and have been archived via the Internet Archive Wayback Machine at https://archive.org/web

Updated digital material and resources associated with this volume are available at https://www.openbookpublishers.com/isbn/9781783742738#resources

Every effort has been made to identify and contact copyright holders and any omission or error will be corrected if notification is made to the publisher.

Birkbeck, University of London, has generously contributed towards the publication of this volume.

ISBN Paperback: 978-1-78374-273-8
ISBN Hardback: 978-1-78374-274-5
ISBN Digital (PDF): 978-1-78374-275-2
ISBN Digital ebook (epub): 978-1-78374-276-9
ISBN Digital ebook (mobi): 978-1-78374-277-6
DOI: 10.11647/OBP.0102

Cover image: CCAC (The Community College of Allegheny County North Library), 'Red, white, and blue books' (2014), Flickr, https://www.flickr.com/photos/ccacnorthlib/14547337031, CC BY-SA 2.0 license.

All paper used by Open Book Publishers is SFI (Sustainable Forestry Initiative), PEFC (Programme for the Endorsement of Forest Certification Schemes) and Forest Stewardship Council(r)(FSC(r) certified.

Printed in the United Kingdom, United States, and Australia
by Lightning Source for Open Book Publishers (Cambridge, UK)

For Siân, Joe, and Caroline

Contents

About the Author ... 1
Style ... 2
Acknowledgements ... 5

Part I: Introduction ... 9
1. Authors, Institutions, and Markets ... 11
2. What, Where? ... 43

Part II: Critique ... 55
3. Aesthetic Critique ... 57
4. Political Critique ... 87

Part III: Legitimation ... 113
5. Sincerity and Truth ... 115
6. Labour and Theory ... 135

Part IV: Discipline ... 157
7. Genre and Class ... 159
8. Discipline and Publish ... 185

Part V: The End ... 205
9. Conclusion ... 207

Bibliography ... 209
Index ... 227

About the Author

Professor Martin Paul Eve is Chair of Literature, Technology and Publishing at Birkbeck, University of London. He is the author of three other books, *Pynchon and Philosophy: Wittgenstein, Foucault and Adorno* (Palgrave, 2014); *Open Access and the Humanities: Contexts, Controversies and the Future* (Cambridge University Press, 2014); and *Password* (a cultural history of the password) (Bloomsbury, 2016). Martin is also well known for his work on open access publishing and especially as a founder of the Open Library of Humanities.

Style

In this work, double quotation marks are used to signify direct quotation of text and speech while single quotation marks indicate terms that merit scepticism or are not the author's own; scare-quotes. Theory is written with a capital 'T' throughout when it refers to literary or poststructuralist schools. Names of people and works that appear in the main text also appear in the index, those in the footnotes do not.

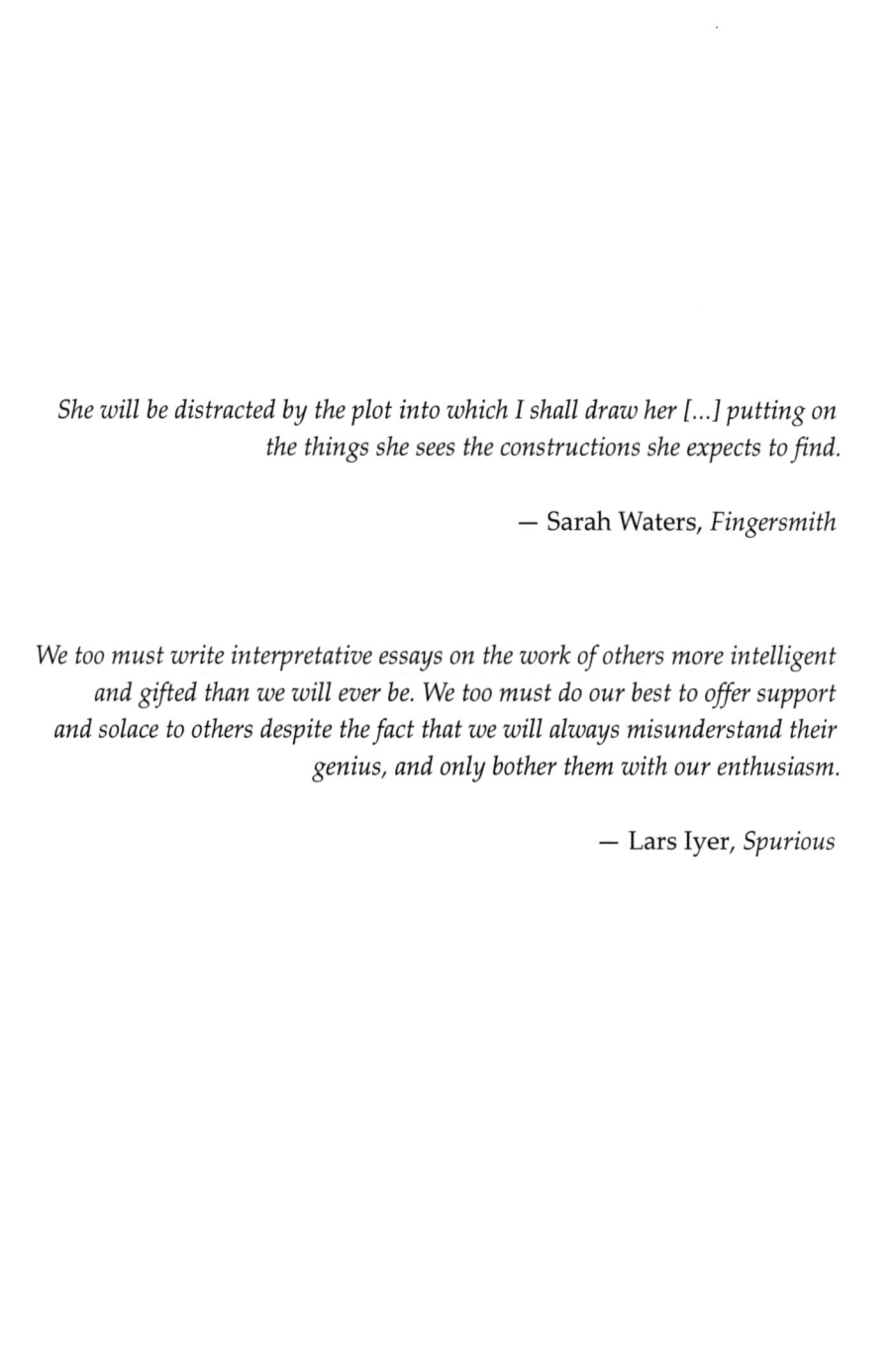

She will be distracted by the plot into which I shall draw her [...] putting on the things she sees the constructions she expects to find.

— Sarah Waters, *Fingersmith*

We too must write interpretative essays on the work of others more intelligent and gifted than we will ever be. We too must do our best to offer support and solace to others despite the fact that we will always misunderstand their genius, and only bother them with our enthusiasm.

— Lars Iyer, *Spurious*

Acknowledgements

This book began life in early 2012 and was meant to be my second book. It is, instead, co-genetic with two of my other books: *Pynchon and Philosophy* and *Open Access and the Humanities*. The former of these books sparked my interest in mutations in metafiction in contemporary fiction, an aspect that was borne out over Pynchon's extensive career as a writer. Reflecting this, earlier drafts of this book were called *Metafiction After the Millennium* and *The Anxiety of Academia*, the latter referring to Harold Bloom's *Anxiety of Influence*. At the same time, in part due to the history of radical politics at the University of Sussex (under constant repressive threat from the administration) where I undertook my PhD, I became interested in the ways in which the public good of the university might be salvaged, even if that was through the instruments of mass technocracy; an aspect that I believe to be furthered by the general, free availability of research material on the internet — open access. These two interests converge in this study of self-aware fiction that plays with the university. I found this book difficult to write and it went through many different drafts until I discovered what I needed to say. My thanks, therefore, must go to everyone who helped me with those other two works and, therefore, in turn, with this.

Three colleagues and friends in particular, though, have been key to this book (in alphabetical order): Siân Adiseshiah, Joe Brooker, and Caroline Edwards. In various ways both direct and indirect I have profited from their wit, wisdom, and kindnesses throughout the process of writing this work and in life more broadly, whether they know it or not. We certainly don't always agree on everything (we probably don't even now, Joe) but in the productive spaces of our discussions, I have found great pleasure and greater understandings that have found their way into this work. This book is dedicated to you. For the stronger parts of the book are due to you. The weaker, to me.

For his erudition and stimulating conversations, I also thank Jake Wilson. It was he who introduced me to the *Tale of the Eloquent Peasant*, which opens this book. Likewise, I thank Adeline Koh for a stimulating conversation in NYC in early 2015. It is thanks to her that I remembered *On Beauty* and kicked myself for ever neglecting it. David Winters introduced me to the work of Lars Iyer, from whom I draw an epigraph, and I have profited from many hours of stimulating conversation with him about fiction after Theory. Thanks must also go to Siobhan Garrigan, who first led me to consider the diary objects in *Affinity* as impossible, while Peter Fifield and Ted Underwood gave invaluable feedback upon my thoughts about digital reading practices. As ever, I thank Ruth Charnock for reading a draft of this work and suggesting improvements (although the remaining faults are all mine).

I also thank Penny Andrews for the cover suggestion and Heidi Coburn for its realisation. At Birkbeck, University of London I would particularly like to thank Robert Atkinson, who helped enormously with budgeting and the book publishing charge. At Open Book Publishers I would like to thank Alessandra Tosi, Rupert Gatti, and William St Clair for their ongoing efforts to ensure that the broadest number of people have access to university research material in the humanities.

Some parts of this work have appeared previously (or are forthcoming) in different article or edited-collection/book chapter form, or are derived from my thinking in other publications. Chapter Three, on Tom McCarthy's C, is partially derived from a different draft of my chapter in *Tom McCarthy: Critical Essays* (Gylphi, 2016), edited by Dennis Duncan (to whom I extend my many thanks for his patient editorial feedback). Chapter Four, on Roberto Bolaño, was originally published open access in *Textual Practice* 29.7 (2015). Part of Chapter Five is under submission to the forthcoming *Routledge Companion to Contemporary Fiction*, edited by Robert Eaglestone. A small part of Chapter Six grew from my article, '"Too Many Goddamn Echoes": Historicizing the Iraq War in Don DeLillo's *Point Omega*', *Journal of American Studies* 49.3 (2015). Parts of Chapter Six appeared open access as '"Structural Dissatisfaction": Academics on Safari in the Novels of Jennifer Egan' in the *Open Library of Humanities*, 1.1 (2015). Chapter Seven, on Sarah Waters, was originally published open access as '"You Will See the Logic of the Design of This": From Historiography to Taxonomography in the Contemporary Metafiction of Sarah Waters's *Affinity*' in *Neo-Victorian Studies*, 6.1 (2013).

Last but not least, and as always, I thank my wife, Helen; my dearest friend and more.

PART I: INTRODUCTION

1. Authors, Institutions, and Markets

For those working in university English departments in the early twenty-first century, these words will probably sound all too familiar: "[t]his man possesses great eloquence. See that he is denied justice for some time and arrange for all his grandiose speeches to be recorded". Yet, despite the plausibility of the scenario, this passage is not a sadistic *diktat* issued from a university administrator to an unsuspecting humanities underling, perhaps enforcing lecture capture or a similar contemporary technology. It comes instead, in rough translation, from a Ninth- or Tenth- Dynasty Ancient Egyptian story called the *Tale of the Eloquent Peasant*. Briefly summarised, this narrative recounts the plight of a peasant who, having been robbed, pleads his case before the high steward and proves to be so articulate that the case is referred to the king. The king's response is that the steward should continue to deny the peasant's petitions in order that the latter's increasingly eloquent speeches on the theme of injustice can be transcribed and recorded. The king orders this delay of justice because he wishes the speeches to be compiled into a literary text for his own future entertainment. At the conclusion, the peasant is eventually given justice (after having his speeches read back to him) and the text is delivered to the king.

We know of the *Tale of the Eloquent Peasant* from a papyrus fragment, now held in the British Museum in London, where the formal legend on the display proclaims that the story represents "a questioning of social and divine justice". For my purposes in this book, however, which will go on to explore the ways in which certain novels play with the institutional authority of university English, this ancient text has two more significant features. Firstly, in a historicist mode, the text demonstrates metafictional tropes well before the first millennium. The text knowingly plays with its own constitution, depicting acts of inscription from *phonos* (speech) to *logos* (written text). Indeed, the self-referential framework at play in this text demonstrates that metafiction is a conceit as old as literature itself, as others have already suggested.[1] Even if I haven't begun here with the more well-known and likely contemporaneous *Epic of Gilgamesh*, the historical placement of the *Tale of the Eloquent Peasant* within the First Intermediate Period gives a starting point for metafiction that defies more recent attempts to situate the form most prominently within a postmodern movement harking back to romanticism.[2] Secondly, in a broader sense, the story focuses on a self-educated and eloquent subject from an outsider class. In the social strata of its time, peasants were not supposed to demonstrate learning through fluent and coherent speech (eloquence). This tale, then, stages a set of complex interactions between class and education, learning and refined talent but also, through its metafictional nature, between what we might see as social/literary 'genre' (codified social/literary/class expectations) and canon (birth right).

Fig. 1 The *Tale of the Eloquent Peasant*. © The Trustees of the British Museum.

---

1   Most notably, Patricia Waugh, *Metafiction: The Theory and Practice of Self-Conscious Fiction* (London: Methuen, 1984), pp. 18–19 suggests that much fiction can be understood as falling on a spectrum of metafictive practice.
2   In this work, I choose not to define the terms 'modernism' or 'postmodernism' *in toto* outright. This is not only because it is tedious to encounter every work that undertakes this task, but more importantly because it is impossible and always selective. I instead opt here to make clear the aspect of (post)modernism to which I am referring at a given moment, be it epistemology vs. ontology *à la* Brian McHale, ludic play, temporal distortion or any of the other characteristics frequently assigned under these taxonomies.

The *Tale of the Eloquent Peasant* is important for me because it historically refracts the interlocking aspects of a twentieth- and twenty-first-century fictional practice with which I will grapple in this book: games of hierarchical power and legitimation played out before backdrops of institutional monopolies on knowledge, all within a self-aware literary domain. This intersection of knowledge, power, and self-awareness can be seen in this particular first instance of the eloquent peasant when the reader of the tale is thrown by the disjunction between the two clauses. One might expect the sentence "this man possesses great eloquence" to be followed by a sentence of praise, of reward. After all, across history it has been common to see eloquence as a virtue. For, as Catherine Packham has deftly traced, eloquence has been core to a quest for the *power* of the sublime from Cicero through to David Hume, with the ancients and the moderns perhaps differing on whether human nature should seek such power.[3]

In more recent days, however, it has become increasingly true that those deemed learned within formalised spaces such as the academy have usually gained their positions of authority through repeated combined performances of eloquence and education: demonstrably satisfying tests, appraisals, accreditations, 'excellence frameworks', and other exercises, usually within strictly codified and prescribed linguistic formulations of academic discourse. In the contemporary academy, the ability to express new knowledge within pre-defined norms of expression (deemed eloquent because the form must efficiently but clearly communicate) is a virtue.

However, despite the fact that eloquence is valued by the king in the ancient tale, there is an unexpected relationship at play in the story's matrix of knowledge, power, aesthetics, and value. This is how the tale derives its startling force: the eloquent peasant is disciplined, engendering an unexpected causal relationship between virtue and chastisement, a situation about which those in the contemporary academic humanities may feel empathetic. In a similar way to many of the fictions that will be examined throughout this book, this tale's shock factor is possible because the text anticipates its readers' expectations

---

3   Catherine Packham, 'Cicero's Ears, or Eloquence in the Age of Politeness: Oratory, Moderation, and the Sublime in Enlightenment Scotland', *Eighteenth-Century Studies*, 46.4 (2013), 499–512, http://dx.doi.org/10.1353/ecs.2013.0043.

and normative value judgements surrounding the charged encounter between class/social situation and eloquence. This expectation is set because the tale takes the parable form of a moral panic about class transgression through non-institutional knowledge and eloquence. Concerned as this text is with justice and class, the *Tale of the Eloquent Peasant* clearly establishes a social and literary generic terrain that is familiar to most readers, even if this set of expectations changes over time. The tale then acts to at least temporarily subvert those literary and social expectations, all framed within a didactic parable of justice and power.[4]

In the crafting of literature, or any kind of rhetoric, there are certain prerequisite factors if authors wish to play this type of game with audience expectations. One must know roughly the identity of one's readers and what that audience group are likely to think, sometimes across heterogeneous discourse communities. In its historical context, the *Tale of the Eloquent Peasant* is a story designed for educated readers, perhaps akin to the early reader-response work of Stanley Fish who speaks of "informed readers".[5] After all, there was no widespread mass literacy in the First Intermediate Period. Although, therefore, it is likely that the tale was communicated in oral form, there is a doubled self-referentiality at work here. On the one hand, the original 'reader' of the tale must have been educated and would probably have been of an upper class, while the contemporary reader of the story may experience the greatest disquiet if he or she identifies with the peasant. On the other hand, though, the content of the story itself has an anti-intellectual bent, a disciplining function designed to keep the eloquent peasants — suppressed by hereditary class-based educational structures rather than any meritocratic system — in their place. I am no ancient historian and the reading here is a contemporary take on a classic. The analogy, though, is striking in the context of my work here: for this is a book about the sometimes hostile reactions to practices within university English that continue to run through a strain of twenty-first-century

---

4 The inversion of order is, of course, temporary. Like Bakhtin's famous carnival, the tale ends with order restored and the normative moral precepts and expectations emerge only strengthened by the momentary misrule.

5 Stanley Fish, 'Literature in the Reader: Affective Stylistics', in *Is There a Text in This Class?: The Authority of Interpretive Communities* (Cambridge, MA: Harvard University Press, 1990), pp. 21–67 (p. 48).

fiction. As with the *Tale of the Eloquent Peasant*, I will argue that the works to which I refer in this volume have a disciplining function, although they are not, now, primarily concerned with institutional royalty in opposition to the commoner. Instead, ironically given the prophecies of much of the anti-humanism and anti-intentionality that dominated post-structuralist literary studies in the 1980s and 1990s, the texts studied in this book inscribe their authors as royalty and academic readers as their peasants. They toy, I will argue, with university English's traditional hierarchies of authority and legitimation while reversing the monopoly on literary-critical speech that academic English has attempted to claim.

This is a book about the way in which a specific sub-form of contemporary fiction interacts with the academy, the story of which is a fascinating power game played between two symbiotic (but heterogeneous) cultural institutions: the university and the novel. Fundamentally, it is a book about contemporary literary fiction's contribution to the ongoing displacement of cultural authority away from university English. In this work I argue for the prominence of a series of novelistic techniques that, whether deliberate or not on the part of the author, function to outmanoeuvre, contain, and determine academic reading practices. This desire to discipline university English through the manipulation and restriction of possible hermeneutic paths is, I contend, a result firstly of the fact that the metafictional paradigm of the high-postmodern era has pitched critical and creative discourses into a type of productive competition with one another. Such tensions and overlaps (or 'turf wars') have only increased in light of the ongoing breakdown of coherent theoretical definitions of 'literature' as distinct from 'criticism'. As the literary works that I cover here then "train their readers in a hermeneutic of suspicion", as Rita Felski puts it, following Paul Ricœur, they also discipline the academy in order to legitimate themselves over and above their critical counterparts from which they do not consider themselves formally discrete.[6] I argue here, then, taking up a challenge issued by Peter Boxall — that such novels exhibit a "resistance to evaluation" — that the "world-making power of prose fiction" in the contemporary era relies upon the ability of the novel to

---

6   Rita Felski, *The Limits of Critique* (Chicago: University of Chicago Press, 2015), p. 43.

"reject or suspend the forms of community that it helps to create".[7] It is the project of this book to ensure that the fact that these rejected or suspended communities are so often *academic* communities does not go unremarked upon.

Secondly, I argue that this disciplinary function is situated amid larger ongoing shifts of legitimation. Indeed, I will go on to show that literature and university English now often find themselves fighting each other within the new world of information-dominated knowledge work described by Alan Liu. For the environment within which university English and the novel now co-exist is one in which "the academy can no longer claim supreme jurisdiction over knowledge", as Liu puts it. It is, though, also an environment in which "the future of the literary" is difficult to foresee in the light of the prominent ahistoricist paradigms of the knowledge economy.[8] In a world that values the constant replacement of the old in the name of innovation, what room is there for tradition to be balanced against the individual talent? For Liu, then, an investigation of the aesthetic value in new paradigms of managerial creation is a "vital task" for "both literature and literary studies", if these practices are to survive in any form.[9] However, here I remain more cynical that such a battle will be fought as allies and chart an alternative narrative in which contemporary literary studies and literature are instead both 'digging in' to protect themselves, trying to reclaim the increasingly scarce conventional authority of their forms, even though it may be too late. Taken together, this set of literary practices betrays what I will come to refer to as an 'anxiety of academia' within the space of literary production.

This trope of 'anxiety' is taken not only from the most obvious referent, Harold Bloom's 'anxieties of influence', in which there is an ambivalent relationship between a text and those texts that influenced it, but also from Ian Hunter's riposte to Jonathan Culler. Hunter asks of Theory and critique: "in what historical or institutional circumstances do people learn to become disdainful of certain knowledges as 'common

---

7   Peter Boxall, *The Value of the Novel* (Cambridge: Cambridge University Press, 2015), p. 11.
8   Alan Liu, *The Laws of Cool: Knowledge Work and the Culture of Information* (Chicago: University of Chicago Press, 2004), pp. 3, 21.
9   *Ibid.*, p. 2.

sense', and to become anxious about themselves for 'taking things for granted'?"[10] I suggest that this anxiety of the self, a kind of competitive desire to be the 'most critical', is playing out between the institutions of the Anglo-American university and the novel in the historical circumstances of the early twenty-first century.

This investigation of fiction and the university does not quite take the form that readers might pre-suppose, though. To dispel any misconceptions from the outset, it is worth stating up front that this volume is not as concerned with campus novels or 'university fiction' as an initial appraiser might infer from the above summary. While it is hardly surprising that academics are interested in fiction that represents the university and that we might expect the challenges of legitimation to play out in such texts, this type of novel has already been expertly documented and remarked upon by Mortimer R. Proctor, John Lyons, Ian Carter, Janice Rossen, Kenneth Womack, Péter Székely, Elaine Showalter, and others.[11] Of course, there are many extant and well-known readings of the campus novel. For instance, Terry Eagleton suggests that a particularly English fascination with the campus novel stems from the fact that it can offer a recuperative setting far-enough dislocated from middle-class existence to an institutional space that

---

10 Ian Hunter, 'The Time of Theory', *Postcolonial Studies*, 10.1 (2007), 5–22 (p. 8), http://dx.doi.org/10.1080/13688790601153123. It also strikes me that many of the anxieties in this space are actually competitive also against the natural/empirical sciences. Hunter and Felski do not go far enough, for my liking, in looking at how the contemporary sciences actually share many of the conditions of negative knowledge. Falsifiability and a desire to militate against false appearance through intersubjectivity are critical to the natural sciences. Of course, both the human, natural and empirical sciences may derive their critical stances from earlier philosophy; its roots can be found in Ancient Greece, not just in the more recent Kantian approaches. But the continuation of the mode feels more like a transformation of natural and empirical scientific practice in another legitimation problem: that of the two cultures.

11 Mortimer R. Proctor, *The English University Novel* (Berkeley: University of California Press, 1957); John Lyons, *The College Novel in America* (Carbondale: Southern Illinois University Press, 1962); Ian Carter, *Ancient Cultures of Conceit: British University Fiction in the Post-War Years* (London: Routledge, 1990); Janice Rossen, *The University on Modern Fiction: When Power Is Academic* (London: Macmillan, 1993); Kenneth Womack, *Postwar Academic Fiction: Satire, Ethics, Community* (Basingstoke: Palgrave Macmillan, 2002); Péter Székely, 'The Academic Novel in the Age of Postmodernity: The Anglo-American Metafictional Academic Novel' (unpublished doctoral thesis, Eötvös Loránd University, 2009), http://doktori.btk.elte.hu/lit/szekelypeter/thesis.pdf; Elaine Showalter, *Faculty Towers: The Academic Novel and Its Discontents* (Philadelphia: University of Pennsylvania Press, 2009).

is both deviant and other while remaining safe, known, and farcical.[12] We also know, though, that the strong influence on contemporary US literary production of professionalised writing training via MFA programmes makes it likely that most authors would have ready first-hand knowledge of a campus background to draw upon (to which I will return later). Indeed, the best joke I have heard on this theme in recent days is that "bad books on writing tell you to 'WRITE WHAT YOU KNOW', a solemn and totally false adage that is the reason there exist so many mediocre novels about English professors contemplating adultery".[13] Rather, then, than re-work the classic formula of complicit laughter at *Lucky Jim* or to take the counter-stance of denouncing the campus novel as inherently conservative, in this book I examine novels that are at once interlinked with the academy and the practices of university English even while, at the same time, these texts are often not engaged in direct representation of the university. These parameters of exclusion and method in my selection of texts are more thoroughly explored in Chapter Two.

Instead, one of the primary ways in which this competitive interaction with the academy is manifest in the works that I cover here, I argue, is through a specific anticipation of an academic discourse-community as an idealised reader-community (with some more words on my echoing of Umberto Eco's famous formulations to follow). That is, as with the *Tale of the Eloquent Peasant*'s anticipation of its educated audience demographic, much contemporary 'literary fiction' is aware of the conditions under which it will be read within the university's literary studies departments and therefore finds itself already one step ahead of its readers. While this paradigm of idealised/model readers harks back to problems of the "hermeneutic cycle" that have been central to debates about critical interpretation for many decades now (and are cyclical in their mutual production of idealised text and idealised readers), the specifically evolved form of academic interaction that I chart here can be seen as a new emergence, or at least a newly realised instantiation of

---

12   Terry Eagleton, 'The Silences of David Lodge', *New Left Review*, 1.172 (1988), 93–102; although, as Merritt Moseley points out, even comedic novels about academics do not have to be, by definition, satiric. Merritt Moseley, 'Introductory: Definitions and Justifications', in *The Academic Novel: New and Classic Essays*, ed. by Merritt Moseley (Chester: Chester Academic Press, 2007), pp. 3–19.

13   Widely attributed to Joe Haldeman.

existing practices.¹⁴ In the novels of Sarah Waters that I explore in the penultimate chapter of this study, for instance, the very narrative path relies on a constriction of interpretation that functions differently when read by academics versed in the work of Michel Foucault. This certainly constitutes a new technique that is different from the paradoxical anti-hermeneutic jibes of, say, Thomas Pynchon's *Gravity's Rainbow* (1973), which may nonetheless mock academic or symptomatic reading practices as onanistic.¹⁵ In this way, this book argues that the academy is woven both more broadly and more deeply into the fabric of the contemporary literary fiction scene than might be supposed were an investigation limited to works that focus on depictions of the university.

In detailing the range of specific thematic uses that such engagements with the academy can serve, it is my contention that some types of fiction now play this game and deploy knowledge of academic discourses and practices as a specific literary and market strategy. While this shares some affinities with the type of "writing back" to the academy that Judith Ryan perceives in the post-Theory novel — and some of the instances studied in this volume do pertain to the deliberate injection of literary-critical and theoretical jargon into texts — I want here to voice a broader hypothesis about the role that this might play in terms of literary legitimation and authority.¹⁶ Whether one considers it in David Mitchell's satire of over-privileged undergraduate life at Cambridge in *The Bone Clocks* (2014), in the high-academic aphoristic style of one of Zadie Smith's sub-narratives in *NW* (2012), or in any of the works discussed in more detail in this volume, toying with academic discourse and reading practices is now a deliberate textual strategy that is used to claim a 'literary' quality for a work.¹⁷ The tacit inscription of the social

---

14 See, Umberto Eco, 'Overinterpreting Texts', in *Interpretation and Overinterpretation*, ed. by Stefan Collini (Cambridge: Cambridge University Press, 1992), pp. 45–66 (p. 64).

15 For instance, this novel accuses the over-interpreting reader of having one's 'hands in your pants', linking over-interpretation to masturbation. This is not a specific technique, though; it is a generalised critique of over-interpretation and an attempt to forestall all meaning even while the text overloads its symbolic register to an extraordinary degree. Thomas Pynchon, *Gravity's Rainbow* (London: Vintage, 1995), pp. 695–96.

16 Judith Ryan, *The Novel After Theory* (New York: Columbia University Press, 2011).

17 For example, see the section entitled 'Ideology in popular entertainment' and its antecedent entry. Zadie Smith, *NW* (London: Penguin, 2013), p. 213.

conventions of English studies into a set of literary conventions is a legitimation strategy for fiction in the era of mass higher education that can be seen as a type of metafictional, generic, and market practice. It is metafictional because this process of interpellating specific 'academic' readerly communities must involve and signal a degree of explicit textual self-awareness. It is a generic practice because we can describe the paradigm in a number of works, as will this book, and because we can then chart how new works might fit this prescription. It is a market practice because, I will argue, the structures of value and accreditation in the academy are now pitched into a type of competition with fiction because of the collapse of viable gatekeeping and canonisation mechanisms. Finally, it is a practice that is particularly relevant in the era of mass higher education because broadened access to training in techniques of critical and close reading destabilises the authority of the academy and of literary fiction.[18]

These three areas of investigation — metafiction, genre, and markets — form the overlapping points of interaction that are explored throughout this book in its engagement with contemporary fiction. These investigations are centred around the institutional form of the university and framed through the lenses of critique, legitimation, and discipline.

Genre, Canons, and Markets

Works of contemporary fiction are 'legitimated' through the overlay of diverse structures of value, from multiple sources (some market, some institution-based), atop the material processes of literary production. For some authors, selling millions of copies will serve as a legitimation of their writing. For others, appearing alongside prominent authors in a literary quarterly, in order to "generate cultural and actual capital" as Amy Hungerford puts it, might suffice.[19] For some, simply appearing in print will be enough. Even just from an authorial perspective, there are, indeed, multiple sources from which literary value can be generated.

---

18 For more on this, see Ronan McDonald, *The Death of the Critic* (London: Continuum, 2007).

19 Amy Hungerford, *Making Literature Now* (Stanford: Stanford University Press, 2016), p. 10.

What, though, is the specific role of the university in the ascription of literary value?

Certainly, the aspects within the novels that I will read here pertain to the university and around university English. This is not, I will hypothesise, because these works have a straightforward desire to belittle academics; this is not a book exclusively about parody, pastiche, or satire, although these elements play a role in the broader function that I posit for such fiction. It is rather because, in one of the narratives that I will trace, university English and other disciplines of literary study form one of the contexts for literary publication and reception. To see a response from fiction to such an environment is unsurprising, especially given the rise of mass higher education and creative writing programmes. A more specific framing of this context, however, is that university English can be seen as the *weaker relation* of the market gatekeeping system for literary fiction, of which publishers form the stronger, obverse side. This weakness contributes towards the oft-touted 'legitimation crisis' in university English.

To understand this observation it is necessary to backtrack to the ongoing influence of the 'canon wars' of the 1980s and 1990s in which traditionalist aesthetic formalists attempted to preserve and defend an overwhelmingly white, male canon against the protestations of Marxist, feminist, and postcolonial schools (among others that might now be said to include critical disability studies), who viewed such a canon as a reflection of socio-historic, rather than aesthetic, conditions. This dilemma over value persists, as has been recently demonstrated by Mark Algee-Hewitt and Mark McGurl in a meta-analysis of various claimed literary canons.[20] Algee-Hewitt and McGurl conduct two separate computational/quantitative analyses in their pamphlet, a product of Stanford's 'literary lab'. After initially appraising a more traditional set of corpora, these social, structural inequalities remain manifest: only 15% of authors algorithmically selected for inclusion were women while a mere 5% were non-white.[21] To this end, the authors then conducted a second analysis with additional corpora contributed by some members

---

20 Mark Algee-Hewitt and Mark McGurl, *Between Canon and Corpus: Six Perspectives on 20th-Century Novels*, Pamphlets of the Stanford Literary Lab (Stanford: Stanford Literary Lab, 2015), https://litlab.stanford.edu/LiteraryLabPamphlet8.pdf.

21 *Ibid.*, p. 13.

of the editorial board of the journal MELUS (Multi Ethnic Literature of the United States), members of the Postcolonial Studies Association, and the editorial board of the Feminist Press (although this revised model still yielded only 10% non-white and 17% female).[22] For the purposes of the current discussion of contemporary fiction, however, what is perhaps most relevant are the principles of value selection that pervade Algee-Hewitt and McGurl's corpora. For their analysis they chose to use four corpora that are publisher/reader selected and only one corpus created by an academic.[23] This is telling and indicative of a broader structural trend. Namely, that the processes that shape value in the literary sphere, even in this appraisal, are mostly based on the market, with academic aesthetic judgement forming only a weaker correlative portion of the gatekeeping system.

My claim that academic value-judgements are the weaker relation of publisher filtering systems is most clear when one considers the processes of market gatekeeping and canon formation for twenty-first-century literary fiction. These questions have been raised most pointedly in recent times not only by James F. English but also by Robert Eaglestone, who writes of the problematic fact that "it is taken as axiomatic that 'serious' or 'literary' fiction is a genre of its own ('Booker' fiction)", a genre that is key to academic study.[24] Furthermore, Eaglestone notes of the publishing market that:

> in the main agents, and trade publishers are very unhelpful and resistant to academics. They do not see the point of us, which is odd as we sell many, many thousands of copies of their books to our students (nearly a captive audience, in fact) and more importantly we create the intellectual and cultural infrastructure within in [sic] which their business grows. ("I studied her in college so I downloaded the new one straight away".) Yet this, too, reveals that one issue in contemporary fiction is what we might

---

22 Ibid., p. 18.
23 Modern Library Board's List of 100 Best Novels of the 20th Century, the Modern Library Reader's List of 100 Best Novels of the 20th Century, the Radcliffe's Rival List of the 100 Best Novels of the 20th Century, Larry McCafery's List of the 100 Best Novels of the 20th Century and the Yearly Best-selling Works of the 20th Century.
24 Robert Eaglestone, 'Contemporary Fiction in the Academy: Towards a Manifesto', Textual Practice, 27.7 (2013), 1089–101 (p. 1097), http://dx.doi.org/10.1080/0950236X.2013.840113; see also James F. English, The Economy of Prestige Prizes, Awards, and the Circulation of Cultural Value (Cambridge, MA: Harvard University Press, 2005).

call the "contemporary history of the book": the ways in which the business of publishing helps to shape and control contemporary fiction.[25]

While I do not attempt in this work to conduct an empirical investigation into this claimed resistance of publishers (as, say, a series of interviews might), I do want to chart a range of complex resistances to and intersections with the academy that are explicit and implicit in much contemporary fiction. I will suggest that these form a new way of considering the relationship between academics, publishers, and authors of such works that centres on a reconfiguration of institutional authority.

Part of this reconfiguration can be voiced through a concern, following Eaglestone, but one that is also linked to Franco Moretti's observations on canon limitation in 'The Slaughterhouse of Literature'.[26] My concern is this: the books that academics working on contemporary novels will consider part of the canon of literary fiction must have already been published and, therefore, pre-filtered. But this is not necessarily the way in which the dissemination of contemporary fiction works or will work in the future. In the realms of science/speculative fiction and other genre forms, the self-publishing movement has gained a great deal of momentum, facilitated by the near-zero dissemination cost (although not labour-cost) per-copy in the digital environment. Yet, as nearly all sources agree, self-publishing in that 'special' yet small genre of prize-winning 'literary fiction', to which Eaglestone alludes, remains extremely difficult.[27] As Felski notes, "the works that we study and teach [...] could never come to our attention without the work of countless helpers: publishers, advertisers, critics, prize committees, reviews, word-of-mouth recommendations, syllabi, textbooks and anthologies, changing tastes and scholarly vocabularies".[28]

---

25 Eaglestone, p. 1096.
26 Franco Moretti, 'The Slaughterhouse of Literature', *MLQ: Modern Language Quarterly*, 61.1 (2000), 207–27.
27 David Henry Sterry, 'Self-Publishing Literary Fiction: The Good, the Bad and the Ugly: Cari Noga Reveals All to the Book Doctors', *Huffington Post*, 20 August 2014, http://www.huffingtonpost.com/david-henry-sterry/selfpublishing-literary-f_b_5695364.html.
28 Felski, p. 170. Felski does attribute "last, but not least, the passions and predilections of ourselves and our students" but I feel that these are subsidiary to the market discoverability factors.

This accounts for at least some of the reasons why publishers might be disdainful towards academics, if Eaglestone's assertion that such disdain exists is, in fact, true. Yes, academics select (value) a subset of a publisher's list for promotion through teaching and research, thereby creating an environment in which such writing can flourish. However, it is only a subset. Publishing remains a business fraught with financial risk in which cross-subsidy must be judiciously applied between works that will sell and those that will flop with no sure-fire predictive technique for determining a novel's reception. The value judgements made by academics to canonise works is not undertaken in advance of publication, which would mitigate this risk to some extent. Instead, academics expect publishers to take the risk of publication and only then will the academy's blessing be bestowed, once this pre-filtering mechanism has been completed. Canons comprise books, not manuscripts. It may also be the case that the role of a commissioning editor is very different to the role of a literary critic. In this case, the academy's labour of value conferral is working in a different space to those of editorial staff and is of no use whatsoever to those gatekeepers at publishing houses who must anticipate the shape of an unknown and potentially unknowable literary market, venturing their own capital, only for academics to reward it after the fact.[29] Academic value judgements may confer a cultural prestige on works but this is at least one step removed from the economic realities and difficulties faced by publishing houses.

In addition to a difference in type of labour, this problem also comes from a shortage of labour in the academy concomitant to the volume of material that must be read (a difference of degree). Let alone an academic career alongside administrative responsibilities, a *human lifespan* is too short to read all the fiction that is now published in the world, not even to speak of work that was rejected by publishers. This bodes poorly for practices of an idealised unfiltered, unaided canon-formation to be core activities in the academy. As Geoffrey Bilder has suggested at many conferences with respect to the related reading

---

29 As my colleague Joe Brooker has said to me many times in informal conversations, attempts to formalise literary value are built on foundations of sand. It's an area where perhaps the most we can say with certainty is that 'different people like different things'.

space of academic research material, university professors have developed sophisticated 'reading-avoidance techniques' to lighten their load. In many types of non-fiction publication, this consists of going first to the index and the bibliography to situate the work and to ascertain whether it must be read. It also involves reading short-form reviews of texts. Most crucially (but also problematically for economic reasons), it can involve using the name of the journal, or the name of the publisher, as a shorthand to denote quality. In the world of fiction, the same can apply. In more extreme cases, such as that voiced recently by Hungerford, a form of "critical not-reading" emerges that could be premised on authorial-biographical or textual misogyny.[30] More typically, that a work has already been published by a reputable press is a prerequisite for a time investment by an academic, with an even more limited subset of works now prioritised through the literary-prize industry.[31] This, though, as before, explains why publishers might be frosty towards academics, particularly if those academics then claim that they ripen the commercial environment for sales of literary fiction. In some cases, publishers take the risks, academics claim the value. A broader and more controversial solution that is posed to this dilemma is to use computational, large-scale corpus-analysis techniques to 'read' at distance, even if this might radically change the value structures of the canonisation process and even if there are substantial technological and legal hurdles to conducting such an approach on contemporary fiction.[32]

There are several reasons why such proposed digital solutions are controversial. When dealing with computational reading methods, it is easy to encounter an aesthetic/teleological opposition to stylometry (the quantitative measurement of stylistic features of texts) from some quarters. Indeed, among the most common questions that are asked

---

30 See Hungerford, *Making Literature Now*, pp. 142–43 for another take on literary 'overproduction', as she terms it. I am not wholly sure what Hungerford means by 'overproduction' here. For what use case is the literature being over-produced? What would be the optimal level of production? Certainly there is more than academics can read, but can this truly be said to be 'over-production'?
31 Again, see English, *The Economy of Prestige Prizes*.
32 See, for example Franco Moretti, *Graphs, Maps, Trees: Abstract Models for Literary History* (London: Verso, 2007); Franco Moretti, *Distant Reading* (London: Verso, 2013); Matthew L. Jockers, *Macroanalysis: Digital Methods and Literary History* (Urbana: University of Illinois Press, 2013); Stephen Ramsay, *Reading Machines: Toward an Algorithmic Criticism* (Urbana: University of Illinois Press, 2011).

by non-stylometrists about its processes are: 'so what?'; 'why should I care?'; and 'what does this actually tell us that we didn't already know?'. In other words, when confronted with mathematical and computational processes for studying texts, the frequent response is to ask what it tells us about a work. The obvious retort is that it tells us neither more nor less than any other study of an aesthetic object; a work of literature. For the study of aesthetics is answerable to nothing except itself at some point in the chain; it is a human pursuit to understand how literary works achieve their affects and sometimes effects.

Yet, as Ted Underwood put it to me in a statement that has haunted my thinking ever since, this challenge of purpose and teleology can be "understood as an aesthetic problem". For literary criticism traditionally makes "fragments of individual experience work to illuminate a big picture" while stylometry takes unexperienced quantitative data to do the same, which feels like an "aesthetic loss".[33] In other words, there is something not-like-reading about stylometry and computational 'reading' that disconcerts people outside of its practices, compounded by a fear held by many that the fundable future of humanities research might compel them into this space against their wishes. Indeed, 'distant reading'/computational 'reading' is actually a non-consumptive use, to use the phrase from American copyright law.[34] It is not actually a form of reading; it is a set of utilitarian techniques for evaluating large-scale corpora. At the same time, though, the common curse uttered by academics working on fiction is that they have already 'lost the ability to read for pleasure'. Indeed, traditional literary criticism always coerces texts into new narrative forms conducive to argument, its practitioners reading to seek case studies suited for exegetic purpose. But we still call this reading.

---

33 Ted Underwood, '@martin_eve Playing Devil's Advocate, obviously. But I think the skepticism is perhaps best understood as an aesthetic problem. One of the +', *@Ted_Underwood*, 2016, https://twitter.com/Ted_Underwood/status/756135378742943744; Ted Underwood, '@martin_eve things lit crit does well is make fragments of individual experience work to illuminate a big picture. When we use evidence+', *@Ted_Underwood*, 2016, https://twitter.com/Ted_Underwood/status/756135767806648320; Ted Underwood, '@martin_eve That isn't "experienced," I think ppl feel that as an *aesthetic* loss. It's not what they *say,* but I think it's felt.', *@Ted_Underwood*, 2016, https://twitter.com/Ted_Underwood/status/756136113115242496.

34 For reasons of space I am here conflating a set of diverse computational practices, but the point still holds.

I wonder, too, whether there is an aesthetic antagonism to literary criticism, as it has existed since the New Criticism and poststructuralist anti-intentional criticism, in computational reading practices. Of course, there have always been archival, biographical, and other more seemingly material literary-critical practices. But one of the legacies of the New Criticism was to turn power to readers, away from authors. The poststructuralist 'Death of the Author' extensions of such New Critical anti-intentionalist practices — even if their practitioners might not have wished them to be billed as such as 'extension' — only strengthened such readerly-centric approaches. It was empowering as a reader to be told that there was nothing outside of the text and that readers could interpret on this basis without a master-author figure undermining such readings.

The features that can be discerned through stylometry and other computational approaches are, though, a disempowerment of the general and academic reader to some extent. Most readers are not likely to notice statistically significant deviations in part-of-speech usage, nor differences in the most-frequently used words within a text. In a way, then, stylometry seems to bring back an authorial subconscious and to read this in a way that counters the aesthetic sense of actual, human reading. It is a type of 'reading against the reader' as other paradigms were 'reading against the author'. The challenge is to connect such findings with the aesthetic experience; to argue why the measurement of linguistic style matters by showing how it connects with the experience of reading.

The other strange aspect that strikes me here, though, is that this 'reading against the reader' is still a facet of much traditional literary criticism. The best literary criticism shocks the reader into a previously unknown and fresh perspective. The best work forces us to see texts in new lights, to bring the shock of the new to the familiar and to critically deform and reform those literary pieces that we thought we knew so well. And this is also a type of 'reading against the reader', for it shows how shallow my own readings were whenever I feel that satisfying jolt of what was previously unseen. It appears to me, however, that the shocks of the new of stylometry do not bring this satisfaction, for the reasons that Underwood has already pointed out: there is nothing with which I can connect them in my experience of reading.

In such a light, computational approaches to valorising corpora of texts differ significantly from more general reading. They do not solve the problem of value judgements in a way that feels commensurate with traditional reading practices, even if they do allow for a more comprehensive literary history. Yet, even with digital methods put aside, the comparative lack of academic engagement with the conditions of possibility for the publication of contemporary fiction — even if it is probably true that the values of the academy do affect publishers' selection criteria in other ways that will become evident throughout this book — can help us to account for the hostility of some contemporary literary fiction towards the university. For, if academics are willing to outsource the assessment of quality fiction to publishers and play no role in its pre-selection for publication (even if the situation for literary prizes is somewhat different), then it is clear that the task of critique of those conditions of production might be situated *within fiction*, not within the academy. This forms one of the initial pre-contexts of my argument: university English has only the most tenuous connections to value-conferral and may be a necessary *but insufficient* condition of possibility for the publication of 'literary fiction'.

Metafiction as Critique

The second pre-context that I want to broach here is that many of the fictions that are closely read in this book — from Tom McCarthy through Roberto Bolaño up to Sarah Waters — possess traits that can be termed 'metafictional'. It is, however, no coincidence that such traits should be prevalent in a study of contemporary fiction's interactions with the academy. This is more than simply a hangover of the fact that contemporary fiction still sits within the shadow of the postmodern aesthetics that dominated the Anglo-American literary scene from the 1960s to the 1990s, even if many, such as Charles Altieri, do now find such forms to be fading or even embarrassing.[35] Rather, it is because metafiction has been defined, by several prominent commentators, in terms of an elision of literary-creative and academic-critical practice.

---

35 Charles Altieri, *Postmodernisms Now: Essays on Contemporaneity in the Arts, Literature and Philosophy* (University Park: Pennsylvania State University Press, 1998), p. 1.

In truth, Mark Currie is right to point out, in his introduction to the literally titled collection on the form, *Metafiction* (1995), that there are problems with the standard definitions of this mode. It is now a well-known fact that the term metafiction arose during the height of the postmodern literary phase in the 1960s and was first ascribed to William Gass. The word is used to describe fiction that is 'self-aware', fiction that knows it is fiction, fiction that draws attention, through various stylistic conceits, to itself as a work of fiction. Major studies of the form include Robert Scholes's *The Fabulators* (1967) and his article 'Metafiction' in the *Iowa Review* (1970); Robert Alter's *Partial Magic: The Novel as a Self-Conscious Genre* (1975); Linda Hutcheon's *Narcissistic Narrative: The Metafictional Paradox* (1984); and Patricia Waugh's *Metafiction: The Theory and Practice of Self-Conscious Fiction* (1984). Each of these works has contributed towards the contemporary understanding that we hold of the term metafiction. From Alter's dialectical framing of *Don Quixote* (1605–1615) as the first realist novel, set in negational opposition to reality, the logical unfurling that fiction must be, always to some degree, about fiction itself began to emerge.

These standard definitions neglect, though, in Currie's argument, the facts that "the idea of self-consciousness is strangely inconsistent with most postmodern literary theories which would attribute neither selfhood nor consciousness to an author" and that "[i]t is not enough that metafiction knows that it is fiction; it must also know that it is metafiction if its self-knowledge is adequate", thus prompting an infinite regress.[36] Currie moves instead, following Robert Scholes, to re-situate metafiction as a critical discourse that "dramatises the boundary between fiction and criticism" within a loose definition of 'criticism'.[37] Currie's argument has merit and his subsequent discussion of the history of twentieth-century literary studies manages convincingly to situate the respective projects of Jacques Derrida and Foucault alongside the metafictive turn, for "[t]he postmodern context is not one divided neatly between fictional texts and their critical readings, but a monistic world of representations in which the boundaries between art and life, language and metalanguage, and fiction and criticism are

---

36   Mark Currie, 'Introduction', in *Metafiction*, ed. by Mark Currie (London: Longman, 1995), p. 1.
37   Ibid., p. 3.

under philosophical attack".³⁸ This is itself an extension of Derrida's well-known rejection of the "formal specificity of the literary work".³⁹ As Raman Selden has put it, Derrida's anti-foundationalist writings are a challenge to disciplinarity that "relentlessly transgress and reject the binary oppositions which govern the protocols of academic discourses" and, in so doing, eradicate "the conventional boundaries between literary and non-literary texts".⁴⁰ Likewise, Eco has claimed that although "according to a current opinion" he has "written some texts that can be labelled as scientific (or academic or theoretical), and some others that can be defined as creative", he does "not believe in such a straightforward distinction".⁴¹

This thinking of a slippage between literary and critical texts has permeated a range of approaches, not just those centred around deconstruction. If, as Boxall notes, "the distinction between creative and critical writing is becoming harder to sustain", then perhaps *the* fundamental recurring question for the discipline of English resurfaces: what is the object of literary studies?⁴² What is special about a 'literary' text? This debate has even spilled over into other ideological areas of literary studies. Various schools of post-Althusserian Marxist literary criticism, as just one instance, have grappled with this question and the relationship of literature to ideology and production. The early work of Terry Eagleton, as another example, extended Pierre Machery's and Etienne Balibar's thinking to triangulate literature at the intersection of various ideologies (such as the authorial ideology) and productive modes (such as the literary mode of production).⁴³ For Tony Bennett, though, even this did not break free of the thinking that 'literature' is its own eternal category, somehow delineated from other types of production. What instead is needed, to Bennett's mind, is an analysis

---

38   *Ibid.*, pp. 17–18.
39   Jacques Derrida, *Positions*, trans. by Alan Bass (Chicago: Chicago University Press, 1981), p. 70.
40   Ramsey Selden, 'Introduction', in *The Cambridge History of Literary Criticism*, ed. by Ramsey Selden (Cambridge: Cambridge University Press, 1993), 1–10 (p. 7).
41   Umberto Eco, 'Reply', in *Interpretation and Overinterpretation*, ed. by Stefan Collini (Cambridge: Cambridge University Press, 1992), pp. 139–51 (p. 140).
42   Boxall, *The Value of the Novel*, p. 5.
43   Terry Eagleton, *Criticism and Ideology: A Study in Marxist Literary Theory* (London: Verso, 1976), pp. 44–63. Eagleton's later work turns away from the category of literature as a homogeneous object of study.

of how literature changes in its re-production and reception over time.[44] Such thinking led, in parallel, to the development of the genetic criticism movement in France, devoted to studying the plurality of *avant-textes* that underpin any supposed final object of study. As Louis Hay put it, "[n]ot *The Text*, but texts".[45] Such work on the *genesis* of texts and the mechanics of writing, though, once again lowers the fences between criticism and literature, manifesting a "deep relation between writing and reading" in which "literature and criticism [are both] really only breathing in the air of modern times".[46] As just one other example, this link between reading and writing and blurring of a distinct critical sphere was certainly also pronounced in the surge of author-critics (Woolf, Eliot, Lawrence, Pound, etc.) in the modernist period.[47] In any case, what is clear here is that debates over the bounding of literature (if such a coherent, isolated category can even exist) are important and central to its study and have been ongoing for some time.[48] Much postmodern metafiction, though, is an attack upon this isolation, staging an incursion or intercession into the critical space and erasing literature as a distinct category set apart from criticism.

There is, however, a troubling aspect to this definition. If metafiction is a mode that elides the difference between criticism and the novel, pitching university English against fiction in a battle for the space of legitimated critical speech, then it is also notable that the form (metafiction) has consistently been held up as trivial or, in its postmodern form, "politically abortive" and "self-indulgent".[49] That said, for every corresponding action there is a reaction, and the assault on metafiction correlates to equal attacks on postmodern and poststructuralist Theory, which have been frequently decried as sophistic and nihilistic;

---

44 Tony Bennett, *Formalism and Marxism* (London: Routledge, 1979), p. 167.
45 Louis Hay, 'Does "Text" Exist?', *Studies in Bibliography*, 41 (1988), 64–76 (p. 73).
46 Louis Hay, 'Genetic Criticism: Origins and Perspective', in *Genetic Criticism: Texts and Avant-Textes*, ed. by Jed Deppman, Daniel Ferrer, and Michael Groden (Philadelphia: University of Pennsylvania Press, 2004), pp. 17–27 (p. 22).
47 McDonald, p. 81.
48 For more on this, see the excellent Celia Britton, 'Structuralist and Poststructuralist Psychoanalytic and Marxist Theories', in *The Cambridge History of Literary Criticism*, ed. by Ramsey Selden (Cambridge: Cambridge University Press, 1993), pp. 197–252 to which much of the above discussion is indebted.
49 David James, *Modernist Futures: Innovation and Inheritance in the Contemporary Novel* (New York: Cambridge University Press, 2012), p. 10; Caroline Levine, *Forms: Whole, Rhythm, Hierarchy, Network* (Princeton: Princeton University Press, 2015), p. ix.

an "association of postmodernism and amorality", as Jane Flax puts it.[50] It could be, then, that metafiction (and particularly postmodern metafiction) aligns only with specific types of critical discourse (high Theory/poststructuralism etc.) and so simply suffers the same ethical attacks.[51]

This co-joined critique remains problematic, though, because if metafiction is a mode that erases, or at least blurs, the boundaries between the critical reading practices of the academy and the reflexivity of fiction, an assault upon metafiction, mounted by the academy, becomes a partially reflexive self-attack.[52] To put this differently: if there is any truth in the affinity or overlap between (if not the exact identity of) fiction and criticism that postmodern metafiction stages, then in accusing metafiction of amorality, many of the academy's own critical practices are also moved into the combat zone. Certainly, specific types of formalist critical practice do not seem to be the target here (despite formalism sharing metafiction's own concern with a critical analysis of aesthetics). It is, perversely, the schools of Theory (Marxist, postcolonial, feminist, critical disability, and deconstructivist) that would usually deem themselves more ethically sound than formalism that seem to be grouped with metafiction in such attacks, thus opening old debates and wounds.

An initial observation on the breadth of the assault on metafiction is worthwhile: I would argue that it is not viable to mount an attack upon postmodernist, metafictive literature on the grounds of amorality without first providing a clear rationale for the ways in which criticism of the period can be clearly delineated from the literature under critique, beyond the fact that the subject of its representation is reflexive. It is clear, after all, that reflexivity is not sufficient: the academy believes that it can study itself without falling prey to political abortion or navel-gazing, as the numerous instances of writing about the contemporary

---

50 Jane Flax, 'Soul Service: Foucault's "Care of the Self" as Politics and Ethics', in *The Mourning After: Attending the Wake of Postmodernism*, ed. by Neil Brooks and Josh Toth (Amsterdam: Rodopi, 2007), pp. 79–98 (p. 80).
51 In historical terms, I feel it might be more accurate to say that postmodern metafiction and its subsequent progeny arise as the logical extension of an ongoing response to a series of ethical dilemmas of representation (the realist novel) to which the form poses itself as a partial, incomplete solution.
52 Flax, p. 80.

university reveal.⁵³ Be it, then, in David Foster Wallace's footnote techniques or in the constant disambiguating regress of *Tristram Shandy* (1759–1767), to critique metafictional practices as trivializing requires an aesthetic theory that positions critical discourse within a communicative framework of rationality against literature.⁵⁴ Put otherwise: to criticise metafiction requires academic/critical discourse to lay a unique claim to an enlightenment function of communication and to sit entirely separately from the artwork that it criticizes. Critical practice would have to stake a monopolising claim for truth, which is certainly difficult given liberal humanist takes on the ethical/moral/didactic function of literature. While we might trace this type of binary disjunction back to the early mechanistic Russian Formalism of Viktor Shklovsky, this is not how most accounts of postmodern metafiction, poststructuralist Theory, or even any formalist criticism that believes its own writing should have aesthetic value would frame it.⁵⁵ Paul de Man put this well when he posited that the "kind of truth" to which philosophy aspires is a literary one and that "philosophy turns out to be an endless reflection on its own destruction at the hands of literature", demonstrating the collapse of this distinction during the deconstructivist phase of Theory in the 1970s.⁵⁶ I might only add that it also works in reverse and that criticism continually aspires to inscribe a philosophical truth inside literature.

There are other ways in which it is possible to push back against these assaults; ways that are important for thinking about a co-incidence of critical and creative thought within the fictions that I contend have

---

53 This could also certainly be linked to the problems of self-representation and understanding that Foucault covers in his anti-humanistic discussion of the empirico-transcendental doublet. The problem that Foucault identifies is how finite beings, such as humans, can consider aspects that are transcendental and, therefore, infinite in scope. Self-reflection is an aspect that must be deemed transcendental to some degree, rather than empirical, because it is impossible to ever wholly objectify self-measurement from within the measuring construct of the self. Michel Foucault, *The Order of Things: An Archaeology of the Human Sciences* (London: Routledge, 2007), pp. 347–51.

54 Such debates have many implications for the teaching of literature, for they imply that if literature does not communicate, it must stand alone. These question the role that communicative exegesis can play. Gerald Graff, *Professing Literature: An Institutional History* (Chicago: University of Chicago Press, 1989), pp. 148–52.

55 Peter Steiner, 'Russian Formalism', in *The Cambridge History of Literary Criticism*, ed. by Ramsey Selden (Cambridge: Cambridge University Press, 1993), 11–29 (p. 18).

56 Paul de Man, *Allegories of Reading: Figural Language in Rousseau, Nietzsche, Rilke, and Proust* (New Haven: Yale University Press, 1979), p. 115.

universities as their institutional contexts. By opening this book with some brief, broad, but specifically framed, historical remarks on metafiction, I aim to show that, in the vast temporal range over which the form can be observed from before Ancient Egypt to the present day, metafiction is ubiquitous and inextricable from the act of writing fiction.[57] As a result of this apparent perpetual affiliation to writing, it becomes imperative to historicize both metafiction's production and reception if the term and its critique are to have any meaning. For a first set of rhetorical questions, then, we might ask: is it true that a correlation can be seen between perceived nihilism of a text and the strength and/or frequency of its metafictional devices? Does not, for instance, the Gospel of John in the Bible, held by many Christian people to be among *the* most ethical of texts, open with meta-textual remarks upon "the Word"? How many metafictional devices does a text have to have, or what proportion of a text must be devoted to such stylistic conceits, before it becomes politically abortive? How are critics who promote this line certain that it is a text's metafiction that causes the nihilism and not other factors?[58] What is so wrong with the ludic mode that leads to such attacks? For many adults enjoy watching or playing professional sports; those childhood pastimes that are now grown up. While, I will here demonstrate a different kind of problematic relationship between aesthetics and power, the interaction of self-referential writing with commitment to issues of class (e.g. Sarah Waters), gender (e.g. Angela Carter) and race (e.g. Percival Everett) also seems to show a turn away from readings of metafiction as nihilistic and/or purely playful. As with any categorical label that can mean everything, without some delineating facet, such taxonomies mean little.

There is, however, a different way of thinking about the self-referentiality of metafiction that complements its position as a discourse that straddles critical and creative thought: metafiction as critique. Critique, as a philosophical term most clearly refracted through Immanuel Kant and Michel Foucault in this volume, refers to

---

57 This itself can be taken as an extrapolation from Patricia Waugh's famous argument that, to some degree, all contemporary fiction is on a metafictional spectrum. Waugh, pp. 18–19.

58 The primary assumption of critics seems to be that art that reflects purely upon itself is too narcissistic, uncommitted, and detached from representation of anything other than itself to gain any ethical purchase.

an analysis of a phenomenon's conditions of possibility. For instance, Kant's *Critique of Pure Reason* (1781) was designed to uncover and schematise a delineation of *a posteriori* experience from a 'pure', *a priori* internal reason. Importantly, though, Kant's critique recognised the fact that it must do so from within the epistemic possibilities that it was charting. By contrast, Foucault's critical histories are toolkits that render our understanding of the present possible only by grasping multiple converging and discontinuous histories from within the contingent present: the historical conditions of possibility. In terms of the *a priori*: as Kant is to epistemology, Foucault is to history.[59]

This leads me to think that there might be a more radical way in which we can consider metafiction. Metafiction is, in fact, aesthetic critique. Metafiction is art that, from within art itself, questions the contemporary conditions of aesthetic and critical possibility for art and fiction. It is not the sole art form that undertakes this endeavour; self-referentiality and a fusion of criticism and aesthetics can be seen in forms of visual art and film. It is, as my opening analysis showed, hardly a new phenomenon. It is only nihilistic and self-absorbed in as much as critique and fiction are nihilistic and self-absorbed, tempered as they are by immanence, and concerned, as they must be, with their own conditions of possibility.

This is why, I will hypothesize in this book, the types of work that interact critically with the university often have prevalent metafictional traits. If metafiction is about encoding a critical affinity within literary texts, then it is a mode that is well-suited to compete with the academy in the re-centring of literary-critical authority within the markets that I detailed above. We should expect to see, in such a limited space, conflicts of legitimation, often played out through metafictional devices, where literary texts jostle with the academy for the authority to comment upon fiction. For it is not clear, as the saying goes, whether this town is (or will remain) big enough for the both of criticism and critical-metafiction. This represents, in some ways, a synthesis of critical and creative labour so that they play with, or against, each other in the same symbolic economies of power.

---

59 The best source that I have read for more on the influence of Kant on Foucault is Colin Koopman, *Genealogy as Critique: Foucault and the Problems of Modernity* (Bloomington: Indiana University Press, 2013), from which this statement derives.

As a note, though: although I claim in this volume that metafiction and the presence of the university is reflected in a paradigm of critique, in some ways this book may be charting the closing of a 'critical' era. That is to say that this book may be positioned at the juncture where 'critique' will be viewed as a historical phenomenon of the study of English and not a contemporary practice. For increasingly (although the trend dates back to at least 2004 when Cathy N. Davidson and David Theo Goldberg suggested that it was time that we "critiqued the mantra of critique"[60]) there is a doubt in the discipline that 'critique' may be the most valuable tool of the future. For the first part, the term has become so diffuse as to be near meaningless. Critique is, certainly, a term used loosely in literary studies to refer to a variety of practices: "a spirit of skeptical questioning", as Felski details it, "or outright condemnation, an emphasis on its precarious position vis-à-vis overbearing and oppressive social forces, the claim to be engaged in some kind of radical intellectual and/or political work, and the assumption that whatever is *not* critical must therefore be *uncritical*".[61] Meanwhile, N. Katherine Hayles has noted that "after more than two decades of symptomatic reading [...] many scholars are not finding it a productive practice, perhaps because (like many deconstructive readings) its results have become to seem formulaic".[62] Amid such diversity of practice and with so many value judgements contributing to each of these sub-practices, it is not surprising that 'critique' has been moved into the 'critical' sights. In more philosophically specific terms, though, Bruno Latour has noted that the mode of critique descended from Kantian philosophy may be "running out of steam". In his prominent article on this topic, Latour criticises much French philosophy/Theory for its anti-foundational and anti-realist modes, using the example of climate-change deniers citing science studies to demonstrate how critique is increasingly turned back against its claimed radical purposes.[63] All of this is to say that, although

---

60 Cathy N. Davidson and David Theo Goldberg, 'Engaging the Humanities', *Profession* (2004), 42–62 (p. 45).
61 Felski, p. 4.
62 N. Katherine Hayles, *How We Think: Digital Media and Contemporary Technogenesis* (Chicago: University of Chicago Press, 2012), p. 59.
63 Bruno Latour, 'Why Has Critique Run out of Steam?: From Matters of Fact to Matters of Concern', *Critical Inquiry*, 30.2 (2004), 225–48.

I believe I am writing about the contemporary, it may turn out that I am writing a history.

However, to summarise the second pre-context for my argument: metafiction has evolved as a form that highlights the artificiality of 'literature' as a coherent category against 'criticism'. Metafiction might also be seen as a form of critique, examining the conditions of possibility for aesthetic practice. In this way, metafictional texts begin to jostle with university English — which is already facing a challenge to its own authority as per my first pre-context — for the legitimate right to critical speech.

Academic Reading Practices

The final pre-context that must be addressed before going further is what it might mean to say that a novel 'has an academic audience in mind' or that a work of fiction has knowledge of 'academic reading practices'. This is in some cases fairly straightforward but in others more difficult. I certainly do not wish to re-pitch a regressive battle between 'common readers' and academics, as exemplified in the structuralism of some Prague School epistemologies.[64] It is also true that there is no single homogeneous and internally consistent method of reading, teaching, or researching literature within the academy. From squabbles among scholars, historians, critics, generalists, philologists, New Critics, poststructuralists, and digital humanists it is clear that the history of the discipline of English comprises a diverse range of techniques and practices.[65] That said, the most basic type of interaction that I would call 'academic' for contemporary fiction is the deployment of specific literary-critical/theoretical terms that originated in the space of professionalised university English. The seepage of this discourse beyond the ivory tower is a historical product of the rise of mass higher education, the popularity/rise of English as a discipline, and the influence of creative writing programmes.

---

64 Roman Jakobson and Krystyna Pomorska, *Dialogues* (Cambridge: Cambridge University Press, 1983), p. 116ff; Lubomír Doležel, 'Structuralism of the Prague School', in *The Cambridge History of Literary Criticism*, ed. by Ramsey Selden (Cambridge: Cambridge University Press, 1993), 33–57 (pp. 38–39).

65 For more on this, see Graff, whose work recurs throughout this book.

On this last point, as I and others have previously noted elsewhere, much American metafictional writing from the 1960s onwards was born within and was co-productive of the context of Theory-saturated writing programmes. To reiterate briefly those previous observations, consider Adam Kelly's argument, building on the important work of Mark McGurl, that "post-war American fiction is inseparable from its institutional contexts" and that, therefore, the "academic context of the post-1960s English program, with its increasing incorporation of theory into the teaching of literature, may be just as materially relevant as the expansion of the creative writing program during that period".[66] While writers of a post-1960s generation were co-productive of such a Theory-intensive mode, subsequent authors, such as many of those appearing in this volume, write immanently to academic theoretical concerns, thereby further complicating a firm delineation between the critical and creative spheres. That said, there are geographical specificities to this argument that cannot be dismissed; the US creative writing programmes simply did not boom in the same way at the same time elsewhere, particularly in Europe (although we see a surge in the popularity of such programmes in the UK at the time of writing). Concomitantly, however, the theoretical paradigms that most strongly influenced literary studies in the global North over this period *were* broad in their reach. To restate this: the entanglement of a strand of contemporary fiction with Anglo-American institutional contexts must be seen through the context of writing programmes in the US but also through literary studies and Theory programmes elsewhere worldwide, of which many writers were graduates. It is more to the latter contexts than to the creative writing programmes that this book is devoted.

With the proliferation of access to a previously elevated space of social and cultural authority — the university — has come a shift in authorial practices. Certainly, a contemporary author of literary fiction can rely on an audience containing a sizable proportion of

---

66 Adam Kelly, 'Beginning with Postmodernism', *Twentieth Century Literature*, 57.3/4 (2011), 391–422 (p. 396); see also J.J. Williams, 'The Rise of the Academic Novel', *American Literary History*, 24.3 (2012), 561–89, http://dx.doi.org/10.1093/alh/ajs038; Mark McGurl, *The Program Era: Postwar Fiction and the Rise of Creative Writing* (Cambridge, MA: Harvard University Press, 2009); Martin Paul Eve, *Pynchon and Philosophy: Wittgenstein, Foucault and Adorno* (London: Palgrave Macmillan, 2014), pp. 1–2.

humanities graduates. This differs from earlier periods. For, around the turn of the twentieth century, as Günter Leypoldt has framed it, a mass readership was emerging, but not one that was entangled with or versed in a professional context of criticism: "by extending the domain of short-lived, low-prestige literary commodities, the emergence of a mass readership raised the practice space of professional writers and artists to a level of sacredness that had formerly been monopolized by more traditional forms of (religious, political) authority".[67] We might also add to Leypoldt's account that the professionalisation of literary criticism had not occurred at this time, before I.A. Richards, F.R. Leavis, Russian Formalism, and many others. To reformulate this: before the era of high modernism, in Leypoldt's history, mass readership with relative scarcity of published material (at least by twenty-first-century standards) and the even sparser canonisation of highbrow writing led to a consecration of a minority through a type of sacred enclave. As the turn to academic valuing of *avant-gard*ism took hold in the twentieth century, followed by the rise of mass higher education, literary fiction, as it came to be called, had to seek ever more ways to elevate itself compared to a professionalized academy and a reading populace that was versed in these ways of literary criticism. The adoption of the academy's own terminology is one such strategy for literary fiction that now contributes to what Michelle Lamont, Rita Felski, and many others have framed as the "legitimation crisis" of English, a core feature of which is an oscillation between professionalization/insulation and deprofessionalization/populism with the commensurate disciplinary de-centerings of evaluative criteria that this entails.[68]

This type of cross-fertilisation of Theory, the target referents of which will be especially apparent to those in the academic humanities but that may be lost on readers outside those spaces, is nowhere so clear as in Zadie Smith's novel, *On Beauty* (2005). Smith is a graduate of King's College, Cambridge, where she read English Literature,[69] and this work

---

67 Günter Leypoldt, 'Singularity and the Literary Market', *New Literary History*, 45.1 (2014), 71–88 (p. 79), http://dx.doi.org/10.1353/nlh.2014.0000.
68 Michèle Lamont, *How Professors Think: Inside the Curious World of Academic Judgment* (Cambridge, MA: Harvard University Press, 2009), pp. 70–79; Felski, p. 14.
69 Stephanie Merritt, 'She's Young, Black, British — and the First Publishing Sensation of the Millennium', *The Guardian*, 16 January 2000, http://www.theguardian.com/books/2000/jan/16/fiction.zadiesmith.

is equipped with a powerful arsenal of critiques of higher education with which it can discomfort the academic reader. Superficially, and like many other 'campus'-type novels, *On Beauty* finds comic relief in its academics; the pathetic anti-hero Howard Belsey (whose name lends the novel its Forsterian through-pun of *Howards End* [1910]) is petty, unproductive, malicious, hypocritical, unfaithful, privileged, socially awkward, ridiculous, and, above-all, pretentious. In such a mode, it would seem clear that Smith's critique is of academia, the well-trodden path of legitimating fiction by issuing *ad hominem* 'prejoinders' to yet-unmade critical points.

Yet Smith's novel showcases so much more self-awareness and literary-critical theoretical knowledge than this reading would credit. Its link to the academy is not superficial parody but is in fact woven into the narrative fabric of the text. For one, its title is derived from Elaine Scarry's well-known essay, 'On Beauty and Being Just'. This essay piece is concerned, as are the events within Smith's novel, with the ways in which the lived, emotional experience of 'beauty' has been steadily devalued by the reading practices of the university and a culture of increasing scientism in the study of aesthetics. This is, itself, situated within a longer lineage of the question of whether beauty and truth are synonymous. For Scarry, "beauty and truth are allied", which is not, she asserts, "a claim that the two are identical".[70] As Alexander Dick and Christina Lupton put it, "[t]he underlying aims of *On Beauty and Being Just* are first to unveil and then to counteract the institutional prohibitions that deprive intellectuals of an enriching language of beauty and render works of art and literature powerless as a moral resource in university life", an aim that intersects with the themes of Smith's novel.[71] *On Beauty*, then, cannot be read as anything but, in some senses, metafictional. It is a book that encodes a critique of the way in which the university studies

---

70 Elaine Scarry, 'On Beauty and Being Just' (presented at the Tanner Lectures on Human Values, Yale University, 1998), p. 38, http://tannerlectures.utah.edu/_documents/a-to-z/s/scarry00.pdf; indeed, others such as Seamus Heaney forcefully made this point: 'I rise to rise to the occasion / And not disgrace my art or nation / With verse that sings the old equation / Of beauty and truth.' Seamus Heaney, 'Anniversary Verse' (1982), *The Harvard Advocate*, http://theharvardadvocate.com/article/376/tribute-to-seamus-heaney.

71 Alexander Dick and Christina Lupton, 'On Lecturing and Being Beautiful: Zadie Smith, Elaine Scarry, and the Liberal Aesthetic', *ESC: English Studies in Canada*, 39.2 (2013), 115–37 (p. 117), http://dx.doi.org/10.1353/esc.2013.0032.

aesthetics, within its own aesthetic form. The cyclicality/paradox is clear, though: those most likely to read the text in the objectifying fashion of scientistic literary studies that Scarry criticizes will turn up this ethical critique through the inter-textual reference, even while discrediting the mode that produced such a reading.

In some ways, as I have already hinted, it is clear that the framework that I am constructing here shares an affinity with Eco's work on semiotics and the construction of the ideal or model reader. In various pieces and with a range of modifications, Eco essentially contends that "a text is a device conceived in order to produce its model reader".[72] The author, for Eco, must "foresee a model of the possible reader (hereafter Model Reader) supposedly able to deal interpretatively with the expressions in the same way as the author deals generatively with them".[73] Every text "is a syntactic-semantico-pragmatic device whose foreseen interpretation is part of its generative process".[74] While I do not here hold with Eco's characterisation of some texts as open and others as closed, I do think that the textual strategies that I detail throughout this volume are designed to interpellate and pre-empt/foresee a specific model reader who has informed access to academico-theoretical tropes through membership of an academic discourse community. This foresight, I contend, is used specifically to condition those readers down particular interpretative pathways.

This kind of 'Theory spotting' among the cadre of novelists that Nicholas Dames calls the "Theory generation" is the easy type of interaction to spot.[75] Nonetheless, some of the work in this book will necessarily take this as a starting point, if never the terminus. The more complex interrelated forms that are explored in this book are literary strategies of critique, legitimation (including a type of "market vanguardism", to appropriate Vincent Leitch's terminology), and discipline.[76] As with my initial reading of the *Tale of the Eloquent Peasant*,

---

72 Eco, 'Overinterpreting Texts', p. 64.
73 Umberto Eco, *The Role of the Reader: Explorations in the Semiotics of Texts* (Bloomington: Indiana University Press, 1997), p. 7.
74 *Ibid.*, p. 11.
75 Nicholas Dames, 'The Theory Generation', *n+1*, 14 (2012), https://nplusonemag.com/issue-14/reviews/the-theory-generation.
76 Vincent B. Leitch, *Literary Criticism in the 21st Century: Theory Renaissance* (London: Bloomsbury, 2014), p. 25.

it is the intersection of hermeneutics with a textual functionalism that here draws my attention.⁷⁷ In other words, as per the second introductory chapter below, the type of text with which I am most concerned here is not the novel that merely explicitly encodes its knowledge of the academy at the thematic level through narrative statements. It is the text that also functionally deploys such strategies for its narrative path in an interrelation of narratorial, metanarratorial, and formal components in the service of critique, legitimation, and discipline. These novels possess an awareness of what Harold Becker styles as the "tricks of the trade" of literary studies.⁷⁸

This forms the final pre-context for my argument in this book: that certain forms of metafiction, which are jostling with the academy for the legitimate right to critique, pre-empt academic reading techniques and thereby subvert the practices of university English. Taken together, these three areas of canon, metafiction, and academic reading practices form the background contexts to the narrative that I will more thoroughly plot throughout this work: namely that, in the contest for *critique*, specific works of metafiction seek *legitimation* over and above university English (and, in particular, criticism) and *discipline* the academy in order to achieve this. The question that I will now answer in the next chapter is: which works?

---

77 In at least some of the senses set out by Wolfgang Iser, 'The Reality of Fiction: A Functionalist Approach to Literature', *New Literary History*, 7.1 (1975), 7–38, http://dx.doi.org/10.2307/468276.

78 Howard Becker, *Tricks of the Trade: How to Think About Your Research While You're Doing It* (Chicago: Chicago University Press, 1998).

2. What, Where?

A few remarks on textual selection, then. To continue a theme from the preceding discussion of scientism and *On Beauty*, a central anxiety for academic literary studies in the contemporary era of scientific dominance pertains to the extent to which groupings, taxonomies, and classifications are methodologically derived and how far they help us to understand literary production. How sound are our methods of textual selection? Are there a set of scientific methods that could aid us in the selection of texts? These questions are important because, regardless of the fact that many defences of the humanities resist the language of science and 'methodology', there is a clear shared history between contemporary literary criticism and scientific practice that emerges from the historical philosophy of idealism. For, at least in the caricature of German idealism, philosophy told us that our senses had only primitive access to an underlying truth and that the structuring forces of our perceptual apparatus overrode that truth, reforming it in its own image.[1] There was more than really met the eye, the story went, and the phenomenon was different to the noumenon. As science went on to show that what we thought were solids are, in fact, mostly air and atoms, symptomatic reading too emerged as a method of 'unveiling' a deeper truth. The idea that textual things must never quite be what they seem in literary criticism is a direct result of this lineage. Some kind of desired access to a further essence or thing-in-itself pervades both science and literary studies to this day.

---

1 See Karl Ameriks, 'Introduction: Interpreting German Idealism', in *The Cambridge Companion to German Idealism*, ed. by Karl Ameriks (Cambridge: Cambridge University Press, 2000), pp. 1–17 for more on why this is a slight caricature.

How, then, do we select and exclude texts for analysis in a world of abundant and overflowing literary production? How do our groupings and classifications come about? Within the discipline, but also in the literary marketplace, we all invariably use and create such classifications as terminological shorthands; from the potential periodicities of (early to post) modern(isms) through to the generic descriptors of sci-fi and cli-fi. However, regardless of whether this is seen in the circular theorisations of genre theory or in bookshop sales categories, literary taxonomies are generated *post hoc* — formulated in the light of observation, rather (usually) than being hypothesized and then confirmed by observation.[2] This was recently described to me by one of my scientific colleagues as HARKing: Hypothesizing After Results are Known.[3] The logic here runs that a hypothesis should not be formulated by recourse to the data against which it will be tested, since this can only ever lead to a hypothesis being true. In statistical disciplines there are a set of procedures (usually a z-test or t-test) for deciding whether or not a sample (in our case, a novel) differs from or is likely part of a larger population (in this case, a genre). For a statistician, the first step would be to define a null hypothesis. The null hypothesis is a statement that we wish to disprove but that here might posit: there is no difference between this novel that we are 'measuring' (perhaps measured by various stylometric factors) and the generic corpus (perhaps 'science fiction'). The alternative hypothesis could be: this text is likely to be very different from the tropes found in science fiction novels. But statistical inferential methods could not be used, after the fact, to posit a different alternative hypothesis (say, 'this novel contains more terms pertaining to rural England than most science fiction novels'), since this would be fishing for an answer that we wanted to find and that we are predisposed to believe might be true if we have already seen the data. The other related methodological 'flaw', at least so far as those versed in scientific methods would see it, is that commonalities between texts are created by *ex post facto* subgroup analyses. Rather, say, than positing a causal

---

2   See, for example Stephen Neale, 'Questions of Genre', in *Film Theory: An Anthology*, ed. by Robert Stam and Toby Miller (Malden: Blackwell, 2000), pp. 157–78.

3   Norbert L. Kerr, 'HARKing: Hypothesizing After the Results Are Known', *Personality and Social Psychology Review*, 2.3 (1998), 196–217, http://dx.doi.org/10.1207/s15327957pspr0203_4.

relationship that might give predictive force to measurable stylometric and thematic contents across all works, classifications are first read out of a corpus and then the data are dredged to select only works that exhibit such characteristics. In other words, again, any 'hypothesis' or theory here contains all the data that could also confirm it; a type of circular 'p-hacking', as the practice is known (the term *p value* refers to a test of statistical significance that denotes 'significance' when there is a 95%–99% confidence that the null hypothesis is incorrect).

But literary studies is not, in most forms of its work, science, even if science can sometimes take 'fiction' to mean 'made up' or 'untrue' in a derogative sense. The methods used as critique in literary studies might not pass muster in a laboratory or a clinical trial, but they have resulted in startling critical insights and fruitful groupings of texts. This is probably because, although statistical methods can be applied to literary works through stylometry, literary works are unique and non-repeatable. The one-time classification of literary works from a single dataset is not always (or even usually) meant to answer future speculation but profitably to understand past production. Criticisms of a limited corpus aside, an accurately drawn taxonomy would have already used the entire available dataset and would, therefore, be using the only source that could either confirm or deny its truth. Accusations of HARKing and p-hacking are only valid within inferential sampling or predictive environments and so do not frequently apply to the work of literary studies. And yet, the nagging voice continues to point out, we do sample in literary studies. As ever, there is always too much to read. Certainly when it comes to close reading, we therefore resort to case studies that are supposed to function as metonymic/anecdotal stand-ins for the broader corpus (inferential samples). As computational, quantified and scientistic approaches to literary study continue to gain traction, I suspect that this methodological debate will only grow louder.

It is not my intention here to resolve these dilemmas through some kind of scientistic turn, which form a broader problem of systematisation for literary studies. I do, however, want to use this speculation as a springboard to consider reflexively the challenges of corpus selection. The first question, then, that I need to broach is: what are the benefits of a classification of 'academic' or 'anti-academic' novels for the argument I am making in this book? The second core challenge is the explicit methodology of how we schematise texts and how we justify the parameters of exclusion, particularly since I have raised the problems of gatekeeping and market determinism.

To begin with the latter component, it is easiest to demonstrate the types of fiction to which I am here referring by example and by negative exclusion. As stated from the outset, I am not, for instance, writing of campus novels in the traditional sense, which have well-documented histories from the 1950s onwards. These texts are certainly the historical predecessors of the contemporary novels that I claim exhibit an anxiety of academia, but their contexts of production and reception are so different to the broader span of contemporary fiction as to render comparison moot. However, even while some of the tropes of these early campus novels persist in the writings studied here (a few of the protagonists or narrators of the texts herein are professors, for example), the majority of the textual action in the type of books on which I focus takes place at sites distant from the university. In some instances, such as in the work of Sarah Waters, there is no formal connection to the university at all. Likewise, in the novels of Jennifer Egan, there is no specified university background setting, although Egan herself noted, after hearing an early version of this chapter, that she had originally intended a far-larger academic presence in *A Visit from the Goon Squad* (2010). What we see instead is an awareness of the practices of the university encoded into these novels' narrative structures. For the novels studied in this book plot a similar phenomenon to that described by Ben de Bruyn in the works of China Miéville as the "academic unconscious", in "books that take us *away from*, rather than *to*, the more or less familiar habitats of students and scholars that feature in campus novels".[4]

The type of reference that I primarily have in mind is sometimes fleeting, off-hand, sly, and, perhaps, demeaning. At once, such novels may imply the form of "pejorative poetics" that Kenneth Womack has charted, even while they are not, themselves, clearly "university fiction".[5] I am looking for fiction that is not about saving the university, but about

---

4 Ben de Bruyn, '"You Should Be Teaching": Creative Writing and Extramural Academics in *Perdido Street Station* and *Embassytown*', in *China Miéville: Critical Essays*, ed. by Caroline Edwards and Tony Venezia (London: Gylphi, 2015), pp. 159–83 (p. 160).
5 Womack, *passim*.

using the university in its own service. As Péter Székely has noted, it is not the *setting* of a text in a university, or the density of its references to academia, that make a text an 'academic novel'.⁶ It is, instead, a type of 'functional deployment'. This functional deployment of the academy is more likely to be seen in novels where the university is marginalised rather than central, I contend, because that is the logical outcome of the disciplinary and critical practices that these texts contain: to project the world that is wanted where the university has lost the competitive battle. The best way that I have found in which to characterise the type of interaction that I see and chart in this book is through the term 'incursion'; moments of seemingly aggressive territorial squabbling in which the creative and the critical fields make 'incursions' into each other's spaces.

Institutional Incursions

As an example of this type of incursion, take, for instance, the moment in Dana Spiotta's *Eat the Document* (2006) where the precocious young character, Josh Marshall, proclaims that he "[doesn't] need some academic hack's introduction to contextualise" a book. This is the type of statement that embodies the complex, double-layered conjunction of metafiction and the academy with which this book is concerned. This is because, on the one hand, it appears as a straight criticism: a character proclaiming his disdain for the university and its empowered community. In a slightly broader context, though, it appears very differently. Josh also states that he "hates books without indexes" and that he simply checks "the indexes to see what the reference points are and sometimes the bibliographies [...] Sometimes I only read the index". Nash scathingly replies to Josh: "[s]ome books of philosophy and social theory from independent small presses didn't have indexes until someone, perhaps an academic hack, added them later".⁷ At the isolated, sentence level, this appears to be a jab at the academy and probably a science vs. humanities, two-cultures-style rhetoric. With only a slightly broader frame, though, it appears that Josh uses the very

---

6   Székely.
7   Dana Spiotta, *Eat the Document: A Novel* (London: Picador, 2007), p. 45.

'reading-avoidance techniques' outlined above in Chapter One that are sometimes favoured by academics: he goes straight to the index to situate the work and to ascertain whether the rest of the book is worth reading within a limited economy of time.[8] Nash's further statement seems also to revalidate the academic stance. However, at the level of the whole text, the scene is once more complicated: Josh betrays the narrative of techno-liberation/idealism that he earlier espoused and turns tail to work for big business. Even if Josh appears to be aligned with the academia that he professes to be against, his eventual "smart cynicism", as Adam Kelly puts it, bodes poorly for the presentation of the university, however it is framed.[9] *Eat the Document* is clearly not a campus novel. This is far from claiming that it doesn't have anything to say about the university, entangled as it is with the politics of '68 and its aftermath.

However, there is a problem of exclusion here beyond the fact that I am not including unpublished works. Just because I am not dealing with the traditional campus novel does not mean that those texts are 'simple' with respect to the university. To proclaim that *Lucky Jim*, for instance, is 'just' a parody of post-war academic life is to do the novel a grave disservice. Likewise, Philip Roth's multi-layered *The Human Stain* (2000) is nominally set on a campus while playing a complex (but perhaps ultimately conservative) game of politics, speech, and race. John Barth's *Gilles Goat-Boy* (1966) is a campus novel, but strongly metafictional and postmodern: hardly a straightforward text. If these texts are also complex and worthy of scrutiny, then why exclude them? There are a conjunction of reasons, practical and theoretical, both pertaining to space.

In a first sense, there is limited space within a book volume. Feeling that many of the complexities of the campus novel have been dealt with elsewhere, they are excluded from this book not purely for reasons of complexity, but rather pragmatically.[10] Everyone has another text

---

[8] Although I promised not to delve too deeply into the campus novel, this is also the exact strategy used by Jim Dixon in Kingsley Amis's well-known text: the protagonist tries "to read as little as possible of any given book". Kingsley Amis, *Lucky Jim* (New York: Penguin, 1992), pp. 16–17.

[9] Adam Kelly, '"Who Is Responsible?": Revisiting the Radical Years in Dana Spiotta's *Eat the Document*', in *'Forever Young'?: The Changing Images of America*, ed. by Philip Coleman and Stephen Matterson (Heidelberg: Universitatsverlag Winter, 2012), pp. 219–30 (p. 222).

[10] See, in particular, Székely which is fairly comprehensive.

that features an academic in some way that I could add to this work. Likewise, everyone has a favourite cynical caricature of an academic in fiction.

On a second front, I have made a decision to investigate in this volume the ways in which university English has seeped into texts that seem far removed from the institutional spaces of the campus. This is undertaken to differing degrees in the various novels here studied but the purpose is to show how the ripples of the academy are often felt at greater literary-spatial distances than might initially be supposed. For this reason, in general and perhaps with the exception of Percival Everett (whose *Erasure* [2001] is too good a work to omit), I will generally exclude from discussion those texts that sit so close to their academic home as to seem embroiled in circular production and reception: written by academics for academics. Examples of this genre might include Stephen Grant's *A Moment More Sublime* (2014), which seems to have landed the author in hot water with his institution, Julie Schumacher's nonetheless marvellous epistolary *Dear Committee Members* (2014), Austin M. Wright's *Recalcitrance, Faulkner, and the Professors: A Critical Fiction* (1990), Adrian Jones Pearson's *Cow Country* (2015) (which caused a furore when Art Winslow suggested that this was Thomas Pynchon writing under a pseudonym), or Sheila M. Cronin's *The Gift Counselor: A Novel* (2014).[11] Indeed, current professional publications for those working in higher education are populated with articles on fiction that supposedly "capture truths about the sector", which apparently range from Thomas Hughes's *Tom Brown at Oxford* (1861), through Nabokov's *Pnin* (1957) and *Pale Fire* (1962), to Howard Jacobson's *Coming from Behind* (1983), and Linda Grant's *Upstairs at the Party* (2014).[12] These texts have much to say about the university and are certainly metafictional. Nabokov, in particular, can be said to be drawing attention to the "parasitic nature of criticism", as Laura Frost put it in the aforementioned *Times*

---

11   Alison Flood, 'Lecturer's Campus Novel Gets Black Marks from College Employer', *The Guardian*, 21 November 2014, http://www.theguardian.com/books/2014/nov/21/lecturer-novel-college-employer-stephen-grant-richmond-on-thames; Alex Shephard, 'The Hunt for a Possible Pynchon Novel Leads to a Name', *The New Republic*, 12 September 2015, http://www.newrepublic.com/article/122802/thomas-pynchon-didnt-write-cow-country-aj-perry-probably-did.

12   John Sutherland and others, 'This Is Your Life', *Times Higher Education*, 20 November 2014, pp. 34–40; Michelle Dean, 'Campus Novels: Six of the Best Books about University Life', *The Guardian*, 29 August 2016, https://www.theguardian.com/books/2016/aug/29/campus-novels-best-books-university-life.

Higher Education article. At the same time, though, she acknowledges that "academics are at once the novel's target and its most devoted followers", thus lending credence to my exclusionary logic. These texts are more insular in production and reception than the other books from which I here draw insights.

These three elements, then, serve as the core touchstones that group the works discussed in this book: they enact more distant critiques of the university; they attempt to discipline the academy; and they have an 'anxiety of academia'/legitimation to some degree. I do not have an overarching neologism to coin for such works but instead see the grouping as fluid. I have clustered these works for the purposes of analysis only so that, when their affinity is noted and has served its purpose, the binding may disintegrate again into its three constituent parts.

As a closing remark before mapping the route by which this book will make its argument, it is worth pointing out the issues of geographical specificity that must be considered when talking about 'the university'. The academy, its academics, its disciplines, and its practices vary from country to country, and even from institution to institution, around the world.[13] In fact, it is a nominal irony that there is no universal university to which all abstracted remarks could be addressed. As with the creative writing programmes, much of the American system differs greatly from its European cousins, for instance, and the British system of funding at this time is radically opposed to that in, say, Germany. In line with this and to ensure a sensible scale of bounding, the particular 'flavour' of the academy that is studied here is the Anglo-American university. That said, the novels treated in this work span American, South American, and British authors and often deal with the globalised nature of twenty-first-century higher education, even if their notion of 'the university' is particular. In this book I will argue, on occasion, that the specific setting has consequences for the treatment of the university. I also, in this work, am dealing with novels as a deliberate selective choice. There is surely also a study to be had on this topic with respect to twentieth-century drama. It was, after all, Samuel Beckett who most famously turned the word "critic" into an insult in *Waiting for Godot* (1953) while Sarah

---

13 Although, notably, even in Bolaño's text it is the Anglo-American university that comes under critique.

Kane's sadistic torturer, Tinker, in *Cleansed* (1998) is the character most obsessed with meaning-making and interpretation: "[y]ou know what that means?", he asks; "I think I — Misunderstood", he says; "I'm not really a doctor", he confesses with a hint of PhD envy.[14]

From here this book is structured into six further chapters and a conclusion. This respectively follows the pattern of two chapters each on critique, legitimation, and discipline. By the conclusion of this book, I will have reversed the order of this formulation to contend that texts discipline the academy so that they may find themselves legitimated to work critically. Until that time, however, I take the inverse pattern to build the argument. Following this introductory section, the next chapter examines the ways in which certain authors invoke the aesthetic value judgements of the academy with respect to literary fiction in order to situate their own work within various canons. In the case of Chapter Three this centres on Tom McCarthy and the lineages of modern and postmodern fiction that are implied, surfaced, and marketed by his extra-mural writings and his literary sales campaigns. In charting this lineage, I demonstrate the ways in which McCarthy's novel *C* (2010) takes on the traditional preserve of the academy, performing the act of self-canonisation that university English usually considers its own right. This is, I suggest, an attempt by the novel to pre-master its own conditions of receptive possibility. Of course, it would be absurd to suggest that *C* is the only text to take on such a task. To claim a lineage is a well-worn tactic of literary marketing. The degree to which *C* plays this game, however, within highbrow discussions of literary history and genre affinity makes it an ideal opening for this work, a specificity from which broader conclusions about this widespread method of patrilineage can be drawn. It is also significant because *C* is not a text that mentions the university in any prominent way. This will give a better sense of the type of incursion of the academy and fiction into each other's labour spaces that I am trying to demonstrate.

Having explored notions of aesthetic critique as a function of metafiction that deals with the academy, the fourth chapter primarily examines Roberto Bolaño's *2666* (2004), a novel that can be situated,

---

14 Sarah Kane, 'Cleansed', in *Complete Plays* (London: Methuen, 2001), pp. 105–51 (pp. 122, 146, 147); I owe this thinking primarily to Dan Reballato, '*Cleansed*', 2016, http://www.danrebellato.co.uk/spilledink/2016/2/24/cleansed.

aesthetically, within the traditions of utopian fiction and the North American encyclopaedic, postmodern novel. This chapter also contends, however, that Bolaño's novel is exemplary of a type of didacticism that cloaks its mechanism behind an overloaded structure of metafiction. One of the explicit targets of this didacticism is the neoliberal university that, in *2666*, is structurally twinned with the police department and is thus complicit in the novel's femicides. This chapter suggests the ways in which Bolaño's novel attempts to perform a type of ethical critique of the academy while also outlining its mode of crypto-didacticism: a political critique. Taking theoretical cues from Theodor W. Adorno and Pierre Bourdieu, I read *2666* as a metafictional work that signals its own desire to teach, thereby once more showing how the space of critique comes to be inhabited by certain types of novel.

The fifth chapter begins the section on legitimation and examines Percival Everett's riotously funny novel, *Erasure*. While *Erasure* is the text with the clearest feel of a 'campus novel' in this work, I here examine its aspects of postmodern play in relation to a legitimation function above academia. This centres around notions of sincerity and irony, as well as the mirror images within the text that tend to pre-empt an academic critique. By demonstrating an awareness of, but disdain for, the theoretical paradigms and strategies for critiquing race, *Erasure* becomes a novel that legitimates itself to speak critically about such matters, even while avoiding propagandist communication.

The sixth chapter examines the recent work of Jennifer Egan, and most notably *A Visit from the Goon Squad*. This novel, which Egan originally intended to feature an academic specifically pontificating on the "great rock 'n' roll pauses", is a text populated by a disproportionately high number of, often unfulfilled, postgraduate researchers: "I'm in the PhD program at Berkeley", proclaims Mindy; "Joe, who hailed from Kenya [...] was getting his PhD in robotics at Columbia"; "Bix, who's black, is spending his nights in the electrical-engineering lab where he's doing his PhD research"; while only Rebecca "was an academic star". In this text, academia seems a place of misery, of "harried academic slaving", and, ultimately, of "immaturity and disastrous choices".

In this book's penultimate chapter, and starting the final section on 'discipline', I note that although, in some ways, Sarah Waters's *Affinity* (1999) looks akin to historiographic metafiction, M.-L. Kohlke has persuasively argued that the text is more accurately dubbed "new(meta)realism", a mode that demonstrates the exhausted potential of the form.[15] This chapter suggests that genre play and a meta-generic mode, dubbed taxonomography, might be a further helpful description for the mechanism through which Waters's novel effects its twists and pre-empts the expectations of an academic discourse community. This reading exposes Waters's continuing preoccupation with the academy but also situates her writing within a broader spectrum of fiction that foregrounds genre as a central concern. Ultimately, this chapter asks whether Waters's novel can, itself, be considered as a text that disciplines its own academic study in the way that it suggests that the academy has become, once more, blind to class.

The final chapter, before this book's conclusion, examines the works of Ishmael Reed, with a particular focus on his most recent novel, *Juice!* (2011). Honing in on the representation of the academic journal *Critical Inquiry* that appears in this text, I argue that the critical representation of scholarly communication paradigms is at once a comment upon narrow circulation and at the same time a critique of over-reading. Taking a paradigm of 'over-reading' to represent incommensurate output compared to authorial input, I note that Reed's critique seems to preclude academic discourse through a triangulation effect in which it becomes impossible to speak. And yet, I finally close, academics continue to write. It may be, I argue, that while we perceive strong links and feedback circuits between university English and the fiction it studies, these loops of behavioural discipline seem to have fewer real-world effects on practice than we might assume.

---

15   Kohlke, M.-L., 'Into History through the Back Door: The "Past Historic" in *Nights at the Circus* and *Affinity*', *Women: A Cultural Review*, 15 (2004), 153–66 (p. 156), http://doi.org/10.1080/0957404042000234015.

PART II: CRITIQUE

3. Aesthetic Critique

It is an often overlooked facet of early university English programmes in the United States that there was greater agreement between academicians on the texts to be taught than on the very rationale for the study of literature. As Gerald Graff has demonstrated, while some felt in the early period that literature could not even *be* taught and simply stood alone as art, those who wanted to professionalise the discipline began prescribing set lists of texts for examination. Surprisingly, as Graff notes, there was consensus on these texts, mostly because this gave the appearance of a coherent object of study for university English, even if this coherence was artificially constructed.[1]

Since that time, Marxist, postcolonial, queer, and feminist schools, among others, have historicised and challenged the value judgements of the academy, culminating in the so-called 'canon wars' of the 1980s. However, as above, the charge persists to this day that the archive consulted by academics studying contemporary fiction remains partial and non-representative; an accusation that has by now been laid at the door of almost every taxonomic grouping, whether national or periodic, and one that continues to induce anxieties of method.[2] This inadequacy is not just because the 'archive' of contemporary fiction

---

1 Graff, pp. 98–100. Graff does point out two features of this that are worth noting: 1) there were two canons, one for breadth and one for depth; and 2) although a canon was prescribed, this prescription could not dictate its teaching and reception; for more on the situation with respect to the homogeneity of contemporary syllabi, see Joe Karaganis and others, 'The Open Syllabus Project', 2016, http://explorer.opensyllabusproject.org.
2 See, for instance, Warner Berthoff, 'Ambitious Scheme', *Commentary*, 44.4 (1967), 110–14.

is ever-growing and reflexively self-modifying, which is true of all archives.³ It is also because this archive is intentionally limited for practical reasons alongside gatekeeping market forces; there is simply too much to read and, for the university, too much to study. As a result, publishers exclude and select, and the academy prioritises and focuses. In the university, these practicalities are best demonstrated in what Ted Underwood has called a "disciplinary investment in discontinuity" where it can be seen that English studies falls back on descriptive period movements (romanticism, modernisms, postmodernisms) from which represented figures are elevated as canonical exemplars (Wordsworth, Joyce, Eliot, Pynchon, Morrison, etc.).⁴

While this periodisation balances the demand for synchronic understanding (the way a text works internally) against diachronic historical development (literary history), the result of this selective periodisation is that from the reservoir of hundreds-of-thousands of published texts, academic value is conferred upon relatively few works, with comparatively little distinction between institutions' taught canons.⁵ As Franco Moretti frames this, "if we set today's canon of nineteenth-century British novels at two hundred titles […] they would still only be about *0.5 per cent* of all published novels".⁶ Yet ever since the first contemporary literature courses were taught in the 1890s at Columbia and Yale, aspersions have been cast about the value and method of literary studies for ascribing worth. As a result, we sit within a present shaped by the "path dependency" of periodisation and/or national literatures.⁷ Anxieties about classification and historical/future value certainly continue to sit at the core of the discipline's identity. A central part of what university English does in its writing and teaching is to discuss and theorize canon formation and literary history.

In this chapter, I examine the ways in which two novels — predominantly Tom McCarthy's 2010 work, *C*, and as a correlative text with less emphasis, Mark Z. Danielewski's *House of Leaves* (2000) — respond to these ongoing debates about canonisation, generic

---

3   For more on this, see Eaglestone.
4   Ted Underwood, *Why Literary Periods Mattered: Historical Contrast and the Prestige of English Studies* (Stanford: Stanford University Press, 2013), p. 170.
5   Even if there is no guarantee that a homogeneous canon will be taught uniformly.
6   Moretti, *Distant Reading*, p. 66.
7   Levine, p. 59.

taxonomies, and questions of value that are central to university English and literary criticism.[8] There are three interlinked points of argument that I seek to make here. The first is that novels like *C* and *House of Leaves* pre-anticipate their own academic and market reception as 'literary fiction' and attempt to place themselves within various aesthetic lineages that confer value, usually through intertextual reference.[9] In McCarthy's case, I will argue, these intertextual affiliations comprise a lineage of modern and postmodern fiction, even when the text is ambivalent about its own relationship to these forms. In this chapter, I particularly focus on the latter camp of postmodern influence since it has been relatively under-studied to date in McCarthy's work. While, then, McCarthy has been read as a "forensic scientist of modernism", I here am more focused upon how these works become 'histories of the present' in terms of literary genre, within a broader intertextual frame that stretches into the postmodern period.[10]

Secondly, this chapter teases out the methods by which these types of intertextual referential strategies functionally act in ways similar to the academic discipline of literary criticism with respect to value

---

[8] The most recent tract on which is Boxall, *The Value of the Novel*; but see also Helen Small, *The Value of the Humanities* (Oxford: Oxford University Press, 2013); *Humanities in the Twenty-First Century Beyond Utility and Markets*, ed. by Eleonora Belfiore and Anna Upchurch (London: Palgrave Macmillan, 2013); Michael Bérubé, 'Value and Values', in *The Humanities, Higher Education, and Academic Freedom: Three Necessary Arguments*, by Michael Bérubé and Jennifer Ruth (New York: Palgrave Macmillan, 2015), pp. 27–56.

[9] The way in which intertexts function is never straightforward and a range of theories have been advanced. I signal this here since some readers may object that intertextuality does not only affiliate but may also be a form of slaughter of antecedents. See Linda Hutcheon, *A Theory of Parody: The Teachings of Twentieth-Century Art Forms* (New York: Methuen, 1985), p. 37; Gérard Genette, *Palimpsests: Literature in the Second Degree*, trans. by Channa Newman and Claude Doubinsky (Lincoln: University of Nebraska Press, 1997); Michael Riffaterre, *Semiotics of Poetry* (Bloomington: Indiana University Press, 1978); Julia Kristeva, *Semeiotike. Recherches pour une sémanalyse* (Paris: Seuil, 1969); Roland Barthes, 'An Introduction to the Structural Analysis of Narrative', trans. by Lionel Duisit, *New Literary History*, 6.2 (1975), 237–72, http://dx.doi.org/10.2307/468419; Harold Bloom, *Poetry and Repression* (New Haven: Yale University Press, 1976); Harold Bloom, *The Anxiety of Influence: A Theory of Poetry* (Oxford: Oxford University Press, 1979); Ulrich Broich, 'Intertextuality', in *International Postmodernism*, ed. by Hans Bertens and Douwe Fokkema (Amsterdam: John Benjamins, 1997), pp. 249–55.

[10] Justus Nieland, 'Dirty Media: Tom McCarthy and the Afterlife of Modernism', *MFS: Modern Fiction Studies*, 58.3 (2012), 569–99 (p. 570), http://dx.doi.org/10.1353/mfs.2012.0058.

ascription and canon formation. In the case of *C* and *House of Leaves*, this manifests itself most notably in the works' allusive self-placements within authority-conferring canons — even when the placement is ambiguous — but also through an implied process of research. In other words, although *C* does not contain overt depictions of academics or universities, its knowing nods to Freud, Derrida, Woolf, Pynchon, DeLillo, and Ballard — alongside its implied archive of historical research and the author's journalistic writings on high modernism — signal that the novel is, at least in part, about the classificatory history of twentieth-century literature. Traditionally, discussing this classificatory history has been the role of the academy but it is also clearly encoded within novels such as *C* and *House of Leaves*.

Thirdly and finally, then, in its network of references I will argue that *C* might be seen as a literary-historical novel; a text that charts the death of realism, the exhaustion of modernism, and the ongoing struggle to classify that which lies beyond the postmodern. With its high-academic, 'difficult' reference points, its implied (but ultimately empty) historically researched archive and its patrilineal authority-conferring self-situation, *C* becomes a text that reveals a quasi-academic process of canonisation through a mirror imprint of university English. I demonstrate these phenomena through a tripartite analysis of *C* as a work of literary history, moving then to explore the under-examined postmodern intertexts for the novel, and closing with some remarks on canon and authority.

McCarthy and Novels About the History of Literature

By way of background, Tom McCarthy is a London-based writer of literary fiction best known for the three novels *Remainder* (2005), *C*, and *Satin Island* (2015), with the latter two of these texts both shortlisted for the Man Booker Prize. He is also the author of a number of less well-known pieces, notably *Men in Space* (2007) and a work of literary criticism, *Tintin and the Secret of Literature* (2006). Furthermore, alongside Simon Critchley, McCarthy is responsible for the founding of the 'Necronautical Society' and has authored a number of 'General Secretary's reports' to the society — *Navigation Was Always a Difficult*

Art (2002) and *Calling all Agents* (2003) — although the precise purpose of this *avant-garde* organisation-of-two is purposefully never specified.[11]

Importantly for my argument here, though, McCarthy has, in recent times, begun to position himself as that rarest of intellectual (although specifically not academic) types: a popular literary critic. Writing on *Ulysses* (1922) and Ballard's *Crash* (1973) in the *London Review of Books* in 2014, as he did on Toussaint in 2010 when *C* was published and on Steven Hall in 2007 to coincide with *Men in Space*, McCarthy makes a concerted effort to showcase his intellectual erudition in public.[12] This would seem to be part of a calculated strategy to tie in with the publication of his new works. For example, the sudden outpouring of *LRB* pieces in mid-to-late 2014, after a four-year hiatus, appears, to the cynically-minded, to coincide with the publication of *Satin Island*, a novel that is of note to this study since it contains apparent references to specific sociologists, such as Sarah Thornton, alongside the philosophers Deleuze and Badiou.[13]

It is not just a general erudition that is at stake here, though. McCarthy's populist criticism, usually on highbrow literary fiction, affiliates his non-academic authorial presence with the high literature of the modernist and postmodernist schools favoured on difficult university syllabi, an aspect that can be seen in his 2015 *Guardian* article, again on Joyce.[14] Unlike, say, the fusion of Homeric and biblical intertexts as canonising sources in *Ulysses*, however, McCarthy's use of modernist and postmodernist referents is not just designed, as Joyce once claimed of his own novel, to keep the professors busy, but to supplant them.[15] Although McCarthy's affiliation with modernist and postmodernist canons is neither straightforwardly one of lineage nor

---

11 I am grateful to David Winters for our ongoing work together on a co-authored article about McCarthy, from which parts of this background sketch derive.

12 Tom McCarthy: '"*Ulysses*" and Its Wake', *London Review of Books*, 19 June 2014, pp. 39–41; 'Writing Machines', *London Review of Books*, 18 December 2014, pp. 21–22; 'Stabbing the Olive', *London Review of Books*, 11 February 2010, pp. 26–28; 'Straight to the Multiplex', *London Review of Books*, 1 November 2007, pp. 33–34.

13 *Idem*, *Satin Island* (London: Jonathan Cape, 2015), pp. 21–22, 30.

14 *Idem*, 'The Death of Writing — If James Joyce Were Alive Today He'd Be Working for Google', *The Guardian*, 7 March 2015, http://www.theguardian.com/books/2015/mar/07/tom-mccarthy-death-writing-james-joyce-working-google.

15 For more on Joyce and the canon, see Robert Alter, *Canon and Creativity: Modern Writing and the Authority of Scripture* (New Haven: Yale University Press, 2000).

of homage, it nonetheless generates an authorial presence with a prefabricated canon lineage behind him, an aspect that almost certainly applies to other public-intellectual writers who deploy such marketing techniques, such as Will Self. McCarthy's identity projection then becomes the author-critic; the figure who is not an academic but who can demonstrably play that game, while choosing to write fiction.[16]

Despite the sense that McCarthy might be one-upping the academy and other centres of artistic authority by supplanting their function, his early career has been blessed with praise from those very university spaces in what almost amounts to a pre-canonisation.[17] His first novel, *Remainder*, famously originally published by Metronome before being picked up by Alma, was deemed to be "[o]ne of the great English novels of the past ten years" by no less a figure than Zadie Smith. In an introduction to a recent edition, McKenzie Wark called the text a "remarkable novel" and read its narrative as one charting historical shifts in mimesis.[18]

To some extent, though, this aura of academic canonisation comes about because McCarthy's works trade in the same themes as literary criticism. For instance, in *Remainder* the narrator is significantly injured in some kind of never-specified accident but receives a large compensatory sum, on condition that he never speaks of the accident again. However, the protagonist of the novel becomes obsessed with paradoxically trying to recapture and re-enact his pre-accident experience of a time when he felt authentic: "it was a performance [...] to make my movements come across as more authentic".[19] Although *Remainder*'s protagonist has an almost psychopathic level of emotional detachment (in common with most of McCarthy's narrators), the focus here on *techne* and mimesis

---

16 As I pointed out in the introduction, it is also notable that the canonical modernist period represented a high point for the author-critic paradigm. See McDonald, p. 81.
17 The acknowledgements in *Satin Island*, which deal with the institutional contexts within which the novel was written, might even be considered parodic, poking fun at art residencies. Also, at the 2011 conference on McCarthy's work, Simon Critchley was somewhat disparaging of an attempt to classify the novels in academic terms, stating that the matter was "of absolutely no interest to him". These two factors at once demonstrate the curious and ambiguous relationship that McCarthy has to institutional settings.
18 Tom McCarthy, *Remainder* (London: Alma, 2015).
19 *Ibid.*, p. 15.

as a path to authenticity, achieved by performance (and presumably also an implied metatextual act of writing) is presented as therapeutic. The protagonist continually 're-enacts' situations in the hope of feeling a pure, unmediated, un-enacted experience. The protagonist seeks literary realism.

Yet representational mimesis gets a bad rap in *Remainder*. It is associated with a detached psychopathy: the protagonist is not upset by the fact that cats are dying in his re-enactments at a "loss rate of three every two days" (140), a euphemism that resonates with the banal yet evil statistical language of industrialized genocide. The mimetic impulse of the protagonist of *Remainder* turns out to be an artistic socio-pathology engendered by a neuro-pathology. Reading in this light, *Remainder* becomes a novel that is about the history of representational art; it works to chart a generic and stylistic history, aiming to bury the realist forms (mimesis seeking authenticity) that are depicted as pathological. *Remainder* can be read as a novel that is *about* literary-historical criticism and one that presents implicit value judgements on various historical forms of the novel.

At least part of this technique of plotting a literary history is extended within McCarthy's later novel, *C*. I will now turn to read in more detail some of the ways in which McCarthy's later novel signals itself in these literary traditions through an analysis of its prose stylistics; through an examination of the way in which text situates itself in a lineage of historical fiction; and through a range of intertexts that strengthen this affiliation.

Quasi-Historical Fictions and Implied Archives

Although it has elicited mixed critical responses, *C* tells the life story of Serge Carrefax, a character born at the turn of the industrial (and interrelated technological) revolution.[20] A figure blessed with analytical rather than emotional intelligence, Carrefax represents the blossoming and abrupt death of technological utopianism. After all, as the text notes

---

20   For such a mixed review, see Peter Carty, 'C, By Tom McCarthy', *The Independent*, 14 August 2010, http://www.independent.co.uk/arts-entertainment/books/reviews/c-by-tom-mccarthy-2049878.html, which notes that "*C* contains numerous framing passages to underline the text's concerns with signals, codes and transmission, and they can become obtrusive".

with supreme irony, there is a belief in Serge's lifetime regarding war that "the more we can chatter with one another, the less likely that sort of thing [war] becomes".[21] C certainly wades deeply in the tradition of postmodern irony.[22]

Like *Remainder*, though, *C* is also a novel that focuses upon a *literary history* through knowingly futile generic re-performances of paradigms such as experimental modernism. In fact, it is partly that *C* continues the project of *Remainder* that makes its re-performance of high modernism problematic; for what would be the difference between the damaged protagonist of *Remainder* seeking to recover a past realism and McCarthy's recovery of modernism in *C*? It is clear that, when read in the context of *Remainder*, *C* cannot be seen as a text that sincerely re-performs modernism any more than it re-performs realism. For the latter genre, this challenge is encoded in the novel's near-plotless structure and emotionally devoid characters; Carrefax "sees things flat" and has a "perceptual apparatus" that refuses "point-blank to be twisted into the requisite configuration" for realism.[23] Yet, McCarthy knows that, by spurning the realist paradigm, his novel will be read in terms of '-modernisms'. Pre-anticipating this reception, McCarthy gives signals that the text should not be read as a re-performance of modernism either. In terms of modernism, Justus Nieland, for example, notes that *C* "stands not as the empty resuscitation of an *avant-garde* idiom but as its crypt, as a way of presiding over modernism's death by reenacting it traumatically, by lingering in the remains of its most fecund catastrophes, which are also those of the twentieth-century itself".[24] This is nowhere better borne out in the text than in the moment when Serge's sister Sophie dies, most likely by suicide of chemical ingestion. Her death occurs in the laboratory, the site of (high modernist and *avant-garde*) *experiment*. In this way, like *Remainder*, and when coupled with McCarthy's own extra-fictional engagements with literary history,

---

21 Tom McCarthy, *C* (London: Jonathan Cape, 2010), p. 48.
22 This type of irony most famously appears in the works of Thomas Pynchon. See for instance, Thomas Pynchon, *V.* (London: Vintage, 1995), p. 245, where the author notes of the numbers killed in the Herero genocide that "[t]his is only 1 per cent of six million, but still pretty good".
23 McCarthy, *C*, p. 39.
24 Nieland, p. 570.

C starts to become a historical fiction of sorts; a historical fiction about aesthetics and literature that signals its own generic placement.

If C should be considered as a history of literary genre, though, then it must also be compared to and contrasted with other forms of the historical novel. When thinking of historical fiction, even if the historical subject is literary history, the subtitle of Walter Scott's most well-known novel, *Waverley* (1814), still forms the basis of a particular conception. The phrase "'*Tis Sixty Years Since*" is the grounding for the rules of the annually awarded Walter Scott Prize for Historical Fiction. This prestigious (and relatively lucrative) award stipulates that the temporal setting of the submitted novel must be at least sixty years prior to the time of writing. In turn, this rule is based on the assumption that, at current human lifespans and levels of productivity, this interval will prove sufficient to exclude the author's direct experience, as a mature adult, of the period in question.

This 'sixty-year rule' is undoubtedly a definition with which many readers would have sympathy and within which the vast majority of texts that we consider 'historical fiction' fall. It is, however, hardly the only conception. For instance, the Historical Novel Society, a UK-based self-confessed 'campaigning group' that was formed to champion historical fiction, puts the figure at fifty years but also includes works "written by someone who was not alive at the time of those events (who therefore approaches them only by research)".[25]

It is also the case that, as with any taxonomy of literature, a cluster of characteristics are expected of the historical novel that are not purely to do with its subject period. For Sarah Johnson, the aesthetics of writing and parameters of reading are generically codified. As she puts it:

> [t]he genre also has unofficial rules that authors are expected to follow. To persuade readers that the story could really have happened (and perhaps some of it did), authors should portray the time period as accurately as possible and avoid obvious anachronisms. The fiction and the history should be well balanced, with neither one overwhelming the other.[26]

---

25 Richard Lee, 'Defining the Genre', *Historical Novel Society*, 2014, http://historicalnovelsociety.org/guides/defining-the-genre.
26 Sarah L. Johnson, 'Historical Fiction — Masters of the Past', *Bookmarks Magazine*, 2006, http://www.bookmarksmagazine.com/historical-fiction-masters-past/sarah-l-johnson.

Likewise, while noting that historical fiction is frequently more of a meditation on the present than on the past, Jerome de Groot shares Johnson's formulaic characteristics of the historical novel:

> [h]istorical fiction works by presenting something familiar but simultaneously distant from our lives. Its world must have heft and authenticity — it must feel right — but at the same time, the reader knows that the novel is a representation of something that is lost, that cannot be reconstructed but only guessed at. This dissonance, it seems to me, lies at the heart of historical fiction and makes it one of the most interesting genres around.[27]

From these observations, a series of commonly-held characteristics of the historical novel can be roughly, but fairly, schematised thus: relative periodisation (the sixty-year rule); writing beyond experience (research); accuracy, heft and credibility (generic conventions); and a suspension of disbelief at enclosed epistemologies of the past (dissonance).

C certainly fulfils some of the criteria traditionally ascribed to 'historical fiction' in the way in which it both plays with genre and represents its historical periods. Regardless of whether one takes the fifty-year or sixty-year rule, the setting of McCarthy's novel in the early twentieth century is well outside of this banding. This even holds if, as I do, one considers McCarthy's work to be a literary-historical fiction (i.e. a text about the history of literary forms). For most, if not all, of the referent texts for his (deliberately failing) re-performance of modernism (and even postmodernism), to which I will turn shortly, are now over fifty or sixty years old. However, in other areas of McCarthy's text, the definitional elements of historical fiction are less pronounced. Consider, for instance, McCarthy's research base for the text and the "accuracy, heft and credibility" of this research.

One of the most significant aspects of the research base for C is the text's cryptic references to the plane of Lieutenant Paul Friedrich 'Fritz' Kempf, against whom the protagonist, Serge, fights in an aerial battle in the later part of the novel. Kempf, a recipient of the iron cross, had the words *'kennscht mi nocht'* painted on the wings of his plane, a fact that C accurately re-conveys, and which, roughly translated, means 'do

---

27 Jerome de Groot, 'Walter Scott Prize for Historical Fiction: The New Time-Travellers', *The Scotsman*, 18 June 2010, http://www.scotsman.com/lifestyle/books/walter-scott-prize-for-historical-fiction-the-new-time-travellers-1-813580.

you still remember me?'.²⁸ This slogan on the aircraft wing is, however, the *only* piece of identifying information that C gives to signal that the enemy pilot is Kempf, who is not a particularly well-known fighter ace.

That said, from this single reference we can begin to dig into the research base and archive. Kempf was a member of squadron Jasta B (which was originally called Jasta 2) and, later, Jastaschule I and was credited with four victories over the course of the First World War, thereby narrowing the potential date for Serge's encounter with him to four specific moments.²⁹ Two of Kempf's takedowns were of Sopwith Camel aeroplanes (on 20 October 1917 and 8 May 1918 respectively) and one a Sopwith Pup (5 June 1917), both types of single-seater biplane, but a victory is also logged to him on either 29 or 30 April 1917 against a two-seater plane (a BE2e).³⁰ At no point in the war that I have managed to find, however, did Kempf down an RE 8 aircraft (of the type in which Serge flies).

Depending on one's level of inclination, it is possible to trace this further into the archive. Given that Serge has a conversation with Walpond-Skinner "one afternoon in January", when he is preparing to lay tunnel mines, it seems probable that the engagement at which Serge fights could be either the Battle of Vimy Ridge (9 to 12 April 1917) or the Battle of Messines (7 to 14 June 1917).³¹ Kempf was in Jasta B between 4 April 1917 and 17 October 1917 (i.e. for both battles) and then again from January 1918 to 18 August 1918. He was, conversely, in Jastaschule I between 17 October 1917 and January 1918 and then from 18 August 1918 to 11 November 1918.³² Even assuming that Kempf was not Serge's sole adversary, or that he was not correctly attributed with shooting down Serge's plane, I have not been able to track down any known victories against RE8 aircraft from 104 squadron by anyone in Jasta B.

As with all historical fiction, however, it is unwise to mistake the aesthetic use of historical detail for a correlation with reality. At some point in all historical fiction the connection with reality is severed.

---

28 McCarthy, *C*, p. 173.
29 Greg VanWyngarden, *Jagdstaffel 2 Boelcke: Von Richthofen's Mentor* (Oxford: Osprey, 2007), pp. 6, 90.
30 Norman L.R. Franks, Frank W. Bailey, and Rick Duiven, *The Jasta Pilots* (London: Grub Street, 1996), p. 179; VanWyngarden, p. 39.
31 McCarthy, *C*, p. 166.
32 Franks, Bailey, and Duiven, p. 179.

It seems most probable that *C*'s dogfight is not based upon any one specific account, although the use of Kempf rather than the 'Red Baron' (von Richthofen) would narrow McCarthy's potential sourcings. This technique, however, also encourages a readerly hunt for a factual underpinning through the curious specificity of its detail. After all, once a reader has linked *'kennsch mi nocht'* to Kempf the next step is to ask what else the novel might not be saying. Pinpointing such data is not, however, the purpose of this historical digression. It is rather to show, by example, that *C*'s aesthetics and content presuppose, or at least insinuate, the presence of an archive, regardless of whether one exists. In terms of its research-base and its accuracy, *C implies an archive* by splicing true *but obscure* details (*kennscht mi nocht*) into a fictional world of quasi-facticity. The fact that this cryptically sown detail of the wing insignia is also a statement *about memory* ('do you still remember me?') and therefore intertwined with the nature of history (historiography) transforms the detail into a *clue* for the reader to decode. The level of specific historical detail here — that the reader is given the markings of one precise plane as Serge's foe — invites a type of paranoid reading that the text must ultimately frustrate. This is not a difference of type or kind to other historical fiction, which always relies on such a withdrawal from fact, but rather a difference of degree as to where a reading becomes 'paranoid', a difference of placement in where the suspension of disbelief is triggered. When this type of historical thinking is applied to McCarthy's literary history, the significance of the holes in the fiction's archive becomes clear. The fact that the history of the text is not fully rooted in a verifiable past, even while the novel signals that there might be a factual underpinning, runs in parallel to McCarthy's relationship with modernism and postmodernism. The signposts are there but the pathway from past to present is blocked.

McCarthy's is hardly the only text in the contemporary period to toy with an implied archive within a framework of genre play and, perhaps perversely, it is one of the texts that does this less overtly and academically than others. At the extreme other end of this spectrum is Mark Z. Danielewski's *House of Leaves*, a novel where the entire plot is based around the reconstruction of an archive. The premise of the book is, at a first outline, a straightforward frame narrative. The narrator,

Johnny Truant, has come into possession of the disorganised archive of the recently deceased character, Zampanò. Through the archive, a book is constructed that at once weaves the day-to-day hedonistic life of Truant into the reconstruction of an academic text concerned with a fictional film called *The Navidson Record*. This metacinematic undertaking details the filmmaking of the eponymous Will Navidson as his family move into a ^{house} that is eerily able to reconfigure its internal space into impossible dimensions, weaving a dangerous labyrinth around them (the word 'house' in *House of Leaves* is always superscripted but also colourized in certain editions). The novel itself is cited as a prime example of ergodic literature, that is literature with a non-linear flow that involves heavy reader involvement. In Danielewski's novel, the text becomes the ^{house}, with the typography on the page breaking down, rotating, fracturing and extending as the dimensions of the building depicted change and as Truant's world also begins to disintegrate, bringing a fresh significance to the material presence of the codex, which must be reorientated and physically manipulated by a reader.

House of Leaves, like David Foster Wallace's *Infinite Jest* (1996), is notable for its proliferation of footnotes throughout. Some of these notes contain Truant's own story at great length while others solely make reference to fictional academic texts, such as "'Naguib Paredes' *Cinematic Projections* (Boston: Faber and Faber, 1995), p. 84".[33] These notes serve a twofold function. In the first place, they act to parody the academy through a structure of empty reference. For the supposed purpose of footnotes in academic texts is to provide a chain of verification. As Anthony Grafton has put it in his study of the footnote: "the culturally contingent and eminently fallible footnote offers the only guarantee we have that statements about the past derive from identifiable sources. And that is the only ground we have to trust them".[34] Yet, it is also an obvious, yet usually unspoken, fact that the vast majority of footnotes go unchecked and merely trusted. Instead, their presence is enough; an indication that, if enough are recognisable and enough are in the work, then their

---

33 Mark Z. Danielewski, *House of Leaves* (London: Anchor, 2000), p. 98.
34 Anthony Grafton, *The Footnote: A Curious History* (Cambridge, MA: Harvard University Press, 1999), p. 233.

accuracy can be assumed. *House of Leaves* plays with this expectation as we cannot check the fictional referents. In the second place, the footnotes in *House of Leaves* work in the same way as McCarthy's *C* in the creation of a fictional archive; an attempt to represent the *structure of facticity* that is knowingly only half true and that the reader knows is unverifiable. This is a transfer to the archival/research space of a sort of postmodern theology in which the structure of belief remains even while it is devoid of content in which to believe.[35]

In this way, Danielewski's fictional archive of academic articles and books deliberately works to undo both of the supposed generic functions of footnotes in a true academic text, thereby simultaneously invoking an academic lineage and parodying/destroying that same line. *C* works slightly differently, parodying less the known conventions of academic writing than toying with the conventions of the historical novel and the decoding paradigms of literary criticism. What both these texts share, though, is a structural affinity with history, cultural lineages, and an implied archive, while also deliberately fracturing an identity with the academic disciplinary form of history by yielding only empty referents, signposts to nowhere.

One final and useful way in which we might understand *C*'s stance on history is by locating it as a work of postmodern historiographic metafiction — a term coined by Linda Hutcheon to denote fiction that highlights its own fictionality while dealing with the *nature of history*[36] — rather than as a more conventional historical novel because of the many meta-narratorial statements within the work that conflate history with narrative. Building on the work of Hayden White, texts such as *C* perform the claim that the predominant difference between history and fiction is the former's claim to truth.[37] Firstly, to make this case, consider that *C*'s historiography is constructivist. In McCarthy's novel, history in its formal sense is written by the victors and usually consists of privileging 'great figures' and wars. This is perhaps most

---

35 See Amy Hungerford, *Postmodern Belief: American Literature and Religion since 1960* (Princeton: Princeton University Press, 2010).
36 Linda Hutcheon, *A Poetics of Postmodernism: History, Theory, Fiction* (New York: Routledge, 1988).
37 Hayden White, *Metahistory: Historical Imagination in Nineteenth Century Europe* (Baltimore: Johns Hopkins University Press, 1975), pp. 93–97.

clear when Serge is flipping through the brochure for the Kloděbrady Baths. We are told, at this point, that "the accompanying text gives the town's history, which seems to consist of a series of invasions, wars and squabbles over succession".[38] Elements of personal narrative and "secrets of the heart", however, are elsewhere revealed to be omitted from the official historical record in C and are referred to as "clandestine history", a gesture that immediately pluralises the truth of a singular historical record and summons a paradigm of 'history from below'.[39] At the same time, however, institutional history as recounted by Laura, a character who "studied history at St. Hilda's College, Oxford", is shown by McCarthy to be entirely concerned with mythological narratives. Laura's 'history' dissertation was on Osiris and consists of recounting the "well-known myth" and "cosmology" of Ancient Egypt from an intra-diegetic perspective that speaks of the ancient gods as though they were factual occurrences: "[t]he sun itself entered the body of Osiris".[40] For Laura, who comes from the heart of formal and institutional academic history at Oxford, myth-making and history-making are similar, if not the same.

As Serge's recording officer demands, then, asking for the history of their recent flight in the First World War section of the novel: "[n]arrative, Carrefax". Serge's reply demonstrates how history, in the formal senses that the novel critiques, elides specificity and is based on subjective reconstruction: "we went up; we saw stuff; it was good".[41] The result of this disjuncture between levels in C — in which we are shown the initial events but then given a reductive 'history' — is "to both inscribe and undermine the authority and objectivity of historical sources and explanations", as Hutcheon puts it.[42] In this way, C critiques the historiographic underpinnings of realist historical fiction through a postmodernist approach. However, since McCarthy is also interested in the way in which texts are classified, it seems to me that, by implication, C also sets its sights on the truth claims of *literary* history.

---

38 McCarthy, C, p. 85.
39 Ibid., p. 290.
40 Ibid., pp. 280–81.
41 Ibid., p. 143.
42 Hutcheon, *A Poetics of Postmodernism*, p. 123.

Canon, Genre, and Intertextuality

C can be considered, then, as a non-referential historical fiction of sorts, one that subverts the form through an emptiness of content (perhaps a 'quasi-historical fiction') but also a text where these remarks on history/fiction apply as much to its theme as to its meta-statements on its own generic placement in literary history. This text, however, also begins to make a further incursion into the same space of critique as university English when this proto-historicity turns its attention to literary genre. Typically, charting or describing literary generic discontinuity and generating a historical taxonomy has been the preserve of university English. As I noted in the introduction, such classificatory activities remain core to the activity of literary history and contextual criticism, even if they are also extremely important to the literary marketplace. The primary way in which *C* makes this incursion, though, is through its complex intertextual signalling by which the text seeks to classify itself.

Novels such as *C* signal their acts of self-classification in literary history in a variety of ways, but do so especially frequently through the intertextual allusions within their narrative and linguistic structures. For readers who can perceive these signals, these intertextual references productively restrict the valid frames of interpretation. As Umberto Eco has put it under his well-known semiotic approach, "in order to make forecasts which can be approved by the further course of the *fabula*, the Model Reader resorts to intertextual frames".[43] Classification and resemblance is to some extent in the eye of the beholder, a negotiated process wherein texts work to place themselves in various lineages and histories through accordance with convention ('genre') before readers decode these contexts to provide a frame for comprehension.

To begin with an obvious example of how this intertextual framing plays out in McCarthy's novel, consider that *C* is, undoubtedly, a disorientating read. As the text itself puts it, in one of its many metatextual moments but supposedly describing the intra-diegetic theatre event, "the next few scenes are confusing".[44] Although not obfuscating in its narrative to the same extent as *Ulysses* or Pynchon's *Gravity's Rainbow*,

---

43 Eco, *The Role of the Reader*, p. 32.
44 McCarthy, *C*, p. 58.

the reader can feel constantly wrong footed, several steps behind his or her authorial guide.[45] Evidently, this places the novel in the tradition of 'experimental' work favoured by the high (post)modernists in which 'difficulty' plays a core role.

Naturally, there are various different lineages of difficult fiction. Some 'difficult' contemporary novels, such as Eimar McBride's *A Girl is a Half-Formed Thing* (2013), evoke modernist minimalism and syntactic experimentation within the frame of late Beckett (as in, say, *Worstward Ho* [1983]), as seen in the text's opening lines: "[f]or you. You'll soon. You'll give her name. In the stitches of her skin she'll wear your say".[46] Others, such as *C*, eschew radical linguistic experimentation and instead aim at the maximalist postmodern canon of proliferation, confusion, and overcoding. In the case of *C*, this is partly a result of the text's contrivance and its high 'clever clever' game-playing to which I will shortly turn. This is additionally linked to the novel's rich linguistic and structural signification, and it is worth briefly evaluating a few aspects of this. For in addition to specific literary resonances/allusions, there are, as always, also broader generic intertextual frames guiding the reader's comprehension in McCarthy's text. How could there not be? In Barbara Herrnstein Smith's words, "no judgement is or could be objective in the classic sense of justified on totally context-transcendent and subject-independent grounds".[47] To demonstrate the rooted contexts that most strongly condition *C*, after charting the ways in which the novel directly invokes the works of Thomas Pynchon, Don DeLillo, and J.G. Ballard (with knowing nods to Woolf's *Between the Acts*), the three core elements to which I will draw attention within the novel might broadly be schematised as: 1) a ludic mode; 2) micro-proplepsis and epistemic play; and 3) differentiated repetition. These elements are key to the way in which *C* attempts to signpost its own literary antecedents and placement.

---

45 Interestingly, *Gravity's Rainbow* begins with a similar metafictional pronouncement about its own structure on its very first page: "[n]o, this is not a disentanglement from, this is a progressive knotting into". Pynchon, *Gravity's Rainbow*, p. 1.
46 Eimear McBride, *A Girl Is a Half-Formed Thing: A Novel* (New York: Hogarth, 2015), p. 3.
47 Barbara Herrnstein Smith, *Belief and Resistance: Dynamics of Contemporary Intellectual Controversy* (Cambridge, MA: Harvard University Press, 1997), p. 6.

To begin this, a set of authorial comparisons can be used to understand the frame of reference for C, which I argue is broader in range than *Remainder* and encompasses an overlooked postmodern canon. The works of Pynchon, for instance, form an apt touchstone given that McCarthy recently reviewed the audiobook of *Gravity's Rainbow* in *The New York Times*.[48] Beyond this, consider, for instance, that mid-way through Pynchon's influential first novel, *V.* (1963), the reader is introduced to Kurt Mondaugen, a wireless radio operator stationed in the colonial German Südwest. Mondaugen is there to investigate the atmospheric disturbances ('sferics') that have been detected and the strange messages thereby conveyed. The most notable of these messages, as decoded by the sinister Lieutenant Weissman (the 'white man' and, later, Nazi, of Pynchon's subsequent novel *Gravity's Rainbow*), reads "DIGEWOELDTIMSTEALALENSWTASNDEURFUALRLIKST". As Weissmann sees it: "I remove every third letter and obtain: GODMEANTNURRK. This rearranged spells Kurt Mondaugen. [...] The remainder of the message [...] now reads: DIEWELTISTALLES WASDERFALLIST". Mondaugen replies, in a fashion as 'curt' as his name, that he has: "heard that somewhere before".[49]

These themes of cryptanalysis, anagrammatic play, modernist (or at least Wittgensteinian) philosophy, and radio waves also find a locus in *C*. McCarthy's text opens and closes, for instance, on themes pertaining to a misunderstood message about "Incest-Radio" and a mis-transposition of messages because of a telegraphic fault, to which I will return shortly.[50] It also contains long Pynchonesque cryptographic strings that invite interpretation and plurality: "BY.NF. BADSAC7 SC-CS 1911; BY.VER. BUC2 SC-CS 1913".[51] Furthermore, the edition of *C* cited in this book even has a blurb that compares the novel to Pynchon. That Pynchon, perhaps the grandmaster of postmodern literary irony, should sit as a central reference point for McCarthy's work is hardly surprising. Pynchon has, after all, made a career out of weaving detailed technological knowledge into the tapestry of novels that exhibit deep

---

48 Tom McCarthy, '*Gravity's Rainbow*, Read by George Guidall', *The New York Times*, 21 November 2014, http://www.nytimes.com/2014/11/23/books/review/gravitys-rainbow-read-by-george-guidall.html.
49 Pynchon, *V.*, p. 278; I first made this point in Eve, *Pynchon and Philosophy*, p. 28.
50 McCarthy, *C*, p. 304.
51 *Ibid.*, p. 178.

technological scepticism, denouncing the neutrality theory that there could be "a good Rocket to take us to the stars, an evil Rocket for the World's suicide".[52]

This connection between the writers runs more deeply, however. For one, as a side link, McCarthy is represented in the United States by Melanie Jackson, the literary agent to whom Pynchon is married. This is certainly of strategic benefit for a writer who wishes to be seen as 'serious' but also 'postmodern'; Jackson is an agent with a fearsome reputation in her own right, handling such eminent figures as Wole Soyinka, Lorrie Moore, and Percival Everett. However, these textual and extra-textual affinities between Pynchon and McCarthy stand for more than their specific relations. As almost the archetypical postmodernist, it is difficult but to read a writer's relationship to Pynchon as a metonym for a relationship to postmodernism, in its many guises, and the affiliated academic critical machines.

This is not all, though. Rather than just 'between the acts', the Woolfian modernist reference point with which C clearly toys in its village theatre scene, we might also consider whether C is a text situated in the 'angle between the walls', that is, a text that is riffing on the postmodern fiction of J.G. Ballard.[53] Take, for instance, the resonance with the geometric perversions of *The Atrocity Exhibition* (1970) that are clearly seen in several of C's passages:

> [m]ore than anything, it's what he hears in Petrou's voice, its exiled, hovering cadences — and what he sees in Petrou's face and body, his perpetual slightly sideways stance: a longing for some kind of world, one either disappeared or yet to come, or perhaps even one that's always been there, although only in some other place, in a dimension Euclid never plotted, which is nonetheless reflecting off him at an asymptotic angle.[54]

It would be possible to select almost any passage from Ballard's experimental novel and to find much of McCarthy's work as a replication,

---

52 Pynchon, *Gravity's Rainbow*, p. 727.
53 A connection previously explored elsewhere in McCarthy's *Remainder*. See Jim Byatt, 'Being Dead?: Trauma and the Liminal Narrative in J.G. Ballard's *Crash* and Tom McCarthy's *Remainder*', *Forum for Modern Language Studies*, 48.3 (2012), 245–59, http://dx.doi.org/10.1093/fmls/cqs017.
54 McCarthy, *C*, p. 251.

or, if feeling uncharitable, a weak parody, of his style. Consider, for instance, the notion that "[t]hese embraces of Travers's were gestures of displaced affections, a marriage of Freud and Euclid", the last clause of which seems perfectly to embody the topological slant to C's curious sexual encounters.[55]

More specifically, C's resonance with Ballardian geometric tropes is ensconced within notions of subjunctivity; of a world hiding behind this world, disallowed from coming into possibility but forever remaining on the cusp of realisation. In Ballard's text, such subjunctivity and ontological instability are engendered through a pluralisation of worlds, as it is in C. For *The Atrocity Exhibition* this is framed through notions of inner and outer worlds, with the inner being primarily concerned with the psyche. Consider that, at the core of *The Atrocity Exhibition* — in a passage that bears close similarity to many of Ballard's own pronouncements on the novel, such as the introduction to the Danish edition — Dr Nathan says that:

> [p]lanes intersect: on one level, the tragedies of Cape Kennedy and Vietnam serialized on billboards, random deaths mimetized in the experimental auto disasters of Nader and his co-workers. Their precise role in the unconscious merits closer scrutiny; by the way, they may in fact play very different parts from the ones we assign them. On another level, the immediate personal environment, the volumes of space enclosed by your opposed hands, the geometry of your postures, the time-values contained in this office, the angles between these walls. On a third level, the inner world of the psyche. Where these planes intersect, images are born, some kind of valid reality begins to clarify itself.[56]

In other words, there is a mediated public sphere; a world of interpersonal relationships; and an inner landscape of the mind. In C this plays out slightly differently with a dysfunctionally narrated broad public and historical plane ("I liked the war"),[57] mediated through a character who is incapable of forming meaningful interpersonal relationships in his localised world ("[t]urn around", he says. "I want to see your back"),[58] and whose interior mental landscape is contoured and rocky (a space

---

55 J.G. Ballard, *The Atrocity Exhibition* (San Francisco: RE/Search, 1990), p. 76.
56 *Ibid.*, p. 47.
57 McCarthy, *C*, p. 214.
58 *Ibid.*, p. 114.

"that seems to have become all noise and signal").[59] *The Atrocity Exhibition* and, to an extent, *C*, attempt to map the intersection of these spaces in new ways that avoid: 1) the sensationalised mediation of the first sphere; 2) the usually sentimentalised depiction of the second; and 3) the conventional Cartesian separation of the inner world from the outer.

Ballard, however, is not the only other point of postmodern anchorage for *C*. Rather, on top of the allusions to Pynchon, one moment in the novel feels particularly motivated by a recreation of the themes of Baudrillardian simulation mirrored in Don DeLillo's wonderful *White Noise* (1985).[60] Towards the end of McCarthy's novel, Abigail relates to Serge her experience of watching tourists at the pyramids in Cairo, tourists who

> got their cameras out and started photographing them, although I don't know why because their photos won't turn out as nice as the ones in the book and brochures either. And they didn't even photograph the things for very long, because there was a buffet laid out on the deck [...] but then of course they realised that they had to show a certain reverence towards the Pyramids, while still not missing out on lunch, so they revered and ate and photographed all at once.[61]

This relates to, but is not directly the same as, one of the most celebrated passages of DeLillo's novel, namely the incident with the "most photographed barn in America":

> [s]everal days later Murray asked me about a tourist attraction known as the most photographed barn in America. We drove 22 miles into the country around Farmington. There were meadows and apple orchards. White fences trailed through the rolling fields. Soon the sign started appearing. THE MOST PHOTOGRAPHED BARN IN AMERICA. We counted five signs before we reached the site. There were 40 cars and a tour bus in the makeshift lot. We walked along a cowpath to the slightly elevated spot set aside for viewing and photographing. All the people had cameras; some had tripods, telephoto lenses, filter kits. A man in a booth sold postcards and slides — pictures of the barn taken from the elevated spot. We stood near a grove of trees and watched the

---

59 *Ibid.*, p. 178.
60 I'm not meaning to imply here that Baudrillard influenced *White Noise*; the historical timelines do not quite match.
61 McCarthy, *C*, p. 262.

photographers. Murray maintained a prolonged silence, occasionally scrawling some notes in a little book.

"No one sees the barn", he said finally.[62]

These two passages, while overlapping, are very different in their outcomes. DeLillo's text is concerned with the displacement of reality and the endless proliferation of simulacra engendered by mechanical reproduction in the era of late capital: "[w]e're not here to capture an image, we're here to maintain one. Every photograph reinforces the aura", he writes.[63] McCarthy's passage, on the other hand, effects the more pedestrian critique that is surely familiar to anybody who has acted as a flâneur among tourists: that the act of photographing supersedes experiencing.

This is not to say that *C* achieves its resonances merely through textual similitude. It is rather that *C* is not confined to the modernist frames that others have suggested; its literary-historical lineage and the contexts within which it pre-anticipates its reception project further forward in time. There are, as I have suggested above, many more generic tropes that McCarthy uses within his work but that nonetheless imply connections to specific, more recent literary histories. For instance, to begin to see evidence of how McCarthy encodes a ludic mode through moments of metafictional reflexivity, usually centred around linguistic games — a trope found in much postmodernist writing — consider, as an example, how the reader is told, early in the text, that:

> Serge gets stuck on words like "antipodean" and "fortuitous", and even ones like "tables". He keeps switching letters around. It's not deliberate, just something that he does.[64]

This instance is just the first of many in which McCarthy distils the novel's totality into a microcosmic metonym at the levels of language, of theme, and of authorship. Firstly, in terms of language and anagrams, when Serge confuses the letters in "tables", McCarthy asks us to consider whether the character might be the 'ablest' (the most competent to deal with the trials of modernity?), in a 'stable' condition (with his stagnation and focus on blockage, to which I will return), whether he might 'be last'

---

62 Don DeLillo, *White Noise* (London: Picador, 2011), pp. 13–15.
63 *Ibid.*, p. 14.
64 McCarthy, *C*, p. 38.

to survive, or whether he is simply playing with a 'lab set', an apparatus that proves so fatal for his sister. Secondly, and as just one example, at the thematic level, this passage connects with the 'tilting' table of the séance later in the novel where Serge rigs a device to interfere with a medium's trickery.[65] In this sense, Serge's early "switching letters around" in the word tables parallels the rearrangement of letters that he later conducts on the medium's table. Finally, in terms of authorship, all moments of metafiction suggest an easy reading in which we might consider whether there is a parallel between McCarthy and Serge; is Serge, in some way, the 'author' of C? McCarthy's novel, I would argue, tends to stop just short of such metatextual gimmickry. After all, the linguistic playfulness does not occur consistently throughout the novel. It seems, rather, that the flattening of diegetic levels that is suggested by McCarthy's metatextual play even demonstrates self-aware of the metafictional tradition and works to signal this.

At the microcosmic level, however, this postmodern style of disorientation and aesthetic swirling is also a result of the text's microprolepsis. By this, I mean the fact that the text makes no concession to the reader's lack of foreknowledge of events only later revealed, in spite of its otherwise overwhelmingly linear, chronological character. Take, as an example, the initial instance at the beginning of the novel where Carrefax senior is sending for a doctor to tend to his pregnant wife and the 'F' and 'Q's in his telegraphy system are substituted ('F' [..-.] and 'Q' [--.-] being inverse codes in the Morse system).[66] This invention of telegraphy is the closest that C ever comes to depicting a wholesale academic environment (despite the fleeting reference to an Oxford historian earlier); a research laboratory. In this instance, though, the context is clearly private, not a public institution, and the text is saturated with mentions of patent races and other commercialisations of the new technologies. This has implications for a representation of the contemporary academic sciences, frequently enmeshed and encouraged in the pursuit of profitable research with commercial aims. The reader is, however, aware at this stage neither that early telegraphy will form a central thematic tenet of the novel nor that such a prototypical system has been developed by the character. Only a few pages later, this is

---

65   Ibid., p. 230.
66   Ibid., p. 6.

explained in more detail to the reader.⁶⁷ The length of stretch between mystery and resolution here is not substantial enough to make the work as taxing as many of the high modernist and postmodernist fictions, but it does immediately call to mind the premise on which their 'difficulty' rests.

However, while epistemic play is a frequent feature of all fiction and may even be intrinsic to its form, particularly within modern and postmodern varieties, *C* is curious in its presentation because it chooses to conceal information from the reader only for brief periods before revealing its hand. It is also an outlier in this respect because the chronological macro-structure of the novel is entirely linear; a mode that does not usually lend itself to abrupt retrospective enlightenment (for a counter example, one could compare the temporal leaps of Graham Swift's *Waterland* [1983] and the moment of grim revelation in that text that is facilitated by its final analeptic shock). Although there are portions of Serge's life that are not narrated (i.e. the text's chapters are non-adjacent in chronological terms), *C*'s quadripartite structure of "Caul", "Chute", "Crash", and "Call" moves definitively forward in time through the life of Serge Carrefax.

Although this may, at first, sound more like a realist mode than a postmodern styling, this structure actually shows, in terms of literary history, why *C* appears to do something different to the forms of modernist epistemic play to which it pays homage. While the dark tone of McCarthy's war-saturated novel might induce a temptation to think that it is a dystopian historical work in which the critical force of history is brought to bear on the present — a didactic text that might warn us of the dangers of the past repeating (which depends upon cycles and historical analogy) — *C* does not seem to be wholly convinced by the logic of cycles and repetition. Instead, its structure is aptly 'C'-shaped. The homophonic titles of the first and last sections of the text ("Caul"/"Call") imply the loop, the cycle, but eventually shy from it in a differentiated repetition. Likewise, the cleansing instructions of Serge's doctor at the clinic are to think in terms of change, not cycles: "things mutate", he notes, "that is the way of nature — of good nature [...] You though, [...] have got blockage [...] instead of transformation, only repetition".⁶⁸

---

67 *Ibid.*, p. 12.
68 *Ibid.*, p. 105.

To reiterate: through the fact that its first and last section titles sound identical ("Caul"/"Call") in conjunction with the above in-text diagnoses of 'repetition', *C* hints that the reader should expect to see parallels and cycles. This extends to the interpretation of the generic structures within which *C* might be read; echoes of and affinities with modernism and postmodernism. However, Serge seems incapable of closing the loop (and such repetition is presented, as above, as a pathology) and so, while his death bears the hallmarks of his childhood, the repetition is imperfect. This changes the focus in the novel from epistemology (in which we would *know* and recognise elements of the past by their resemblance to the present) to one of ontology (in which the present is a newly transformed world and way of *being*). This is the classic shift in dominant — from epistemology to ontology — charted by Brian McHale and that he claims defines the postmodern novel, situated at the heart of *C*'s historiography.[69]

To demonstrate this ontological mutation, which is reflected in McCarthy's language, consider the textual collocation of "incest" with the name of Serge's sister, "Sophie" (imperfectly repeated as "Sophia"), at the end of the novel that harks back to the familial near-voyeurism and his sister's use of his penis as a telegraph key in the life of young Serge.[70] Yet, at the moment of Serge's death it is not the term "incest" that appears, but rather we see that term, which characterises his childhood and where it "all began", transformed into an "insect" bite.[71] Through such moves, McCarthy's text invites literary-critical "pattern-making and pattern-interpreting behavior" from its readers (by implying an affinity between chronologically distant moments in the text) only to frustrate such text-processing (by showing and stating that such affinity is always imperfect in its analogy), a trope of interpretative refusal that, again, McHale famously ascribes as a core feature of the postmodern novel.[72]

---

69 Brian McHale, 'Change of Dominant from Modernist to Postmodernist Writing', in *Approaching Postmodernism: Papers Presented at a Workshop on Postmodernism, 21–23 September 1984, University of Utrecht*, ed. by Douwe W. Fokkema and Hans Bertens (Amsterdam: John Benjamins, 1986), pp. 53–79.
70 McCarthy, *C*, pp. 22, 60–61, 253.
71 *Ibid.*, pp. 252, 304–10.
72 Brian McHale, 'Modernist Reading, Post-Modern Text: The Case of *Gravity's Rainbow*', *Poetics Today*, 1.1/2 (1979), 85–110 (p. 88).

The same observation can, once more, be extended to literary taxonomy and canon formation. In the endless proliferation of '-modernist' suffixes that are now applied by the academy as terminological markers, it is clear that the same phenomenon is at work: a failed differentiated repetition. All new genres of the serious novel must be, under this logic, related to modernism, the category of serious experiment. At the same time, they are not allowed to be the *same* as the high modernism of 1922. They must still make it new, but not too new. McCarthy's play on differentiated repetitions, while depicting the modernist 'period', within a work that situates itself within (post)modernisms, exemplifies and echoes the problems of canonising taxonomies of the academy.

Auto-Canonisation and Aesthetic Critique

As I noted in the introduction, *C* is hardly the only text that takes on this role and function of charting its own literary-historical placement (in this particular case, David Foster Wallace's 'Westward the Course of Empire Takes Its Way' [1997] also springs to mind). It is in fact common over a diverse body of texts in a range of styles. One could, for example, think of the explicit references throughout Alison Bechdel's *Fun Home* (2006) to *Ulysses*, among many other works. In one sense, this archival construction is a mediation and historicization of Bechdel's own life. As Heike Bauer has put it, "[v]ia books — including British, Irish, and U.S. texts and European writing in English translation — Bechdel's memoirs historicize her family and interrogate the queer entanglements of her own lesbian life with the lives of parents who are trapped in a damaging emotional void forged during the socially repressive and sexually persecutory Eisenhower era".[73] In another more formalist sense, though, it is a validating move, a self-situation by Bechdel of her work within a high literary tradition.

By contrast, some writers, such as Jonathan Franzen, use this technique counter-intuitively both to affiliate and to disaffiliate themselves from various traditions. For instance, in *Freedom* (2010), Franzen's rock-star character, Richard Katz, is first introduced reading a copy of Pynchon's

---

73 Heike Bauer, 'Vital Lines Drawn From Books: Difficult Feelings in Alison Bechdel's *Fun Home* and *Are You My Mother?*', *Journal of Lesbian Studies*, 18.3 (2014), 266–81 (p. 267), http://dx.doi.org/10.1080/10894160.2014.896614.

V. This allows Franzen at once to validate his work as 'serious', high fiction that knows its antecedents, while also serving to complicate the canonical status of such novels, due to Katz's ambiguous status within that text. Indeed, Richard Katz in *Freedom* is a deeply flawed character, one who causes a great deal of pain to Walter through his affair with Patty. Nonetheless, he is educated, articulate, and emotionally sensitive to a far higher level than many other of Franzen's characters.

This dis- and re- affiliating stance towards canon is one that Pynchon had himself explored in *V*. For, at one point therein, Rachel Owlglass remarks, of the Whole Sick Crew, that "that Crew does not live, it experiences. It does not create, it talks about people who do. Varèse, Ionesco, de Kooning, Wittgenstein, I could puke".[74] Yet, as I have previously pointed out, "Rachel Owlglass is a conflicted character who has an erotic encounter with her car, but who is 'disgusted' by Jewish girls undergoing plastic surgery to erase their Jewishness, and, most prominently, is the chief protagonist in the campaign to intercept Esther and Slab on their way to a Cuban abortion clinic".[75] Intra-fictional veneration of a canon, voiced through a double-edged or ambiguous character morality, serves to affiliate but also to question the works that are targeted.

What we do see is that in the combination of historical and/or academic-discursive forms encoded within fiction, we tend towards works that begin to jostle with the academy for the right to speak about literary history; the conditions of aesthetic possibility. This interpretation is given further credence if we return finally to Danielewski's novel, which begins increasingly to use the names of real academics and novelists throughout. For instance, in addition to *The Navidson Record* another fictional artefact within the book is a film of supposed interviews called "What Some Have Thought". The transcript of this 'film' features a range of fictional figures: "Jennifer Antipala" for example is claimed to be an "Architect and Structural Engineer", although I have been unable to locate a record of such an individual.[76] By contrast, other figures 'interviewed' are real and include: the French poststructuralist philosopher, Jacques Derrida; the professor of cognitive science,

---

74 Pynchon, *V.*, p. 380.
75 Eve, *Pynchon and Philosophy*, p. 44.
76 Danielewski, p. 355.

Douglas R. Hofstadter; the American feminist critic Camille Paglia; the (very different) gothic/horror novelists Anne Rice and Stephen King; Hunter S. Thompson, the celebrated journalist; the filmmaker Stanley Kubrick; the co-founder of Apple computers, Steve Wozniak; and the American university professor perhaps most associated with the role of academia in canon formation, Harold Bloom.[77] It would be possible, but tiresome, to recount the ways in which this act of naming real people simultaneously gestures towards extra-textual realities while maintaining a separate intra-textual representation; this approach has been done to death. In fact, Danielewski's copyright page contains a humorous variant on the standard disclaimer:

> [t]his novel is a work of fiction. Any references to real people […] are intended to give the fiction a sense of reality and authenticity. Other names, characters and incidents are either the product of the author's imagination or are used fictitiously, as are those fictionalized events and incidents which involve real persons and did not occur or *are set in the future*.[78]

What is perhaps more relevant, for the discussion at hand, is the way in which Danielewski selects the academics here as the most probable generators of frameworks within which his own work might be read. Derrida, for example, is an easy target for parody. It is also likely, though, that a work that plays on the bounds between fiction, its construction, spatiality, and the archive would be read, in an academic context, through Derrida. In parodying Derrida, Danielewski somewhat invalidates such a reading. A similar approach might be taken with each of the figures here cited, but I'll only pause, finally, to examine the specific instance of Harold Bloom.

Bloom is well known not only for his book *The Anxiety of Influence* (1973), which is the work that Danielewski here parodies and which is concerned with the ways in which writers feel and channel the burden of tradition into their creations, but also for his writing on the Western canon. Without wanting to recount the entire history of the 'canon wars', which is far better covered elsewhere, in *The Western Canon: The Books and School of the Ages* (1994), Bloom defended the value structures that

---

77   Ibid., pp. 354–65.
78   Ibid., p. imprinture, emphasis mine.

had produced the traditional canon against various schools of feminist, Marxist, postcolonial, and poststructuralist approaches. Bloom refers to these projects as the 'School of Resentment', claiming that the members of these communities wish to modify the canon to include aesthetically inferior works in order to advance their own political purposes. Bloom's analysis is, in many ways, dubious as it presupposes an apolitical environment prior to cultural studies; it seems to imply that all was well when straight, white men were the pure arbiters of quality, anointing their brethren. To then brand those who work on redressing the historical imbalance of the canon as 'resentful' is troubling.

This seems reflected in Danielewski's depiction of Bloom, which is perhaps a caricature from the author's own time at Yale.[79] In a possibly legally-actionable passage (despite the aforementioned disclaimer), the Bloom represented here is extraordinarily patronising. The interviewer, Karen Green, is referred to as "my dear girl" by Bloom, throughout, which is probably a reaction against his dismissal of the feminist literary schools. The Bloom character also then goes on to describe the house as being "endlessly familiar, endlessly repetitive [...] pointedly against symbol". Danielewski's Bloom thinks that this means that through creating this "featureless golem, a universal eclipse", *The Navidson Record* (and, by extension *House of Leaves*) works to "succeed in securing poetic independence". In the parody that is enacted, however, Bloom comes across as at once simply a figure of "academic onanism", as the text later puts it, and at the same time a representative of canonisation processes.[80] In this way, *House of Leaves* gives the clearest signposts yet for a discussion of intertextuality as a process of canonisation.

Novels that Act Like Academics

In this chapter, I have argued that *C* and *House of Leaves* begin tentatively to show us the ways in which works of fiction can speak over the academy by pre-anticipating their own reception (through intertextual frames) and by working as novels that obliquely chart literary histories. Both of these novels contain gestures towards or even

---

79   Hayles notes that Danielewski attended Yale. Hayles, p. 237.
80   Danielewski, p. 467.

representations of taxonomies of literary history that university English would typically call its own preserve. Both texts also play with the structure of academic writing, yielding empty referents and a quasi-facticity that has the structure of literary history but not necessarily the content. Both novels and in the case of *C*, the author, are also concerned with canon and the ways in which value is ascribed within the academy. In this way, both these novels perform a type of aesthetic critique and self-situation within literary history. The fact that the histories in these texts are a broken chain, though, achieved through a set of postmodern historiographic tropes, casts doubt upon the act of literary placement/ classification typically enacted by the academy.

It is this type of activity, I contend, that begins to pitch fiction and university English into a kind of legitimation struggle. If fiction can claim to depict literary history better than the academic descriptions, at a time when university English feels itself under threat, then it is unsurprising that certain anxieties should begin to emerge. In many ways, though, these texts are formalist critiques of aesthetic modes. What I would like to turn to now is the flip side of this: texts that seem to play in the same ballpark as the political and ethical critiques of the academy.

4. Political Critique

If, as shown in the previous chapter, *C* can be considered a text focused on aesthetic critique (i.e. an interrogation of its own conditions of aesthetic possibility and self-situation within a specific literary history and/or taxonomy, independently of the university), then this is the type of metafiction that is *most* vulnerable to the accusation of political nihilism. A purely formalist mode, after all, whether in the university or in fiction seems to disavow politics, even if *Remainder* does make an ethical critique of representational art.[1] While certain texts exemplify an aesthetic critique of the process of canonisation, taking this element far from the university, others, such as Roberto Bolaño's *2666*, to which I will now turn, work very differently. In fact, if one wanted an easy divide between the forms of critique enacted by these two texts, *C* would conduct aesthetic, formalist critique while *2666* could be said to practice political critique. The two are inseparable to some extent; the content/form dichotomy is clearly false. For the purposes of thinking about these two areas, however, it is clear that various metafictions respectively focus more strongly on aesthetic or political critique.

By 'political critique' in this chapter I mean that texts such as *2666* thematically represent ethical and political issues that intersect with the interests of the academy. There are some challenges inherent in this mode. Fiction and the academy may independently reach the same conclusions about issues of ethical import in the present. For instance, it is no coincidence that postcolonial and ecocritical themes should arise in a world recovering from the British Empire and one in which the threat

---

1   In the limited reading that I have presented, *C* comes across as an apolitical novel, which is perhaps a little unfair.

of climate change looms as an unparalleled global catastrophe. Yet we also could say that, for literary criticism, there might be a link between the spaces. It could be that literature responds to the ethical issues of the day and criticism responds to the literature. In the time of the 'novel after Theory' this becomes more complex. Novels such as *2666* contain representations of academics (in fact, specifically literary critics) while also dealing with a set of topical ethical themes, emerging from a set of South American authors who take a similar approach.[2] These texts therefore demonstrate a metafictional process in which they are aware of the way in which such ethical and political tropes will be read back out of their pages. As Judith Ryan puts it, such novels "write back".[3]

As an initial word of caution, though, it might be worth asking in advance what it actually means to call a literary text 'political'. It can mean that we see formal and mimetic affinities with political theories. If we think that politics might consist of a fusion of ethics and influential power, then fiction might well possess those qualities. We might also want to ask, however, what type of influence literature has, what audiences it can reach and, perhaps most importantly: how do, or even just *do*, political elements of short stories, novels and poetry, amid other hybrid forms, translate into action? Is it enough, we might ask, for a text to present an ethical worldview? What about action? There is clearly a persistent and widespread social anxiety about the potential political power of literature and its translation into action. Think only of Hilary Mantel's controversial short story about a fictional assassination of Margaret Thatcher and the media storm that it generated.[4] Look only at the list of books challenged every year for censorship in the US education system.[5] We should be careful, though, not to overstate the power of literature in the mind and in the academy against the power of action on the street. Academics are, like anyone else, subjectively biased and prone to making such assumptions; it would be nice to imagine that

---

2   For just one example, see César Aira, *The Literary Conference*, trans. by Katherine Silver (New York: New Directions, 2010).
3   Ryan.
4   Michelle Huneven, 'Hilary Mantel's Short-Story Collection Long on Controversy', *Los Angeles Times*, 3 October 2014, http://www.latimes.com/books/jacketcopy/la-ca-jc-hilary-mantel-20141005-story.html.
5   American Library Association, 'Frequently Challenged Books', http://www.ala.org/bbooks/frequentlychallengedbooks.

there are leagues of politicised students who leave literature courses every year and who go on to change the world. The evidence shows otherwise. For the most part, the pedagogy of debt incurred by studying literature in the academy teaches students that they must get jobs, enter the 'real world' and leave the realm of political literature in that other space: on the page.

I choose, nonetheless, to call this interrelation of ethical themes 'political' because rather than purely being about ethics, meta-ethics, morality, and so forth, it is the way in which these ethical concerns are translated into a socio-textual power practice for the distribution and arrangements of the exercise of authority in which I am most invested. This is explicitly not to situate 'politics' and 'aesthetics' in opposition to one another. As Caroline Levine has noted, politics itself can fall under the discourse of formalism.[6] In the novels that I write of in this chapter, however, it is specifically the textual *polis* — the authored textual architecture or city — that works to influence the ethical route through which its hermeneutic denizens — its readers — walk.

Roberto Bolaño and *2666*

2666 has been heralded as phenomenal, an especially remarkable feat given that it remained unfinished at the time of the author's death. Impossible to do justice to its size and scope, Bolaño's novel interweaves five narratives concerning: a set of self-absorbed literary critics; the university professor Oscar Amalfitano; a journalist called Oscar Fate; Bolaño's fictional reclusive author Archimbaldi; and a central section on 'the crimes'. All of this is spread across a one-thousand-page epic that was originally published in Spanish in 2004 and then translated into English in 2008, with both versions appearing posthumously. These 'crimes' form the dystopian centrepiece with which the novel batters its reader: the sequential, gruelling description of the bodies of the female victims of sexual homicides around the fictional town of Santa Teresa, a thinly veiled rendition of the ongoing, horrendous reality in Ciudad Juárez.[7] It is a near-unending "repetitive cataloguing of bodies" that,

---

6 Levine.
7 For more on the novel's space, see Jeffrey Gray, 'Roberto Bolaño, Ciudad Juárez, and the Future of Nativism', *Pacific Coast Philology*, 49.2 (2014), 166–76.

as Camelia Raghinaru puts it, "rewrite[s] the general expectations of detective fiction".[8]

In terms of its literary aesthetic, *2666* is an explicitly metatextual artefact that situates itself within two traditions: the utopian work and the encyclopaedic novel, in the latter case particularly of the North American variety, despite arguments to the contrary.[9] This can be seen twofold in the text itself. Firstly, in response to its own representations of violence, the work overtly queries utopian premises when it asks of the author of the original *Utopia* (1516): "why Thomas More [...]?"[10] Secondly, Bolaño aims for his novel to be the "great, imperfect, torrential [work]" that struggles "against something, that something that terrifies us all, that something that [...] spurs us on, amid blood and mortal wounds and stench", thus invoking debates about autonomous and committed art forms within a vast structure; the link between aesthetics and politics explored by incarnations of the postmodern encyclopaedic novel.[11]

Bolaño's novel, then, is an example of contemporary writing that exhibits a strong ethical core even amid aesthetic structures that hark back to (supposedly amoral) postmodern metafiction. It is also, I will argue, a text that achieves its ethical payoff through a focus on matters of 'teaching'. As a result, I think of *2666* under the remit of a category that I term 'crypto-didacticism', a phrase denoting fictions that appear vast and chaotic but that nonetheless aim to school their readerships in ethics. In this light, I suggest that those in the academy given the task of 'teaching contemporary fiction' should be aware that they might also on occasion read such a statement in its adjectival form: contemporary fiction that teaches.

The broadest signal given by *2666* that it should be considered under such a mode, but also the key indicator of the target audience

---

8 Camelia Raghinaru, 'Biopolitics in Roberto Bolaño's *2666*, "The Part About the Crimes"', *Altre Modernità*, 15 (2016), 146–62 (p. 150), http://dx.doi.org/10.13130/2035-7680/7182.

9 Sharae Deckard, 'Peripheral Realism, Millennial Capitalism, and Roberto Bolaño's *2666*', *Modern Language Quarterly*, 73.3 (2012), 351–72 (p. 369), http://dx.doi.org/10.1215/00267929-1631433.

10 Roberto Bolaño, *2666*, trans. by Natasha Wimmer (London: Picador, 2009), p. 193.

11 *Ibid.*, p. 227.

that the text seeks to educate, is that the university is awarded a central place — and is indeed explicitly depicted — in this novel. It is my contention in this chapter that 2666 is a text that trains its didactic strains back upon the academy in a utopian mode that, while intensely critical, still sees a limited potential for redemption. This chapter proposes that 2666 is a novel that attempts to teach, and perhaps redeem, the academy, a reading for which Sharae Deckard has already paved the way in her assertion that the first two portions of the text can be defined as "didactic 'set pieces'".[12]

Linked to this pedagogical mission, it is also worth considering the aesthetics of 2666 within a tradition of what could be termed 'fictions of process', a brand of metafiction that asks the reader to value the journey, rather than the arrival, the reading, rather than the having-read. 2666 exhibits these characteristics (being composed of several, anachronistic, practically autonomous sub-books and without a clear arc of narrative progress: a 'shaggy-dog story') and can be seen as a novel that instead seeks to effect change through subjectification processes whereby the aim is to encounter an anticipated reader who can then be hailed and altered: an "experience book" as Timothy O'Leary might term it.[13] Such a conjunction of process and subjectification has an internalising pedagogical function in which the reader believes him or herself to be an autodidact, even though, in fact, the text presupposed its particular teachings in advance. The philosophy adopted by such works, I contend, is that the best form of teaching makes the student — or, in this case, the reader — believe that it was his or her idea in the first place.

This chapter seeks, therefore, to interrogate the political didacticism of Bolaño's novel while also exposing the role that is assigned to the university in this text, with particular emphasis upon its structural affiliation to the police and their co-facilitation of mass murder. 2666 is a text that enacts a political critique of the university *and* fiction through a novelistic representation of university English.

In order to effect this argument, this chapter is structured into two distinct parts. The first ('Crypto-Didacticism, Utopia, and 2666')

---

12 Deckard, p. 357.
13 Timothy O'Leary, *Foucault and Fiction: The Experience Book* (London: Continuum, 2009).

presents a more abstract and theoretical background to ideas of pedagogy and didacticism within the novel. It begins by exploring the fact that interpretations of Bolaño's text are frequently premised on the same, perhaps reductive, ethical narrative, which invites the question of why such a lengthy text is necessary if *2666* really is a novel with a core 'message'. Noting, however, that Bolaño takes explicit measures to avoid conflating empathy and pornography (thus demonstrating a nuanced approach to its depiction of horror), this section then moves to examine both the political 'commitment' of the novel and the particular implications of the fact that Bolaño's world is not its real-world correlative; the impact of distancing seen in utopian fictions.

The second part ('*Quis custodiet ipsos custodes*?: Critiquing the critics and the university in *2666*') examines Bolaño's explicit representation of the university in the novel. Noting that the university in *2666* is structurally twinned with the police force and also that the text ridicules purely aesthetic interpretations of literature, I argue that Bolaño depicts the university as deploying 'strategies of condescension' in its ethical readings of literature that sit in conflict with the academy's own societal position. This leads to a double bind within the text calling almost for a silence of exegesis from the academy. Finally, through a reading of the conflicting temporalities of the novel's title I note in conclusion that Bolaño's critique is designed not to silence, but rather to raise reflexive awareness and to alter critical subjectivity; there is a redemptive potential. In the novel's ultimate demand that people 'keep writing', despite a flawed subject position, a more self-conscious conjunction of pre-compromised ethics and aesthetics seems to emerge. In this way, *2666* performs a political and social critique from within a novelistic environment saturated with academia. Like Andreea Marinescu, I believe that *2666*'s "capacity to generate discourse about its place within the conformity/resistance binary is ultimately the important aspect".[14] This capacity is built, however, on a critique of both the academy's and the text's own ability to speak meaningfully on such political and ethical topics.

---

14 Andreea Marinescu, '"I Can't Go On, I'll Go On": The Avant-Garde in the Works of Roberto Bolaño and Raúl Ruiz', *Romance Notes*, 54.3 (2014), 391–98 (p. 393), http://dx.doi.org/10.1353/rmc.2014.0071.

Crypto-Didacticism, Utopia, and *2666*

2666 is a novel that lends itself to a range of ethical readings that all share a common narrative core. This is, I contend, a result of the fact that it anticipates the reading methods of the academy and plays a complex game of schooling in which it attempts to foresee and guide the academic response, a mode that I term 'crypto-didacticism'. I use 'crypto-didacticism' to denote a subform of the encyclopaedic novel that hides an essential moralising purpose amid a lengthy, overloaded structure. The *modus operandi* of a crypto-didactic novel is to cloak its purpose within a super-dense structure so that, by the necessary intellectual capital that the reader is forced to expend in comprehension, its fundamental normative ethical propositions are all the harder for the reader to reject. This function is, as Adorno put it about the inadequacy of the concept in *Negative Dialectics* (1966), at once "both striking and secret".[15] It is also, as Bourdieu might note, an aspect that most readers of such hyper-dense works would wish to deny.

This seems to be bound to a false collective renunciation of the fact that the cultural expertise necessary for comprehension of such works can also be seen as interchangeable with other forms of power and material capital, derived from educational prestige: "fundamentally the work of denial which is the source of social alchemy is, like magic, a collective undertaking".[16] The way in which such novels work is through a repetitive overloading of imagery (such as 'the crimes' in *2666*) within a broadly metafictive framework, a technique that is, I argue, designed to avoid the phenomenon of "beliefs in collision" charted by Smith.[17] Rather than challenging through confrontational evidence, crypto-didactic texts suggest self-modification and reflexivity (through their metafictional elements) while showing the reader bodies (sometimes literally) of evidence that suggest a specific conclusion.

At a reductive level, then, the specific ethical conclusion that can be deduced from *2666* can be expressed thus: four hundred women have been tortured, raped, and murdered, the police do nothing about

---

15 Theodor W. Adorno, *Negative Dialectics*, trans. by E.B. Ashton (London: Routledge, 1973), p. 153.
16 Pierre Bourdieu, *Outline of a Theory of Practice* (Cambridge: Cambridge University Press, 1977), p. 195.
17 Barbara Herrnstein Smith, p. 38.

it because the victims are marginalised working class women and, to quote Bolaño directly, "nobody noticed".[18] Amid rampant "gynophobia" and omnipresent misogyny: "the women here aren't worth shit".[19]

A brief literature review of work on *2666* reveals that these basic propositions are the foundation for the majority of critical writing on the novel's ethics, even when such readings are executed with specifically nuanced angles. It is also clear that in drawing an ethical perspective from the novel, critics usually posit a balancing act between an implicit 'teaching' function of such literature and a critical skill in the perception, extraction, and explication of such teachings (a balance between an intent of the author/novel and a focus on reader reception). For instance, although very different from the reading advanced here but also premised upon a fundamental 'teaching' within the text, Grant Farred, alongside Patrick Dove and Sol Pelaez, has argued that Bolaño's true focus in this ethical setup is upon a critique of postcolonialism's entanglement with neoliberalism (focusing upon the marginalisation of the labouring victims), a critique that, nonetheless, further strengthens the notion of a crypto-didactic text.[20] Likewise, Peter Boxall notes that "Bolaño's fictions contain a kind of darkened image of a common world that is the closest the novel today can approach to imagining democracy", thereby situating *2666* within an ethical framework of globalisation that teaches us of the ills that it darkly reflects.[21] Daniela Omlor writes that "the murders of women recounted in the fourth part underpin all other narrative threads", thus interweaving the novel's teaching with its ethical premise.[22] For Fermín A. Rodríguez, "that the figure of exclusion in these novels has the face of a woman, that the biological body of the population is the body of young female workers, and that violence as

---

18 Bolaño, *2666*, p. 372.
19 *Ibid.*, pp. 382, 318.
20 Grant Farred, 'The Impossible Closing: Death, Neoliberalism, and the Postcolonial in Bolaño's *2666'*, *MFS: Modern Fiction Studies*, 56.4 (2010), 689–708; Patrick Dove, 'Literature and the Secret of the World: *2666*, Globalization, and Global War', *CR: The New Centennial Review*, 14.3 (2014), 139–61, http://dx.doi.org/10.14321/crnewcentrevi.14.3.0139; Sol Pelaez, 'Counting Violence: Roberto Bolano and *2666*', *Chasqui*, 43.2 (2014), 30–47.
21 Peter Boxall, *Twenty-First-Century Fiction: A Critical Introduction* (Cambridge: Cambridge University Press, 2013), p. 209.
22 Daniela Omlor, 'Mirroring Borges: The Spaces of Literature in Roberto Bolaño's *2666*', *Bulletin of Hispanic Studies*, 91.6 (2014), 659–70 (p. 660), http://dx.doi.org/10.3828/bhs.2014.40.

a condition of the workings of a power exasperated by the market is fundamentally a continuous violence exerted upon a feminine body".[23] Laura Barberán Reinares writes that "Bolaño's monumental last novel" is one in which the "writer sheds a tenebrous light on the way in which transnational capital, patriarchy, and the state have enabled the vicious deaths of subaltern 'disposable' women".[24] As with Bolaño's repetitious depiction of the crimes in the novel, the list of critical appraisals that draw attention to these same factors continues to grow, as though in some kind of perpetual re-enactment.[25] (And I, too, am here guilty.)

To state this concisely: readings of the ethics within complex, lengthy metafictions such as 2666 tend, in the academy's model of an ethical turn, towards a specific didactic hermeneutic in which the novel is seen as a disciplinary text that attempts to interpellate subjects within its own moral framework. It is, however, surely the predictability of such interpretations that has led Rita Felski and others to feel dissatisfied with symptomatic readings, regardless of how ethically sound such approaches may continue to seem. In any case, it could be, for these novels, as 2666's Florita Almada puts it, that "teaching children", or even literary critics, "might be the best job in the world, gently opening children's eyes, even the tiniest bit".[26]

As with many other encyclopaedic, or even simply vast or 'maximalist', fictions, Bolaño sets about opening his readers' eyes through a structure of length and overloading.[27] In 2666, it seems, to leap straightforwardly to the endpoint is to miss the subject-forming aspect of these texts and negate the internalisation of such teachings. Hence, the textual politics

---

23 Fermín A. Rodríguez, 'Fear, Subjectivity, and Capital: Sergio Chejfec's *The Dark* and Roberto Bolaño's 2666', *Parallax*, 20.4 (2014), 345–59 (p. 345), http://dx.doi.org/10.10 80/13534645.2014.957550.

24 Laura Barberán Reinares, 'Globalized Philomels: State Patriarchy, Transnational Capital, and the Fermicides on the US-Mexican Border in Roberto Bolaño's 2666', *South Atlantic Review*, 75.4 (2010), 51–72 (p. 53).

25 I do *not* mean in this sentence to draw a parallel between some kind of literary-critical 'crime' of repetition and the crimes that Bolaño details. Such a reading would degrade the horror of the crimes. I also somehow feel, despite its repetitiveness, that criticism *should* continue to draw this reading from the novel. It is important, ethical, and worthwhile.

26 Bolaño, 2666, p. 456.

27 For more on these terms, see Stefano Ercolino, *The Maximalist Novel: From Thomas Pynchon's* Gravity's Rainbow *to Roberto Bolaño's* 2666, trans. by Albert. Sbragia (London: Bloomsbury, 2014); Edward Mendelson, 'Encyclopedic Narrative: From Dante to Pynchon', *MLN*, 91.6 (1976), 1267–75.

of the novel are encoded in such a way that the reader must invest intellectual energy, or capital, in the interpretation and comprehension of the sprawling text in order to 'purchase' the ethical payoff. However, such a reading practice, in which the reader invests effort to come to an interpretation felt to be his or her own, is the *modus operandi* of university English, particularly since the modernist and poststructuralist turns away from the intentionalist schools that situate the author as a centre of meaning. To teach active interpretation on the reader-side is one of *the* fundamental activities of university English/literary criticism in its contemporary mode. This mode, though, must contain within it the potential for misinterpretation, at least in the mind of a controlling author. On this front, Deckard has already noted how Bolaño adeptly connects his intellectuals' lack of political engagement (and obsession with aesthetic interpretation) to the historical situation of the Holocaust.[28] Through this type of link that resides in the structural obscurantism of this torrential, imperfect work, *2666* also implicates the reader who misinterprets. In fact, the mis-readings of the academy add a layer of memory fog (functionally similar to that found in Kazuo Ishiguro's *The Buried Giant* [2015]) that would only become complicit with Bolaño's Eichmann-esque figure, Sammer, who reminds his gravediggers that "the idea isn't to find things, it's to not find them", a more-than-clear, pointed jibe at literary-critical interpretative practices.[29]

Even putting selective readings and misreadings aside, this paradigm of interpretation that I am sketching presents a problem for theoretical literary research upon such work. In novels such as *2666*, to jump to a pre-formulated end result would degrade the utopic, critical power of this type of fiction. Even while such texts ridicule the processes of literary criticism and interpretation, they simultaneously rely on such processes. These texts are reliant on what those in educational communities refer to as 'active learning' in which readers must go through the process of reading and decoding a work for themselves, even if — as per my above literature review — this leads us to a set of interpretations that mostly share a common understanding.

To some extent this is the same problem that explication creates in any form, for as Louis Marin writes in his study of Utopics: "[t]he

---

28 Deckard, p. 359.
29 Bolaño, *2666*, p. 764; Kazuo Ishiguro, *The Buried Giant* (London: Faber, 2015).

benefits of pleasure the textual word play triggered were capitalized into analyses and theses. An authoritative power settled at the very spot of what is not capable of interpretation [...] It may simply be impossible to write and speak about utopia".[30] Exegesis through criticism is thereby placed in its first double bind in Bolaño's novel: pedagogy against comprehension; utopia (as an active and unending unfurling) against misreading and capitulation into pre-formed knowledge structures of analyses and theses. Put differently: to write literary criticism about the ethics of a novel such as *2666* is to claim reductively an "authoritative power [...] at the very spot of what is not capable of interpretation" by reducing the process of reading to "analyses and theses" as though they were a 'message'.[31] On the other hand, to read the novel oneself is to succumb to its teachings and its potential ethical/political utopianism and it seems that those who write criticism of the text come to the same 'analyses and theses'. This is what I mean by saying that Bolaño's novel seems to value 'process' for its political teachings.

In this problem of explication/criticism against utopian (and pedagogical) function, it is profitable to consider the theoretical paradigms within which the ethics and politics of Bolaño's work can be situated. With this in mind, it is worth examining the way that *2666* stages Theodor Adorno's ideas of autonomous and committed art while considering Bolaño's last novel within two opposed critical frameworks: as political and as utopian, for the contemporary university. These frameworks are useful when thinking about didacticism and the university but are nonetheless opposed because, in the instance of political success, the critical utopian function of the artwork is destroyed. As Marin puts it, this is when utopian thinking comes "to the awareness of its own process" as "revolutionary *praxis*".[32] As utopian or dystopian literatures project worlds that contrast with our own — in ways either positive or negative — they call for a translation into action and become politics. When they do so, under some theoretical paradigms they might no longer be considered as 'art'.

---

30   Louis Marin, *Utopics: The Semiological Play of Textual Spaces* (Atlantic Highlands: Humanities Press International, 1990), p. xx.
31   *Ibid.*
32   *Ibid.*, p. 279.

Adorno's essay 'Commitment' (1974) presents a specific response to Sartre's notion of committed literature that is relevant to the discussion at hand. In his writing, Sartre makes the distinction between prose and poetry, arguing that the author of the former can demonstrate political commitment to a cause and for an act of communication, while the latter is a mode that cannot. For Sartre, the prose writer is one "who makes *use* of words" to convey a message.[33] Although Adorno is highly critical of the term 'commitment' for its coercive mode of non-freedom in existentialist philosophy — a point he outlines in *The Jargon of Authenticity* (1964)[34] — in the essay piece 'Commitment' he posits two different polarities of non-commodified literature: committed art that has an overt and specific political aim, but that "strips the magic from a work of art that is content to be a fetish"; and autonomous art, or "art for art's sake", that falsely denounces its own "ineradicable connection with reality" and therefore subconsciously espouses a political aim nonetheless.[35] These positions, in which each dialectically "negates itself with the other", constitute the space in which all art, according to Adorno, has lived; a space located somewhere between the utopian/aesthetic and the political/mimetic.[36] Of relevance for an analysis of *2666*, the example that Adorno uses to demonstrate his thesis comes from the work of Bertolt Brecht.

Adorno stresses that Brecht's original intention, in which Adorno believes he failed, was to practice an art that "both presents itself as didactic, and claims aesthetic dispensation from responsibility for the accuracy of what it teaches".[37] For Adorno, Brecht's work simultaneously claims that it is political while nonetheless also stating that it can claim for itself an artistic detachment or abstraction from political reality. The first part of this problem for Brecht, as Adorno sees it, is that his works are too saturated with overt political messages and information: "the

---

33   Jean-Paul Sartre, *What Is Literature?*, trans. by Bernard Frechtman (New York: Philosophical Library, 1949), p. 19.
34   Theodor W. Adorno, *The Jargon of Authenticity*, trans. by Knut Tarnowski and Frederic Will (London: Routledge and Kegan Paul, 1986), pp. 34, 69–70.
35   *Idem*, 'Commitment', in *Aesthetics and Politics*, trans. by Francis McDonagh (London: Verso, 2007), pp. 177–95 (pp. 175–76).
36   *Ibid.*, p. 176.
37   *Ibid.*, p. 183.

more preoccupied [he] becomes with information, and the less he looks for images, the more he misses the essence of capitalism which the parable is supposed to present".[38] The second dialectical point is that, in Brecht's downgraded metaphors — in this case the substitution of a "trivial gangster organization" for "a conspiracy of the wealthy and powerful" in *The Resistible Rise of Arturo Ui* (1941) — "the true horror of fascism is conjured away".[39] Adorno goes on to argue that "[f]or the sake of political commitment, political reality is trivialized".[40]

2666 is, in many ways, also susceptible to such critiques. A work of epic theatre that nonetheless "has no epic pretensions", Bolaño's novel seeks to "make men think", in Adorno's phrase, but it also potentially falls prey to the traps of 'commitment'.[41] As one example, Bolaño's novel must beware Adorno's association of committed literature with pornography. This is not the more recent idea of 'empathy fatigue' espoused in the wake of mass-media culture, but rather that, for Adorno, "[t]he so-called artistic representation of the sheer physical pain of people [...] contains, however remotely, the power to elicit enjoyment".[42] While Carolyn J. Dean points out, in her critique of this argument, that this strain of thought has a heritage as far back as Diderot in the eighteenth century, and substantially increased in usage around the 1960s in reference to the Holocaust, Bolaño recognises this conflation of sexuality and power that can occur in artistic representation and so constantly reminds the reader that this pornographic mode is also potentially one of sexual violence.[43] Thus, every time that we might be tempted to forget the affinity between the modes, the text reminds us that many, if not all, of the murder victims piled up in *2666* have been both vaginally and anally raped. Furthermore, in *2666*'s discussion of snuff films, Bolaño gives the reader a strong metatextual clue as to where the novel sits, reminding us of both the mimetic fallacy, but also the pornographic potential that, it seems, the novel wishes to avoid: "the snuff industry, in this context,

---

38   *Ibid.*
39   *Ibid.*, p. 184.
40   *Ibid.*, pp. 184–85.
41   Farred, p. 692.
42   Adorno, 'Commitment', p. 189.
43   C.J. Dean, 'Empathy, Pornography, and Suffering', *Differences*, 14.1 (2003), 88–124 (p. 89).

was just a symptom".[44] To rephrase this: Bolaño appreciates the fine line between empathy and pornography in ethically 'committed' literature and metafictionally signposts this so that, each time the trap is open, the reader is pointed around the pitfall. Bolaño, like Dean, wants to express "something quite a bit more complicated than the conventional notion that pornography represents an unspeakable association between sexuality and murder", but is aware of this link and warns the reader of their potential complicity.[45]

As a text that seeks, then, to explore ethically the power of fiction in the wake of mass murder, it is worth considering in more detail how *2666* fits within a utopian tradition (by which I am referring also to dystopian traditions) and also how it resonates with other twenty-first-century novels. This is important; the purpose of Thomas More's original *Utopia* was, at least in part, to reflect critically on the current environment in England, while also parodically schooling its audience in the routes to a perfect world. It turns out that this utopian function is linked, in several ways, to the mode of didacticism that *2666* employs. In the study of literary utopia, fictions (such as Swift's *Gulliver's Travels* [1726]) are usually not deemed important so much for the specific *topoi* they present — although these are undoubtedly of enormous real-world significance — but rather for their more generalizable qualities of ongoing (uncompletable) dislocation and reformulation; a literary distancing from the real-world analogies to which mimesis aspires. In such a model, in addition to exhibiting internal incoherence, utopian *and* dystopian worlds aim to expose a rift between what could be (realms of subjunctive possibility) and what merely is and, therefore, the preconditions of its possibility; critique. In both cases, this is a matter of perspective. Dystopia takes the elements of the present that look most threatening or dangerous and amplifies them in a projected future. Utopia, on the other hand, takes those elements that loom large (such as politics) in our world and makes them seem petty by resolving their debates in an instantiated but dislocated space.

---

44 Bolaño, *2666*, p. 536. This approach might be contrasted with the depiction of snuff films in American fiction of the brat pack generation, such as Bret Easton Ellis's *Less Than Zero* (1985).

45 C.J. Dean, p. 106.

In *Gulliver's Travels*, for instance, this is exemplified in the way in which Gulliver's perspective is changed between the different worlds that he visits. In Brobdingnag, he is small amid a land of giants and the ugliness of the world is (misogynistically here) amplified, shown in his disgust at seeing the pores in the skin of the women lifting him up. The small cracks in the world are made large. In Lilliput, though, the Big and Little Endians fight their war over which end of a boiled egg should face upwards — and here, Gulliver is a giant who views such politics as literally petty. This well-rehearsed idea of dislocation and reformulation, a subjunctive thinking-otherwise, is a key concept in utopian fiction.[46]

2666 deliberately signals itself in this mode. Its city is not the real-world Ciudad Juárez but an emphatically insisted-upon intra-textual reality: "Santa Teresa. I'm talking about Santa Teresa".[47] The potentially dangerous essentialism that is engendered by this dislocation and abstraction — the creation of a "floating signifier", as Sarah Pollack has put it — conversely again lends itself to a pedagogical function at the expense of specificity; a 'teachable moment' as the present lingo might have it.[48] This is, once more, the challenge of which Adorno wrote: as Bolaño dislocates his environment from the mimetic reality it gains political force, but perhaps only somewhat at the expense of the specific suffering in the real place of Ciudad Juárez.

That said, Bolaño even announces that we should read *2666* in a critical dystopic mode through his mapping of the city space. In this aspect of the text, Bolaño reworks Marin's formulation that the utopian city "gives not a possible route, or even a system of possible routes, but articulations signaled by closed and open surface spaces" in the fact that his city is mapped by the dead, closed (but openly violated) female body, navigated by the male police officials, and mediated through the intersubjective shifts of narration in the novel.[49] To evoke Borges, as does Marin, and following Boxall's reading: *2666* is a one-to-one map of the abstracted necropolis narrated with the body-as-text, rather than a

---

46 For more on this, see Tom Moylan, *Demand the Impossible: Science Fiction and the Utopian Imagination* (New York: Methuen, 1986).
47 Bolaño, *2666*, p. 459.
48 Sarah Pollack, 'After Bolaño: Rethinking the Politics of Latin American Literature in Translation', *PMLA*, 128.3 (2013), 660–67 (p. 663).
49 Marin, p. 208.

particular, specific space of lived horror. Yet, just at the moment when Bolaño's abstraction seems to go too far, the transnational features of the text, with clear representations of global economy and travel, return to lend a specificity to the location. Santa Teresa is also Ciudad Juárez but, in its fictional abstraction, Bolaño is saved from the purely political/mimetic and allowed to play with the utopian/aesthetic.

This questioning of societal independence in art, in conjunction with the idea of the utopian tradition in 2666, prompts a return to Marin and his reading of May '68 and the university. Bolaño clearly signals that the function of the university, or rather its breakdown, is crucial to his investigation through the satirical portrayal of the literature professors and the pretentious high-literary writing of his fictional author, with a cult academic following, who trails sentences thus: "then, too, then, too, then, too".[50] As Farred puts it: "2666 satirizes the cult status that the Archimboldians of all theoretical stripes have assigned the elusive, Pynchonesque author".[51] In fact, one of the key didactic purposes of Bolaño's novel is an attempt to evaluate critically the academy: the neoliberal university as a site of revolution, teaching, and resistance. Examining these sites in his theoretical work, Marin asks: "[w]asn't this the place where the relationship between teacher and student, authorized and institutionalized, could be deconstructed through this relationship's very content?".[52]

The university was proposed, in '68's grim optimism, as a "'properly' utopic space", but how much we had to learn of utopia in order to see the "proof of the project's failure", writes Marin. Most academics are, by now, more aware of the university's socio-disciplinary, as opposed to esoterically cultural, function than they would like. We are now beyond the age of innocence when we could imagine an academy free from interdependence with the dominant ideology, be that in its mirroring of the "capitalist industrial system" or of the labour practices "linked to the most insidious forms of cultural exploitation".[53] Bolaño's critique of the institutional structure is, however, more complicated than this straightforward, plaintive protesting would suggest.

---

50   Bolaño, 2666, p. 661.
51   Farred, p. 699.
52   Marin, p. 4.
53   Ibid., pp. 4–5.

Quis Custodiet Ipsos Custodes?: Critiquing the Critics and the University in *2666*

Bolaño's text, I have argued, is one that can be seen as crypto-didactic; a novel that is slyly pedagogical in its ethical precepts, using a history of utopian fictional techniques to underwrite this. As can now be explored in more detail, the dystopia of *2666* brings a specific focus to the structure of the university and the text appears to mount several critiques of this institution. The entanglement of the university in the dystopic critique of *2666* is furthered through the statements that show, not a site of pure learning divorced from the horrendous events that are charted throughout the novel, nor even one on the correct side of the events of 1968, but instead an institution connected by blood. In fact, the most transparent of these signposts is the family bloodline: Don Pedro Negrete, head of the ineffectual and corrupt city police in the text, is the "twin brother of the university rector".[54] The scorn poured on the university here is not a simple case of an anti-academic authorial jibe (although such institutions are also depicted as "breeding grounds for the shameless"), but an insinuation that the entire mechanism of the university is paired with the corruption of the police force that permits mass rape and slaughter; twinned representations of Louis Althusser's state apparatuses.[55] Bolaño shows that the idea of the university as a site of detached, utopian purity is deeply flawed through an almost idealist mode that separates appearance from essence.[56] This is achieved through the fact that the surface appearance, or depiction, of the critics in the first part of the novel is as eccentric and pedantic, formalist individuals obsessed with their texts; merely isolated, but harmless. Their essence, however, is one of violence. This is most clearly revealed when they savagely beat the taxi driver who objects to their polyamorous interest in Liz Norton. At this point the text suddenly veers into discourses of

---

54 Bolaño, *2666*, p. 606.
55 *Ibid.*, p. 787; Louis Althusser, 'Ideology and Ideological State Apparatuses (Notes towards an Investigation)', in *Lenin and Philosophy and Other Essays*, trans. by Ben Brewster (London: NLB, 1971), pp. 121–73.
56 For more on this interpretation of German idealist traditions, see Ameriks; Paul Guyer, 'Absolute Idealism and the Rejection of Kantian Dualism', in *The Cambridge Companion to German Idealism*, ed. by Karl Ameriks (Cambridge: Cambridge University Press, 2000), pp. 37–56.

national and religious hatred. Bolaño's text is instantly peppered with "English" vs. "Pakistani" and the violence is purported to embody the insults:

> shove Islam up your ass [...] this one is for Salman Rushdie [...] this one is for the feminists of Paris [...] this one is for the feminists of New York [...] this one is for the ghost of Valerie Solanas, you son of a bitch, and on and on, until he was unconscious and bleeding from every orifice in the head, except the eyes.[57]

The invocation of feminism as justification for racial violence is particularly pertinent not only to the femicides in Mexico, thereby implicating the critics, but also to a wider discussion regarding occidental neo-colonialism, Islamophobia, and intersectionality. In this instance, it is the university, through the critics, that appears central to this violence. This is important. As will be seen, literary criticism in Bolaño's novel may be depicted as onanistically detached, but its ethics and elements of hypocrisy *do matter*. In fact, it matters to such an extent that Bolaño connects it directly to the misogyny of the central and most prominent portion of his novel.

As Bolaño gives no straight out-and-out reasoning for why the university can be seen as totally complicit with this violence, it seems most straightforward — by the law of Occam's razor — to link it to Farred's reading of a postcolonial critique of neoliberalism within the text and the academy's growing entanglement with big business.[58] This is seen in the function of exclusivity and marginalisation in the university structure. When the critics first meet Amalfitano "the first impression" they had "was mostly negative, in keeping with the mediocrity of the place", a statement that draws a parallel between geo-specificity/location and assumptions of merit.[59] The exception to the group here is Liz Norton, an educated and intelligent character, but one who is less tightly bound to the academic institution: "[a]ll they knew about Liz Norton was that she taught German literature at a university in London. And that, unlike them, she wasn't a full professor".[60] Despite

---

57   Bolaño, *2666*, p. 74.
58   For more on the place of the university within neoliberalism, see Wendy Brown, *Undoing the Demos: Neoliberalism's Stealth Revolution* (New York: Zone, 2015).
59   Bolaño, *2666*, p. 114.
60   *Ibid.*, p. 12.

sharing her surname with an early literary elitist and generalist literary professor, unlike the other critics, Norton sees the human being rather than the competitive academic association of individuals with national placement: her "impression was of sad man whose life was ebbing slowly away".[61] Yet, "[w]hen Amalfitano told them he had translated *The Endless Rose*", one of the fictional author's (that is, Archimbaldi's) novels and likely a play on Umberto Eco's *The Name of the Rose* (1980), "the critics' opinion of him changed".[62] The structures of value and worth that Bolaño's academy co-opts, in keeping with all neoliberal, late-capitalist (for whatever those terms are worth) vocational careers, is one of 'excellence' amid competition, but also one that privileges the preoccupations of the occidental university. When Amalfitano shares the interests of the Anglo-American critics, his worth is increased. To distinguish oneself from the mediocre mass is the aim, but the 'mediocre' mass of people, in *2666*, are being sequentially murdered.

The fundamental critique of the university's entanglement with neoliberalism is now well-known and rehearsed, particularly in humanities departments. As far as the term 'neoliberal' is useful to denote a political rationality of free-market-based systems operated on a nominal insistence on transparency and underwritten by fixations on quantification and measurement, this is well summarised by Sheila Slaughter and Gary Rhoades:

> [p]ublic colleges and universities are exemplars of neoliberalism. As with neoliberal regimes worldwide, U.S. public higher education assigns markets central social value. Public colleges and universities emphasize that they support corporate competitiveness through their major role in the global, knowledge-based economy. They stress their role in training advanced students for professional positions close to the technoscience core of knowledge economies.[63]

Clearly, from such critiques, and many others that frequently circulate, the direct threat to the liberal Enlightenment humanist educational

---

61 *Ibid.*, p. 114; for more on Charles Eliot Norton and his belief that he was defending against cultural barbarism, see Graff, pp. 82–83.
62 Bolaño, *2666*, p. 116.
63 Sheila Slaughter and Gary Rhoades, 'The Neo-Liberal University', *New Labor Forum*, 6 (2000), 73–79 (p. 73).

project through entanglement with the market is the main objection.[64] This prompts two responses that are pertinent to 2666. The first is a counter-objection that, as Stephen Billet puts it, "the provision of vocational education through universities has long existed, and has always been largely directed towards occupational purposes, despite the contrary often being claimed".[65] The fact that these vocations are well paid and in intellectually demanding areas is often overlooked in the denunciation of the university's claimed secession to the needs of society. The second is that, if we are to see the university and the police as twinned, as Bolaño's novel implies, then the function of the university that is under critique shifts slightly: the university must work, as with late-Foucault's reading of the police, to create a "live, active, productive man" but also to totalise, discipline and, in the next phase, control.[66]

2666 presents, from this, an academy divided against itself. As revolutionary praxis, it is failure: there has only been a further entrenchment of the academy in neoliberal models of commodified education and societal discipline. As a utopian project, to follow Marin's schema, the university also falls down: the supposition of the university's function as pure and discrete from commerce or the aims of society leads to segregation and implicit complicity through inaction with the exploitation (and in Bolaño's text, murder) of lower class women. This is clearly seen in the fact that the bumbling literature professors, alongside the rector who looked "as if every day he took long meditative walks in the country" (implying a life free from cares, a stereotyped and outmoded presentation of academic life), form a group whose exegesis of Archimbaldi's texts as a "Dionysian vision of ultimate carnival" (aesthetic critique) sits in opposition to another

---

64 See, for more critiques, among others, Thomas Docherty, *For the University: Democracy and the Future of the Institution* (London: Bloomsbury, 2011); John Holmwood, *A Manifesto for the Public University* (London: Bloomsbury, 2011), http://dx.doi.org/10.5040/9781849666459; Andrew McGettigan, *The Great University Gamble: Money, Markets and the Future of Higher Education* (London: Pluto, 2013); William Davies, *The Limits of Neoliberalism: Authority, Sovereignty and the Logic of Competition* (Thousand Oaks: SAGE, 2014); Brown.
65 Stephen Billett, *Vocational Education: Purposes, Traditions and Prospects* (London: Springer, 2011), p. 8.
66 Michel Foucault, 'Pastoral Power and Political Reason', in *Religion and Culture*, ed. by Jeremy R. Carrette (Manchester: Manchester University Press, 1999), pp. 135–52 (p. 149); Gilles Deleuze, 'Postscript on the Societies of Control', *October*, 59 (1992), 3–7.

group's readings of "suffering" and "civic duty" (political critique) in the writer's works.[67] While there has long been a stereotype of the literature professor as a "kind of internal émigré" from broader cultures, it is the eponymous critics' anarchic aesthetic and formal approaches that prevail in the text's narrative.[68] In their isolated apolitical obsession with aesthetics, rather than an integration with the social, the suffering of individuals is erased. As was seen in the preceding chapter, this function can also be taken away from the university by novels that seek to supersede university English in this area. Bolaño's critique, though, is very different to McCarthy's. Rather than critiquing the role of university English in the canonisation process and in the conferral of aesthetic value, Bolaño seems to brand this very activity as the height of self-obsessed nihilism or narcissism; the same accusation that some in the academy level at metafiction.

When viewed in this light, the role of the university as represented in *2666* brings Bolaño's project back full-circle to notions of commitment and didacticism. By remarking on formalism as opposed to ethical readings the text begins to signal the acceptable interpretations through which it can be read by university professors and the degree to which their position is pre-compromised. In this way, *2666* demonstrates a knowledge of the ways in which it will be approached by academics and metafictionally steers the reader; a crypto-didactic function. Firstly, it seems clear that the novel ridicules purely aesthetic interpretations divorced from social reality as affordable only to an apolitical, privileged class group. For a literary-critical reading of Bolaño's work to adopt this stance, therefore, would place its arguments in logical contradiction with the text. Secondly, though, the text also pre-invalidates sociological approaches of the academy towards literature on the basis of the social position that the university occupies; twinned with the police. To speak on behalf of the subaltern through institutional practices that the text depicts as married to violence suggests that literary criticism, in Bolaño's take, would do better to remain silent than to adopt a self-profiting strategy of condescension.

---

67 Bolaño, *2666*, pp. 111–12.
68 For more on the narratives of humanistic resistance to corporate culture through elitist retreat, see Alan Trachtenberg, *The Incorporation of America: Culture and Society in the Gilded Age* (New York: Hill and Wang, 2007); Graff, pp. 82–86.

To expand upon this a little, 'strategies of condescension', in the sociology of Pierre Bourdieu, are "those strategies by which agents who occupy a higher position in one of the hierarchies of objective space symbolically deny the social distance between themselves and others, a distance which does not thereby cease to exist". From such a situation, the dominant party in a power relationship "can use objective distances in such a way as to cumulate the advantages of propinquity and the advantages of distance, that is, distance and the recognition of distance warranted by its symbolic denegation [denial]".[69] Bolaño demonstrates that his literary critics are deploying such a strategy in their 'defence' of Liz Norton. At once, the critics espouse feminist values (while not truly valuing Norton's intellectual contributions and instead wanting to sleep with her), while concurrently shunning notions of equality as it applies in other spheres of liberal tolerance. In this way, Bolaño makes his critics benefit from an ethical payoff in outwardly supporting feminist equality from their privileged position of patriarchal authority while also showing that their underlying racism is intensely problematic for any kind of inclusivity or intersectionality. The benefit to the critics in outwardly collapsing the distance between their patriarchal position and supporting Norton is transparent. The same is true, however, of their critical reading practices. While benefiting from a supposed history of liberal humanism and civic purpose, the critics choose to explore aesthetics over ethics. Conversely, it is also true that the rival critics, who do enact ethical readings, do so from a socially elevated position, and so themselves benefit from their critical, ethical reading.

To digress briefly, these particular strategies of condescension are prevalent in many contemporary novels that deal with the academy but perhaps appear nowhere so explicitly as in the aforementioned work by Zadie Smith, *On Beauty*. Near to the close of this text, the reader is presented with the most detailed portrait of Howard Belsey's friend, Erskine, that the novel will offer. At this moment, Smith explicitly signals that she is working with strategies of condescension. Erskine's "great talent", we are told, lay "in making people feel more important than they actually were". From this, Smith writes, "[i]t might seem, when Erskine praised you or did you a professional favour, that it was

---

69 Pierre Bourdieu, 'Social Space and Symbolic Power', *Sociological Theory*, 7.1 (1989), 14–25 (p. 16), http://dx.doi.org/10.2307/202060.

you who were benefiting. And you might indeed benefit". However, "in almost every case", she continues, "Erskine was benefiting more".[70]

This is of particular relevance for a comparative reading with Bolaño's novel. In *2666* it is clear that the moment I have been detailing, in which the male critics collapse distances of power for their own benefit (a strategy of condescension), is inextricably linked to race. The critics amplify their racism in order, supposedly, to downplay their misogyny while all the while profiting from this act. In *On Beauty*, the specific context is the moment when Carl is appointed to the (newly fabricated) post of 'Hip Hop Archivist' in order to circumvent the impending prohibition on discretionary students attending Wellington College's classes, an aspect that intersects with the different political polarities of the novel's various black characters: the conservative Kipps against the liberal Erskine. In this particular instance, the benefit to Erskine in concocting a job for Carl is to avoid entering into the spirited debate about affirmative action and the historically conditioned elements of inequality within a supposed meritocracy that problematically circle his outward show of generosity. While very different works, it is nonetheless of note that this practical, strategic move in *On Beauty*, is also linked to issues of race within a context of an academic humanities department, as it is in *2666*.

To return to Bolaño's novel, though, this problem, in which criticism is scarcely possible and in which art struggles to speak of politics, is reflected in another didactic contradiction of the text: the temporal disjunction of its name. As with most utopian fictions that have to dislocate their settings, Bolaño certainly re-spatializes his work to a fictional Santa Teresa. However, the novel's temporality is arguably located amid a fluctuation between the past, the contemporary, and the future. This is especially clear when the novel's title is read through the well-known reference in Bolaño's previous novel, *Amulet* (1999), to "a cemetery in the year 2666, a forgotten cemetery under the eyelid of a corpse or an unborn child, bathed in the dispassionate fluids of an eye that tried so hard to forget one particular thing that it ended up forgetting everything else".[71] Treating the title as a year, based on the

---

70   Zadie Smith, *On Beauty* (London: Penguin, 2006), p. 371.
71   Roberto Bolaño, *Amulet*, trans. by Chris Andrews (New York: New Directions, 2008), p. 86.

Amulet reference, Henry Hitchens pointed out that this could correspond to certain datings of the Exodus story occurring 2666 years after the *creation*, thus placing the novel's key reference point in our now-distant past.[72] Conversely, as a year based on the Christian calendar, the text implies a dystopian future; a direction in which humanity is headed as the bodies of the present pile up and are forgotten. Amid these temporal poles lies the novel's present, which has to try not to forget moral lessons, learned either from the text's future projection of a dystopian cemetery or from its redemptive past reference point. In either case, the conception of time and forgetting is curious but can be linked back to a schooling purpose within the novel; the temporal dislocation and its relation to the present mark a demonstrable example or case study of the novel's space and time.

What seems to emerge from this setup is that the issues of commitment that *2666* frames do not appear to be concerned solely with artistic practice; Bolaño does not seek just to teach art how to represent. Instead, broadly speaking, the text's teachings are turned upon the academy. Bolaño's novel, in its treatment of the critics, seems designed to discipline, train, and encourage critics and the academy to write sociologically engaged criticism while concurrently negating the validity of those readings as strategies of condescension and encouraging reflexive thought on the societal position of the university. That this metafictional signalling is designed to teach and to alter critical subjectivity is made clear through a conversation between two of Bolaño's characters:

> "That's a pretty story. [...] A pity I'm too old and have seen too much to believe it".
> "It has nothing to do with belief [...] it has to do with understanding, and then changing".[73]

This has ironic consequences because, under such a mode, Bolaño's novel takes on utilitarian characteristics: it is itself as entangled in the neoliberal web of 'use' and 'utility' of art as the objects of its own critique.

---

72 Henry Hitchens, 'The Mystery Man', *The Financial Times*, 8 December 2008, http://www.ft.com/cms/s/0/7c4c7cd2-c264-11dd-a350-000077b07658.html.
73 Bolaño, *2666*, p. 716.

In this environment, it might be concluded that Bolaño's critique of the university is one designed to shut down literary criticism. As either a hypocritically positioned critical entity, or an ineffectually aesthetically obsessed body, what hope can the university and university English offer in a space where "the victims of sex crimes in this city" number "[m]ore that two thousand a year. And almost half of them are underage. And probably at least that many don't report being attacked. [...] every day more than ten women are raped here"?[74] Yet, as Catherine Belsey puts it: "[a]ssumptions about literature involve assumptions about language and about meaning, and these in turn involve assumptions about human society. The independent universe of literature and autonomy of criticism are false".[75] Bolaño also tells us, through the previous Biblical reference in the novel's title, that all is not lost; it is not too late to begin a journey to a promised land. Redemption might still be possible. Although this doesn't get us out of Adorno's theoretical problem that, in the false world all praxis is false, Bolaño espouses an ethics that asks us to believe once more in the political, utopian and didactic function of writing, both critical and creative. Critics must not, though, be didactic. Bolaño makes it clear enough that this task is to be left to fiction, for otherwise the critics become "like missionaries ready to instill faith in God [...] less interested in literature than in literary criticism, the one field, according to them — some of them, anyway — where revolution was still possible".[76] Despite the criticism of the critics, however, Bolaño also makes it clear that he does not want a vacuum: "[w]hat is it I want you to do? asked the congresswoman. I want you to write about this, keep writing about this. [...] I want you to strike hard, strike human flesh, unassailable flesh, not shadows".[77]

---

74 *Ibid.*, p. 563.
75 Catherine Belsey, *Critical Practice* (London: Routledge, 2002), p. 27.
76 Bolaño, *2666*, p. 72.
77 *Ibid.*, p. 631.

PART III: LEGITIMATION

5. Sincerity and Truth

Although slightly older than the commonly-supposed professionalising Arnoldian origin, the discipline of English studies is relatively young, having come into being as "English language and literature" in 1828 at the University of London (now UCL rather than the federated research university that currently takes the name University of London).[1] Over the course of the discipline's short history, however, a range of aspects has remained ever-present and unsatisfactorily resolved under the heading of 'value'. As John Hartley traces it, these debates can be subdivided into three phases (simplifying for reasons of comprehensibility). The first is to chart the lineage of Matthew Arnold to F.R. Leavis, in which it was consistently argued that "English Literature was the moral centre of the school curriculum" with "militant opposition to the supposed deadening effects of mass culture" resulting in a canonised high elitism. The second phase comes with Stuart Hall's Marxist-inflected approach at the Centre for Contemporary Cultural Studies (following Richard Hoggart) opening the doors to popular culture. The third phase is concerned with governmentality and the use of culture, seen clearly in the work of Tony Bennett pertaining to discourses of "the creative industries" and other phrases used by the state to recuperate the arts.[2]

As was examined in Parts One and Two, these shifts in value structures are charted within various aesthetic, political, and moral contexts in

---

1   See, in particular, Underwood, *Why Literary Periods Mattered*, pp. 81–113; Graff; Franklin E. Court, *Institutionalizing English Literature: Culture and Politics of Literary Study, 1750–1900* (Stanford: Stanford University Press, 1992).
2   John Hartley, *A Short History of Cultural Studies* (London: SAGE, 2003), pp. 32–37.

contemporary fiction. As the authority of the academy to canonise on grounds of high aesthetics wanes, the idea of literary fiction is born and works begin to situate themselves within this paradigm. Conversely, as the authority of the academy to canonise on grounds of morality fades, certain strains of work take on the task of moral education and politico-social critique, even amid a relativistic paradigm far from the Victorian didacticism of a previous age.

Having examined in Part Two the ways in which aesthetic and political critiques of the academy are respectively enacted in a set of very different texts, this third section will now turn to the strategies through which such works legitimate themselves over and above the discipline of literary studies. For this first chapter on this topic, I turn to one of the clearest examples of a work of twenty-first-century metafiction that blurs the boundaries between criticism and fiction, knowing the reading methods of the academy: Percival Everett's *Erasure*. Certainly, the author can claim to know a thing or two about academics: Everett is a Distinguished Professor of English at the University of Southern California. In the finest tradition of biting the hand that feeds, though, *Erasure* offers not only a charged satire of the literary market's racial pigeon holing, but also an insider critique of the academy. In fact it is hardly controversial to say that the creative writing programmes are key to Everett's literary identity.[3] Playing on this lineage, through an authorial claim to insider knowledge and then through an intricate parody of the academy's practices, *Erasure* is a novel that brilliantly demonstrates the type of outflanking of the academy undertaken by much contemporary metafiction of this nature. While I confess that the inclusion of *Erasure* marks a departure from the concept of works sited solely at distances from the academy, the opportunities it yields for opening a discussion of legitimation techniques will, I hope, excuse this.

Erasure, as with many of Everett's works, offers the story of a quasi-autobiographical figure (several of his novels feature a character called "Percival Everett", such as in *I Am Not Sidney Poitier* [2009]). In this case, Thelonius 'Monk' Ellison (transparently fusing Thelonius Monk

---

3   Ramón Saldívar, 'Speculative Realism and the Postrace Aesthetic in Contemporary American Fiction', in *A Companion to American Literary Studies*, ed. by Caroline F. Levander and Robert S. Levine (Hoboken: Wiley, 2011), pp. 517–31 (p. 518), http://dx.doi.org/10.1002/9781444343809.ch32; see also, of course, McGurl.

and Ralph Ellison) is a highly-articulate, educated, *avant-garde* author struggling to place his most recent inaccessible reworking of Ancient Greek legend with a publisher. One of the core reasons for this is that the market-driven system of literary sales as depicted within the novel always categorises the character's fictions as 'African-American writing', rather than evaluating the work on the basis of aesthetic merit. Faced with a mounting crisis in his home life as his mother succumbs to Alzheimer's disease and as his sister is murdered because of her work as an abortion clinic doctor, Ellison's financial situation becomes dire. Around this time, a rival author's book is enjoying a runaway success. Entitled *"We's Lives in Da Ghetto"* — and evidently modelled on Richard Wright's *Native Son* (1940)[4] as well as Sapphire's *Push* (1996) and its subsequent film adaptation[5] — the novel is, according to Ellison, every worst "display of watermelon-eating, banjo-playing darkie carvings and a pyramid of Mammy cookie jars".[6] In a fit of anger at the fact that stereotypical representations of illiterate, criminal, sexualised, irresponsible African Americans are the only depictions to achieve commercial success, Ellison writes his own pseudonymous parody of *"We's Lives in Da Ghetto"*, initially entitled *"My Pafology"* but later antagonistically renamed *"Fuck"*. Predictably, the horrific story (of an irresponsible, sexually violent, uneducated dropout who ends up on a *Jerry Springer*-like show to be confronted by his four children by four mothers) is praised by the publishers and film rights are secured. The novel then goes on to win a major prize, presenting a dilemma for Ellison, who sits on the jury. At the cliffhanger ending in which the narrator must choose whether or not to reveal himself, Ellison's personal finances are saved but his parody is lost on the market and his artistic integrity is gravely compromised.

As much other work has pointed out, *Erasure* plucks upon metatextual strings. The text relies, as Judith Roof notes, upon the "collapse of a perceived difference between author and narrator", an aspect that is both promoted by Everett's own subject position and the explicit

---

4 Dave Gunning, 'Concentric and Centripetal Narratives of Race: Caryl Phillips's *Dancing in the Dark* and Percival Everett's *Erasure*', in *Caryl Phillips: Writing in the Key of Life*, ed. by Bénédicte Ledent and Daria Tunca (Amsterdam: Rodopi, 2012), pp. 359–74 (p. 362).
5 Saldívar, p. 522.
6 Percival Everett, *Erasure* (London: Faber, 2003), p. 35.

depiction of the narrator's dilemma in accepting a literary prize at the end of the text. Most notably for the topic of this book, however, and as with the previous discussion of *House of Leaves*, the novel also introduces "other discourses into its narrative in the form of a scholarly paper".[7] The first section of *Erasure*, for example, is predominantly concerned with the narrator's arrival in Washington to give a paper to the *Nouveau Roman* society. This paper, an extract from a 'novel', is a work of high Theory, obsessed with aesthetic form above and beyond intelligibility "which treats this critical text by Roland Barthes, *S/Z* (1970), exactly as it treats its so-called subject text which is Balzac's *Sarrasine* (1830)". As the narrator's sister remarks: "I just can't read that stuff you write".[8]

This is far from the point. Once the actual paper has been given at the conference, it is clear that the literature professors in the audience have taken nothing from Ellison's academic work. Instead, they anticipate the controversy of his remarks in advance and then react violently despite the fact that, in Ellison's words, they "hadn't understood a word of what I had read".[9] To be clear, though, Ellison himself is depicted as disparaging towards his literary-critical work, describing it as "dry, boring, meaningless stuff" that he "only barely took seriously".[10] This derision of literary criticism finds its apogee in the character Davis Gimbel, apparently "the editor of a journal called *Frigid Noir*".[11] Gimbel is depicted as existing in a "disturbed, certifiable, and agitated postmodern state", a fact that is also signalled when he jumps out at the narrator while yelling the opening lines to Pynchon's *Gravity's Rainbow*.[12] Gimbel claims, in the ensuing argument, that the aesthetic and political projects of postmodern literature (which the text only vaguely outlines) were "interrupted", presumably by a resurgence of mimetic realism. Concurrently, however, the character also states that postmodernism and any other *avant-garde* form that "opposes or

---

7   Judith Roof, 'Everett's Hypernarrator', *Canadian Review of American Studies*, 43.2 (2013), 202–15 (p. 212).
8   Everett, *Erasure*, p. 8.
9   Ibid., pp. 17, 22.
10 Ibid., pp. 40, 44.
11 Ibid., p. 17.
12 "A screaming comes across the sky. It has happened before, but there is nothing to compare it to now". There is also another oblique reference to "an incredibly dense novel from a well-known, reclusive writer of dense novels", probably referring to Pynchon's *Mason & Dixon* (1997). *Ibid.*, pp. 42, 259.

rejects established systems of creation" *must* remain unfinished (the type of logic of 'fictions of process' that I outlined in the preceding chapter). The problem for Gimbel and other postmodernists, according to the narrator, is that he believes himself to be "saying something that makes sense", when the opposite is true. Finally, Ellison resorts to the real-world, common-sense approach when bombarded with supposed academic nonsense: "[m]an, do you need to get laid", he says.[13]

That said, and as Ramón Saldívar notes, the character Ellison is a postmodern writer who is ashamed of his realist work and the types of certainty that are required to write populist, mimetic fiction.[14] For Saldívar, the representation of these two poles, *sous rature*, "parodies both the modern and postmodern ways of thinking about race", making the novel both "postracial" and post-postmodern.[15] While I will not reiterate the thorny problems of the label postracial, which has a tendency to imply the erasure of continued systemic racism, as Saldívar is well aware, it is questionable whether the aesthetic characteristics of Everett's novel can be said to advance beyond postmodernism. Consider, for instance, the technique of *écriture sous rature* that seems central to the novel's conception of race and after which the text is named.[16] Although, in this instance, the take may be sophisticated, the specific strategy originates in Derrida's infamous 1967 inflection of Heidegger's technique at the height of poststructuralism in which presence and absence are simultaneously gestured towards.[17] To claim that the use of such a method — which was formed within the co-generative emergence of poststructuralism and postmodern fiction — constitutes a novel aesthetic strategy beyond the postmodern seems somewhat far-fetched.

Furthermore, the technique by which the novel dislocates the sincerity of Ellison's outer narrative is one of layered relation. The text of the parody novel, *"Fuck"*, fully interrupts the main flow of Ellison's story for approximately sixty pages and constitutes the main satirical

---

13 *Ibid.*, pp. 44–45.
14 Saldívar, p. 525.
15 *Ibid.*, p. 529.
16 Peter Boxall even claims that the "difficult play between inscription and erasure" may be "a constituent element of realism itself". Boxall, *The Value of the Novel*, p. 61.
17 Jacques Derrida, *Of Grammatology*, trans. by Gayatri Chakravorty Spivak (Baltimore: Johns Hopkins University Press, 1998), *passim*.

device of the work. However, as is clear from the history of postmodern, nested narratives, these digressive sub-tales are most often taken as *mise-en-abyme*; that is, reflections of the master works within which they sit. *Erasure*'s most subtle move is quietly to alert the reader that the parody within the novel signifies that the narrative within which it is encapsulated is also a parody. In other words, alongside its clear parody of useless academics, *Erasure* is a text that relies, to some degree, upon the expectations of literary tradition and knowledge of the techniques by which it will be read in order to show that the entire novel is parody. Everett knows that he can signal that Ellison is a parody by nesting a parody within the work. This is part of the way in which the novel plays with the concept of sincerity and legitimation, which I will now outline more thoroughly.

Sincerity

The well-rehearsed argument goes that fiction presents a type of untruth that is nonetheless honest (and perhaps, in some accounts, even *more truthful* than non-fiction) in its claim to distort.[18] Criticism, on the other hand, purports to be truthful and sincere, but is often accused of sophistry. Criticism and fiction are, therefore, involved in a kind of legitimation struggle over the truth. Notions of 'sincerity' in fiction, however, are difficult to discuss because there are different views on what, exactly, 'sincerity' means. The interpretation I advance here is but one among many definitions. As an opening note, though, it is worth pointing out that the term is clearly closely linked to, but separate from, 'authenticity'. So what is the difference? Is there a difference? Elizabeth Markovits and others deny that such a divide exists, or at least is of little use for many discussions.[19] However, in a distinction first taken seriously in the contemporary era by Lionel Trilling, authenticity is usually thought of as an exact correlation between one's hidden inner

---

18   See, for instance, Elizabeth Bowen's remarks on the how the novel 'lies', in Elizabeth Bowen, 'Notes on Writing a Novel', in *The Mulberry Tree: Writings of Elizabeth Bowen*, ed. by Hermione Lee (London: Virago, 1986), pp. 35–48.
19   Elizabeth Markovits, *The Politics of Sincerity: Plato, Frank Speech, and Democratic Judgment* (University Park: Pennsylvania State University Press, 2008), p. 21.

'self' and one's outer assertion and behaviour; a mode in which "there is no within and without".[20]

Unfortunately, if authenticity is about the erasure of a divide between an individual inner essence and its outer expression, a number of difficulties emerge. For one, this authenticity can only be seen as true if one knows one's own inner essence. However, does this 'inner essence' even exist and what is it? Such questions show that authenticity is actually embroiled in the difficulties of knowing oneself that are inherent in any age after psychoanalysis, although these queries also reach back to the slogan of the Delphic oracle. After all, how can one be true to an 'inner self' or 'essence' if one cannot wholly know oneself? That said, most people have a belief that they do know how they feel and also possess an internal representation of themselves — a self-image — that could be said to constitute their authentic self.

Sincerity, on the other hand, is seen in antiquity as a "moral excellence" deriving from Book Four of Aristotle's *Nicomachean Ethics* wherein a person is deemed sincere if he or she will "avoid falsehood as something base".[21] Sincerity is, in the interpretation that I will advance here, a type of honesty that is not merely concerned with accuracy in one's *statements* to others but is rather based upon checking future actions against previous speech and behaviour.[22] Although this differs somewhat from Trilling's definition of sincerity as "a congruence between avowal and actual feeling", this is unavoidable: the only way in which "actual feeling" can be seen is through action that is verified in a social situation.[23] If you say you will do something, do you make every effort truthfully to follow through on it? If you state a belief, do you truly mean it and can this be publicly seen in your subsequent actions?

Of course, it is possible and frequently necessary to *believe* someone else is speaking sincerely before one has seen the public proof that he or she will follow through on his or her words — it would be a grim world

---

20 Lionel Trilling, *Sincerity and Authenticity* (Cambridge, MA: Harvard University Press, 1972), p. 93.
21 Aristotle, *The Nicomachean Ethics*, trans. by David Ross (Oxford: Oxford University Press, 2009), sec. 1127b, 1–5; note, though, that Plato's concept of *parrhesia*, later explored extensively by Michel Foucault, could also be seen as intimately related to notions of 'sincerity'. See Markovits.
22 One also has to be careful that this appraisal of consistency is local and specific, though; a type of appraisal that Markovits calls 'trustworthiness'. Markovits, p. 204.
23 Trilling, p. 2.

were it otherwise. We have all developed strategies for dealing with this unknowable future and lack of proof, using, for example, a person's past record for truthfulness and the persuasiveness of his or her avowal as signifiers; '"I love you", s/he said'. However, any future betrayal of this sincerity will mean that such a belief was misplaced. Sincerity is, therefore, a social phenomenon pertaining to trust that unfolds between a faith in the present performance of avowal (a belief in a person's words and intentions) and the empirical verification of future action (the proof that they have made good on their words). Sincerity is an ongoing negotiation between trust, public performance, and proof, between the rhetoric of the present and the action of the future.

As ideas of sincerity and authenticity are not unchanging but differ from culture to culture, a few examples will serve to demonstrate the differentiation between sincerity and authenticity as they currently exist before I return to Everett. Firstly, assuming that authenticity really exists, it is possible to behave authentically, but insincerely. If one's authentic self is a liar and one makes a promise that is subsequently unfulfilled, one was insincere but authentic. Secondly, in an example that I owe to Orlando Patterson, one can be sincere but inauthentic. Patterson notes that people may be authentically prejudiced but that this does not prohibit them from behaving according to negotiated standards of society, decency, and public self-consistency (sincerity):

> I couldn't care less whether my neighbors and co-workers are authentically sexist, racist or ageist. What matters is that they behave with civility and tolerance, obey the rules of social interaction and are sincere about it. The criteria of sincerity are unambiguous: Will they keep their promises? Will they honor the meanings and understandings we tacitly negotiate? Are their gestures of cordiality offered in conscious good faith?[24]

This could lead to a type of sincere inauthenticity. The other permutations (insincere inauthenticity and authentic sincerity) are also possible but I will refrain from laying these out in detail here. The take-away point, however, is that the terms 'authenticity' and 'sincerity' are linked as they both focus1 on a truth to oneself, but they are also fundamentally distinct in the interpretation I am advancing: only an individual can

---

24 Orlando Patterson, 'Our Overrated Inner Self', *The New York Times*, 26 December 2006, http://www.nytimes.com/2006/12/26/opinion/26patterson.html.

tell whether they are being authentic (if even they can) but sincerity is a societal, public virtue that can be verified and judged by others. It is also true that the choice of prepositive or postpositive adjectival modifier (authentic/inauthentic/sincere/insincere) in each permutation of this matrix may affect the specific reading that is taken.

Table 1: the sincerity and authenticity matrix

	Sincere	Insincere
Authentic	Authentic sincerity Sincere authenticity	Authentic insincerity Insincere authenticity (postmodern fiction?)
Inauthentic	Inauthentic sincerity Sincere inauthenticity (realist fiction)	Inauthentic insincerity Insincere inauthenticity

As a final note, Trilling's thesis is that, when he was writing in the 1970s, contemporary society had become fixated on notions of authenticity at the expense of sincerity. Since that time, however, there has been another reversal back to sincerity (although critics might question whether these shifts are true movements or simply different priorities of classification). This shift back to sincerity from the late-1980s, as Markovits reads it, finds its clearest articulation in Jürgen Habermas's project of communicative action. Under such a theory, sincerity forms a new cornerstone in the field of so-called discourse ethics. As I intimated earlier, 'mutual trust', fostered through sincerity, is a crucial prerequisite to any kind of societal cooperation, in Habermas's formulation.[25]

This shift back towards a focus on sincerity can also be seen in various artforms. Consider, for example, the 1993 film *Groundhog Day*, in which Bill Murray is doomed to repeat the same twenty-four hours over and over until he comes to a more ethical existence. In the film, Murray's character, Phil Connors, at first behaves insincerely in his attempts to win over Andie MacDowell's character, Rita; he tries to learn her desires and to feign a set of false coincidences in their interests so that she will

---

25 Jürgen Habermas, *Moral Consciousness and Communicative Action* (Cambridge, MA: MIT Press, 1990), p. 136; Markovits, p. 20.

sleep with him. As the film progresses and it becomes clear that this will not work — and also that Phil cannot die — he decides to spend his energies ensuring that, for one day, he does nothing but help other people, thereby improving himself. As a result of this, his authentic self is changed and Rita falls in love with him. Once more, this demonstrates Trilling's thesis that authenticity is privileged. However, Phil is also no longer insincere; he avows, feels and acts without irony. His inner self has been changed so that he has no desire to be insincere any longer. He is a straight-talking, sincere (and now loveable) character. In this way, he becomes authentically sincere and the two are once more linked. What this means for contemporary fiction, however, requires some unpacking.

To understand the literary turn towards sincerity in the last twenty-five years, it is crucial to trawl back through the history of a certain mode of literary fiction that came to prominence in America in the 1960s and with which this book is prominently concerned: postmodern metafiction. As is seen most prominently in David Foster Wallace's 'manifesto' documents, the primary targets against which the sincerity group act — at least in the sphere of literary fiction, rather than poetry — are a series of, for the most part white, male writers whose writings were the subject of intense academic critical scrutiny from the 1970s onwards, namely: John Barth, Thomas Pynchon, Jorge Luis Borges, Don DeLillo, E.L. Doctorow, Robert Coover, Donald Barthelme, William H. Gass, William Gaddis, Kurt Vonnegut, and Richard Powers; and, on the other side of the Pond, Umberto Eco and John Fowles.

For the discussion at hand, the predominant stylistic and thematic characteristics of this subset of postmodern literature can be summarised as: irony; reflexivity and metafiction (fiction about fiction or the act of writing itself); reworkings of history; a playful mode that teases the reader; paranoia; and non-linearity (both of narrative and of the chronologies represented). These authors embrace and extend the project of high modernist experiment with often-lengthy and fragmented works that seek new modes of representation to counter the perceived failings of literary realism, namely that the supposedly objective and linear aspects of the nineteenth-century realist novel are not commensurate with lived experience. The undoing of the linear chronology and categorical moral certitude of the nineteenth-century realist novel finds its climax in the representations of a fragmented, complex, and overlapping body of literature that the postmodernists might claim more accurately represents fractured contemporary life.

To understand sincerity in literature, as we shall see shortly with a return to Percival Everett, one of the core components that needs to be analysed is the supposition that the irony of postmodern literature "is parasitic on sincerity", a claim that Markovits complicates.[26] In fact, those contemporary authors seeking new ways of engaging with sincerity in their fiction are not rejecting all aspects of postmodern literature; the complexity, fragmentation, and even the historical subject matter often remain. Instead, the core facet that these authors of the (New) Sincerity reject in their aesthetic is postmodern irony while in their philosophy they retain a postmodern incredulity at the idea of an authentic self. This complicates any narrative of a swing from authenticity to sincerity but is rather focused on the way in which irony, framed as an incongruity, is antithetical to a sincere public ethic.[27] It is worth, however, taking a few moments to consider how this might appear in a literary sense; after all, from my above examples, it seems clear what it could mean for a person to behave with differing degrees of sincerity, but it is less obvious what the literary equivalent of this might be. In order to understand this transcription of a behavioural description to the literary realm, it is important to think about two different spheres of 'action', both within narrative and without: authorship and intra-textual voice.

To begin with the author's position with regard to sincerity, I can think of no better example than the one already furnished by Adam Kelly who has perhaps written more on this 'New Sincerity' movement than anyone else and whose forthcoming and highly-anticipated *American Fiction at the Millennium: Neoliberalism and the New Sincerity* promises to strengthen this debate. Kelly notes of Wallace's short-story 'Octet' that it is extremely difficult — or even impossible — for a work of fiction to interrogate the truth of its own performance.[28] This is because, for an author of fiction to be sincere, he or she should communicate in

---

26   Markovits, p. 36.
27   Jill Gordon, 'Against Vlastos on Complex Irony', *The Classical Quarterly*, 46.1 (1996), 131–37 (p. 90); Markovits, p. 90.
28   Adam Kelly, 'David Foster Wallace and the New Sincerity in American Fiction', in *Consider David Foster Wallace,* ed. by David Hering (Los Angeles: Sideshow Media Group, 2010), pp. 131–46 (p. 143).

some way within a text that he or she is aware of the falsehood inherent to literary representation; fiction should be, at least to some extent, self-aware metafiction. However, as noted in the introduction to this volume, metafiction's self-knowledge is always inadequate and prompts an infinite regress.[29] This leads Kelly to conclude that "in Wallace's fiction the guarantee of the writer's sincere intentions cannot finally lie in representation — sincerity is rather the kind of secret that must always break with representation".[30] The first half of this statement — that fiction cannot represent the writer's sincere intentions — seems uncontentious and forms the basis of the many reading methods that disregard authorial intent, such as those of Roland Barthes, that have their roots in the New Critical movement. The second half, though, is more difficult. In the definition of sincerity that I outlined above, sincerity is always *only* about a trade-off between belief and representation and its future self-consistency; whether or not the hidden inner state of an 'authentic' self is truly represented in that consistency can be seen, as does Patterson, as irrelevant. Like Wittgenstein's "private object", it may exist but it "drops out of consideration".[31]

These limitations of fictional representation are well laid out by David Shields who, in *Reality Hunger: A Manifesto* (2010), appears sceptical of the novel's future (and instead seems to champion a type of literary-collage-journalism). Instead, Shields signals the interlinked problems of authenticity and sincerity that the novel will never wholly master (and that literary journalism should instead honestly face): "[w]hat does it mean to set another person before the camera, trying to extract something of his or her soul? [...] Do you promise to tell the truth, the whole truth, and nothing but the truth?"[32] The novel never can.

In this sense, a sincere author can never be represented within the text. This does not mean, however, that nothing can be done because, in at least one reading, the consistency of a text's 'truth to itself' can stand in for this function. This is distinctly *not* to mean that a text cannot contradict itself; to contain Walt Whitman's famous multitudes is the

---

29 Currie, p. 1.
30 Kelly, 'David Foster Wallace and the New Sincerity in American Fiction', p. 143.
31 Ludwig Wittgenstein, *Philosophical Investigations: The German Text, with a Revised English Translation* (Oxford: Blackwell, 2001), sec. 293.
32 David Shields, *Reality Hunger: A Manifesto* (London: Hamish Hamilton, 2011), pp. 79–80.

prerogative of literature. It is instead to say that fiction must drop any claim to the representation of an author's inner truth: literature is always an outward performance, a representation. Instead, to be sincere, literature must make good on its function to represent well (to engender *belief* in the reason for its avowals — even when metaphorical and implausible) and to represent in a manner consistent with its subject (which stands in for future verification of the avowal, even when contended through varying interpretation). Literature that persuades the reader of the necessity of its aesthetic composition is analogous to the individual who convincingly says: 'I promise'. Whether the promise is borne out is deferred, perhaps indefinitely, into the future.

There are many instances in literary history that do not hold up to this standard of sincerity or occasions when the understanding of a text's sincerity has changed. Consider, for instance, the failure of *Jane Eyre* (1847) that is made clear in the many postcolonial readings of the novel: the disjunct between Charlotte Brontë's statement that "conventionality is not morality" and the subsequent need for the death of Bertha Mason in the novel that allows Jane to marry. Likewise, in a very different epoch of the novel, the sincerity of Vonnegut's *Slaughterhouse-Five* (1969) is cast into doubt when his deeply sardonic text can only write its counter-narrative of the Dresden bombing through denigration of the Holocaust and the research work of a Holocaust-denier.[33] There are, therefore, problems here of interpretation, ambiguity, reader reception, and authorial intention (or otherwise). That said, sincerity in literature, decoupled from authenticity, is — at least in part — about appropriateness and consistency of representation.

Writing Under *Erasure*, Sincerity and Legitimation

Sincerity, while usually thought to be an ethical virtue, is frequently opposed to *strategy*, the means by which ethical projects are practically realised.[34] Strategy, and particularly rhetorical strategy, consists of making utterances not for the sake of truth, or later verification of intent,

---

33 Philip Watts, 'Rewriting History: Céline and Kurt Vonnegut', *The South Atlantic Quarterly*, 93.2 (1994), 265–78.
34 For more on this, see Ben Golder, *Foucault and the Politics of Rights* (Stanford: Stanford University Press, 2015).

but rather for the anticipated practical effect that such words will have upon a particular audience group (speech acts). This is not to say that a person with sincere intentions cannot use strategic rhetoric to achieve a practical end. It does seem, though, that the purity of the sincerity is somewhat compromised by such strategic thinking. This implies two important aspects for a reading of sincerity in Everett's novel. Firstly, sincerity is only possible as a concept because it can be contested and misconstrued as strategy.[35] If there were no possibility of sincerity actually being strategy, we would be more akin to Swift's Hounyhyms, the horse-like race who have no word for 'lie'. Strategy, likewise, can only function when an audience group believes that the rhetoric is sincere and will be fulfilled in verification at a later stage. Because sincerity is based upon a track record of truth and verification, the falsehood of strategy deprecates the symbolic worth of a speaker's future utterances. While, then, sincerity earnestly asks for an investment of trust in the present to be paid off in the future, thereby accumulating faith, strategy dishonestly spends the future reputational capital of sincerity to serve the fulfilment of its goals in the present (which may be either virtuous or malign). This is not to say that sincerity itself cannot be a strategy; far from it. Most contemporary politics of transparency (sincerity) are predicated upon the knowledge that appearing (or actually being) sincere is a good strategy for winning power.[36] In the terms of the above matrix, this is a kind of sincere inauthenticity. Secondly, strategy relies on a believed foreknowledge, or anticipation, of reception. If one cannot anticipate how one's discourse will be understood, it is impossible to manipulate rhetoric to serve a strategic end. In fact, this is the most dangerous situation because the surface effects of discursive utterances cannot accurately be predicted under every condition and so may backfire entirely. Fiction is placed very strangely with regard to this type of scenario if it aims to coerce interpretation, as was seen above in the discussion of Roberto Bolaño. For now, though, let us consider *Erasure*.

---

35 Although this reading may strike some as overly binary and structuralist, this can be eased if one considers a spectrum of strategies, truths, and motivations, as I will now go on to discuss.

36 One need only look at the Liberal Democrats' broken pledge in the United Kingdom regarding university tuition fees and the subsequent demolition of their future election chances.

Erasure is a novel that is at once sincere and strategic in various measures. For one, on the side of sincerity, its aesthetic, formalist decisions are congruent with its conflicted subject matter. To effect a dual parody centred around a non-binary, deconstructionist take on race — one side parodying eloquent, literary black struggle and the other denigrating stereotypically white-perceived black stereotype — Everett needs to deploy irony. While irony is typically thought of as the parasitic opposite of sincerity and is usually considered more applicable to strategy, in this instance Everett seeks to depict a gross social irony and so, therefore, his ironic aesthetic is verifiably congruent with the object of representation. In other words, this irony is sincere. This irony that is core to the novel lies in the tension between a supposed post-racial line within the text, as in Saldívar's argument, and the fact that this can only be represented, within the novel, by a hyper-focalisation upon issues of race.[37] Indeed, if one takes the line that *Erasure* is a text that seeks to move beyond identity determination by race ("the society in which I live tells me I am black")[38] then the largest irony of the novel is that it is read, in almost every piece of critical work upon it, as being concerned with race; the novel deploys quasi-deconstructionist techniques in which it is impossible to extricate an absence of race identity from thought about and speech on the subject of race identity.

This is a problem that is inherent within many identity-based movements and centres around the problem of strategic essentialism. Stemming from the fusion of Western Marxism and French Nietzschianism that fed into the anti-humanist schools that emerged in the 1960s and 1970s, subjects were relativized. Most prominently in the thought of Althusser and Foucault, 'the human' becomes not an atemporal unchanging subject, but a historically conditional (discursive) formation. This thinking then leads, in a theoretical lineage, to movements that relativize other more specific sub-identity formations: 'woman' (gender), 'black' (race), 'English' (nation). For instance, in her well-known 'Cyborg Manifesto', Donna Haraway writes that "[t]here is not even such a state as 'being' female, itself a highly complex category constructed in contested sexual scientific discourses and other social

---

37 Saldívar.
38 Everett, *Erasure*, p. 3.

practices".³⁹ Such a situation creates a problem within environments of inequality. Even if it is known that the underlying identity formation is socially constructed and therefore flawed, to reject the category of, say, 'female' leads, perhaps pre-emptively, to a form of post-feminism in which there is no available discourse through which to redress remaining manifest inequalities.

This problem led Gayatri Chakravorti Spivak to formulate the contentious notion of "strategic essentialism", which she later disowned.⁴⁰ This pragmatic move is well summarised by Razmig Keucheyan who defines it thus: "[t]he concept of strategic essentialism maintains that the provisional fixing of an essence known to be artificial can in some instances be strategically useful. Alternatively put, anti-essentialism can only be theoretical".⁴¹ This is the dilemma that ideas of post-race face: strategy vs. sincerity. Postcolonialism works by removing the grim mask of imperial universality from the specific to reveal identities as constructed or even assigned. While such identities are used and assigned, though, the legacy of inequality persists. *Erasure* continues to stage this dilemma of an environment free of racial identity while, at the same time, doing so by strongly re-inscribing a discursive focus on race as a real and practical identity aspect.

Where academics sit within this discourse is difficult to place, but the parodic depiction of the university — even while the text fights over a critical terrain landmarked by subjectivity, identity, and race — pitches the novel into competition with the academy. The two narratives of the text (Ellison vs. Van Go) are supposed, in some senses, to be polar opposites. However, as already noted, the form of nested narratives implies a correlation and mapping between the two literary spaces, rather than pure opposition. This can be seen in the parallels between the discourse of the academics within the outer narrative and the discourse of the parodically 'stereotypical' black characters within

---

39   Donna J. Haraway, 'A Cyborg Manifesto: Science, Technology, and Socialist-Feminism in the Late Twentieth Century', in *Simians, Cyborgs and Women: The Reinvention of Nature*, by Donna J. Haraway (London: Routledge, 1991), pp. 149–81 (p. 155).

40   Sara Danius, Stefan Jonsson and Gayatri Chakravorty Spivak, 'An Interview with Gayatri Chakravorty Spivak', *boundary 2*, 20.2 (1993), 24–50, http://dx.doi.org/10.2307/303357.

41   Razmig Keucheyan, *The Left Hemisphere: Mapping Critical Theory Today* (New York: Verso, 2013), p. 203.

the inner. After Ellison has given his paper at the *Nouveau Roman* society, Gimbel throws a bundle of keys at him and yells "[y]ou bastard!" and then "moved towards" the narrator "as if to fight".[42] This hardly seems so far from the 'ghetto' characters seen later in the novel:

> "I'm gone kick you in the ass, you don't shut up".
> "Fuck you", he say.
> "Fuck you", I say.
> "Fuck you", he say.
> "Fuck you", I say.

On its own, this would merely be another instance of the way in which the outer narrator, Ellison, as a proxy for Everett, disparages academia. However, *Erasure* is not a text wherein any narrator can directly substitute for, or speak on behalf of, the author. Ellison is also a parody, even if not to the same extent as Van Go. The question, for the evaluation of academics here, then becomes one of double negation and the nature of perspectivized caricature in the novel. This is a matter of double negation because, when a parody is effected within a novel by a character that is, itself, a parody, it is unclear whether the end result is a parody or whether the effect of the parody is thereby lessened (negated). The answer to this is undoubtedly complex and bound up with any reader's phenomenological experience of reading the text. For instance, the realisation that Ellison is also a parody may come too late for a reader to even consider the nested layers of parody and the logical negation that this might entail. Building on this, however, it is unclear whether Everett's parody is working on such a nested paradigm of negation. Put otherwise: is *Erasure* a novel wherein a negative of a negative becomes a positive?

This does not seem to be the case in any straightforward way. Instead, it seems clear that the novel's central parody of white-mass-market black stereotyping is meant. The outer narrative is harder to place, though. Everett is, himself, an academic and bound up in the structures that he parodies. He is also a recipient of many literary awards and honours, an aspect finally parodied in the novel as an incestuous community of experts re-validating themselves. Among others, Everett has received the PEN Center USA Award for Fiction, the Academy Award in Literature

---

42 Everett, *Erasure*, p. 22.

from The American Academy of Arts and Letters, the Hurston/Wright Legacy Award for Fiction, the New American Writing Award, the PEN Oakland/Josephine Miles Literary Award, an honorary Doctorate in 2008 from the College of Santa Fe, the 2010 Believer Book Award and the Dos Passos Prize in 2010. Although hypocritical, this actually gives credence to the argument that there is a degree of sincerity present in the political critique of the outer narrative of *Erasure*, boosted by the aesthetic critique of the congruence of ironic form with ironic subject.

This argument is bolstered when James English's analysis of literary prize culture is added to the equation. In English's argument, using Bourdieu's notions of interchangeable forms of capital, literary prizes are bodies that award material, social, and symbolic capital (money, support, and prestige) to authors who are legitimated by the prize's judges' cultural capital (knowledge and judgemental skills) and its sponsors' material capital (their money). In turn authors bestow symbolic capital back on prizes (whether they accept or scandalously refuse) through their own now-validated cultural capital.[43] In this compelling model of the regulation of symbolic exchange, the most important fact to realise is that such a system is normative because the valorisation process is cyclical. Authors produce work, good authors are judged worthy of prizes (sometimes by judges who are academics, although always after the fact of publication, as in Chapter One), good authors accept or reject literary prizes, good prizes are affiliated with good authors (sometimes regardless of whether they accept or reject the honour), prizes award money and prestige to authors (giving them income to work), and then authors produce work. Now, this is not to say that literary prizes cannot make awards to truly experimental work but rather to reiterate that they *tend* towards the reproduction and legitimation of forms that are already valued, especially in a market context. As with my remarks on the role of academics in canonisation earlier, prizes have the easier job of judging work that has already been published. To return to a previous example, Eimar McBride's *A Girl is a Half-Formed Thing* won multiple prizes after its publication. That book, though, went unpublished for nine years as no publisher foresaw its merit.

---

43 James F. English, 'Winning the Culture Game: Prizes, Awards, and the Rules of Art', *New Literary History*, 33.1 (2002), 109–35.

This symbolic economy of self-replication and conservatism is exactly the scenario that *Erasure* depicts with respect to Black American literary culture. The populist nature of the award ceremony, as it is shown in Everett's novel, sees the inner book (*"Fuck"*) validated by the characters in the outer narrative (*Erasure*). The economies are connected, though. Everett is an academic who writes an academic character who ends up complicity ensnared in potentially awarding the prize to his own parody book that was a product of his anger at the system. What was meant as an act of symbolic refusal and scandal once more serves only to re-enforce the economy that it attempted to denigrate and against which its anger was directed. The attempts of academics to escape this system always seem bound to end in complicity.

At this point, any attempts to locate Everett's novel at the poles of sincerity/strategy or parody/critique break down. In the multiple layerings of intentionality we find a clear example of the core strategies of methodological inflections of deconstruction; never binaries, but overlayed erasures. Even this reading, though, can be taken to a higher plane. In giving his novel the title *Erasure*, Everett signals, in advance, that he is aware of the interpretative strategies that the academy will deploy to read his work. The title, though, is ambiguous. It can, in one instance, be seen as an instruction: read this book through the lens of a Derridean legacy. In the other, it outflanks the reader who does so: the text knows what such a reading will entail and has laid a trail for the reader.

In this way, *Erasure* becomes a novel that centres on race, while framing itself as a text of a 'post-racial' climate even as it knowingly demonstrates the falsity of such a cultural supposition. *Erasure* is an extremely clever puppeteer of the academic reader, exploiting postmodern ambiguity (and the concerns of high Theory) to portray accurately the contradictions in the present legacies and continuations of racial discrimination. It is also a text that uses its superiority and knowingness over an academic discourse community to its own advantage: the novel legitimates itself through a foreknowledge of reading techniques, an outflanking of definitive interpretation, and a collapse of the outer academic/critical (truth-claiming) discourse and inner-fictional spaces. This is not a nihilistic plurality, as was said of the earlier works of Pynchon. It is, rather, a game of regressions, of metafictions where the text can only be read by backing away from pluralities and seeking meaning in the fact that the singular topography of the novel contains multiple hermeneutic responses, even while the fiction disparages such an attitude. In this blurring of the creative and critical spaces, however, the claims for sincere truth-telling spill over into the fiction. In the critique of the critical space enacted by the creative, a legitimation claim is raised that centres on the monopolization of discourse that can speak the truth. It is a 'regime of truth', as Foucault might put it.

In this way, *Erasure* is a text that brilliantly highlights the problems of legitimation against academia faced by much contemporary metafiction. On the one hand, if art is to have a critical societal role, it must supplant criticism in staking ethical claims. In the case of Everett's novel, the text would have to 'say something' about race and authorship (sincere but didactic ethics as opposed to strategic and apolitical aesthetics). If university English remains the most prominent space where such strategies of meaning-making in fiction are validated, however, and if the didactic function that was explored in the preceding chapter on Bolaño holds, then the contest for legitimation arises. Fiction is usually perceived as the more viable market force in such a contest; the mass-market paperback of George Orwell as societal critique while universities are converted into factories to defer employment and incur debt. On the other hand, 'serious' fiction finds itself bound to the academy as the foremost, but not the only, training school for reading literary fiction. Such fiction, it would seem, wants to have its cake and to eat it. It wants readers who are perceptive and, most likely, trained in a background of literary Theory. It then wants such readers to lose their academic trappings. It wants them to climb the ladder and then to discard it. Even while they dangle the toys of childhood in front of a reader, such works seem to say that it is time to grow up. Time to leave school. In their desire for an erasure of the academy, we might term such works "~~academic~~ fictions".

6. Labour and Theory

Although it may be unwise to speak of the 'career' of a writer so evidently in full-flow as Jennifer Egan, it is nonetheless true that certain trends can already be seen over the arc of her writing since 1995. Whether the foremost of these areas is the emergence of new technologies and the way in which they shape our concepts of (re)mediation or in Egan's seemingly broader interest in the place of affect in experimental fiction will remain a topic for a scholarly debate that is only beginning to give Egan her due. It is also apparent, however, that certain institutions and spaces are given quantifiably more space within Egan's work than would be merited under strict societal mimesis, even if they do not occupy a huge proportion of Egan's novels, and that, in line with a broader concern of postmodern fiction, one such space is the university. From even Egan's earliest published fiction, her acclaimed *The Invisible Circus* (1995), it can be asserted that the academy plays a key role, even if that action remains offstage and invisible.

As much of this book has pointed out, satire of the university through fictional representation is hardly a new phenomenon. In Sean McCann's reading of the role of Theory/academic discourse in these types of text, however, we begin to be able to account for some of the complexities of contemporary fiction beyond the postmodern period; the use of Theory becomes a legitimation strategy in which "Roth and the many writers who resemble him […] assume that the only route past bureaucratic confinement of various sorts is to embrace a level of sophistication and expertise that enables them to trump the restrictions that detain more pedestrian minds". Ultimately, in this reactionary stance, although the university "epitomizes the worst features of a manufactured society", it "also becomes the indispensable launching pad for the effort to imagine one's way beyond its limits".[1]

It is clear, with this context and periodisation in mind, that Egan's treatment of academic life should be viewed with some caution and most probably delineated from ideas of the traditional campus novel. It is equally apparent, however, that in this specific generic genealogy, the high frequency of instances of the academy cannot be dismissed as an incidental detail. Over the course of this chapter I will demonstrate that, in fact, Egan's critique of the university is, in some ways, and as with Everett's, an immanent meta-critique. While the history of the campus novel is often premised on hermetically sealing the campus, Egan's novel seems to play on bursting the very notions of inside and outside that facilitate this genre. By depicting these dichotomies, Egan brings Robert Scholes's definition of metafiction to a new, twenty-first century juncture as she, once more, blurs the boundaries between fiction and critique. However, she also simultaneously critiques the structures of labour upon which much of the academy is founded. This is, I contend, an extension of the legitimation techniques that meld aesthetic and political critique that we saw in the preceding chapter on Everett.

Approach and Avoid: Jennifer Egan's Pre-*Goon Squad* Academics

In an anonymously penned 2010 exemplar of a utilitarian evaluation of higher education, *The Economist* noted several aspects that form a worthwhile enframing context for this thematic study, despite the cynicism of the piece. Firstly, the author points out that in 2010 America produced 64,000 doctoral degrees, a figure that includes foreign students.[2] More tellingly, however, the 2010 US Census on educational attainment notes that only 1.2% of Americans hold a doctoral qualification, just over one in every hundred people.[3] This is of

---

[1] Sean McCann, 'Training and Vision: Roth, DeLillo, Banks, Peck, and the Postmodern Aesthetics of Vocation', *Twentieth Century Literature*, 53.3 (2007), 298–326 (p. 302), http://dx.doi.org/10.1215/0041462X-2007-4006.

[2] 'Doctoral Degrees: The Disposable Academic', *The Economist*, 18 December 2010, http://www.economist.com/node/17723223.

[3] Camille L. Ryan and Julie Siebens, 'Educational Attainment in the United States: 2009. Population Characteristics', *US Census Bureau*, February 2012, p. 6, http://files.eric.ed.gov/fulltext/ED529755.pdf.

note because, by any account, Egan's novels feature an unusually high proportion of PhD candidates ("grad students") that is certainly out of kilter with the number of completed doctoral degrees. As a second peripheral construct, *The Economist* piece correctly points out that "armies of low-paid PhD researchers and postdocs boost universities', and therefore countries', research capacity". This is not limited to the United States. A recent survey of higher education institutions in the United Kingdom revealed that universities and colleges are over twice as likely to use so-called 'zero-hours contracts' than other types of workplace, revealing that the 'life of the mind' is often precarious and balanced on a knife-edge.[4]

This sociological documentation is an important starting point for the depictions of academia in Egan's novels. Although it is not the intention here to demonstrate that Egan's mimesis of the academic environment is 'accurate', or at least not the sole intention, there is a more important critical function of her approach that requires this real-world backdrop for any purchase. Academics — taken here to mean those working (paid or unpaid) at universities ('the academy') in a research capacity (staff or research students) — have featured, at least peripherally, in all of Jennifer Egan's novels, with different functions. Given the fact that *A Visit from the Goon Squad* is not alone in dealing with this subject, it is first of all necessary to examine the background to academia that emerges from Egan's other works of novelistic fiction: *The Invisible Circus*, *Look at Me* (2001) and *The Keep* (2006).

Across her entire oeuvre, Egan's literary techniques for highlighting academia can be classified as postmodern.[5] In her first novel, *The Invisible Circus*, however, this primarily takes the form of "approach and avoid".[6] Be it the 1960s, drug culture, free love, political radicalism, or the inter-linked contexts of academia that are explored in this text, Egan pushes her core, informing, historical moments to the margins; they are an invisible circus. While these contexts are frequently referenced in passing, the text elects, at least on its surface narrative, to focus on

---

4 UCU, 'Over Half of Universities and Colleges Use Lecturers on Zero-Hour Contracts', 4 September 2013, http://www.ucu.org.uk/6749.
5 A lineage that Egan herself explicitly acknowledged in a 2009 interview on *The Keep*. Here 'postmodernism' is primarily referring to the metafiction of the 1960s to 1980s. Charlie Reilly, 'An Interview with Jennifer Egan', *Contemporary Literature*, 50.3 (2009), 439–60 (p. 446), http://dx.doi.org/10.1353/cli.0.0074.
6 To appropriate a phrase from Pynchon's *V*.

personal tragedy and a quest for closure. The best individual instance of this is the student of the University of Turin, Pietro, whom Phoebe, the questing protagonist of *The Invisible Circus*, meets on the train to Reims while on her European quest to follow in her sister, Faith's, final, fatal footsteps.

Due to the contextual background within which *The Invisible Circus* sits, the introduction of Pietro is layered within a complex system of overwriting and an intricate double-falsehood. The third-person narrator informs the reader that "[h]e was Pietro, a student at the University of Turin", presumed to be relating the information that was given to Phoebe. Immediately after this, Phoebe responds to Pietro with an untruth: "Phoebe blithely explained that she was making her way toward Italy to meet her older sister. The lie came so effortlessly, bringing with it such a bolt of delight that she wondered why she ever told the truth". Because she has begun with a lie Phoebe is, naturally, suspicious of others and, in this case, questions Pietro: "[y]ou seem older than college" to which Pietro guiltily replies "[a]h. Yes" before revealing that he is actually now beginning training as a Catholic missionary in Madrid. Although it is unclear as to whether Pietro's initial introduction is a deliberate falsehood or is simply the outcome of a complex series of inter-institutional arrangements, the structural progression here is the same: Pietro is introduced; Phoebe is introduced; Pietro's introduction is complicated/undone; Phoebe's introduction is complicated/undone.[7] This structure of promises and re-written falsehoods is important for the political backdrop to *The Invisible Circus* and also for its representation of the university and students. One of the key lines in the text pertaining to this neatly sums up the interrelation between history and forgotten utopian promises: "[f]or all that surrounded her now was barely real. What about Faith? she would remind herself, walking the smudged halls or eating her lunch alone in the hospital-smelling cafeteria; what about the student strike of 1968? All that was forgotten".[8]

Most significantly for her next novel, *Look at Me*, in *The Invisible Circus* Egan seamlessly slides from the (invisible) student groups into the left-wing terrorism of the Baader-Meinhof gang:

---

7 Jennifer Egan, *The Invisible Circus* (London: Corsair, 2012), pp. 150–57.
8 Ibid., pp. 72–73.

> [h]er articles were getting more and more radical—she was sympathetic to these student anarchist groups that were starting to use violence. [...] "Students?" Phoebe said. "Like my age?" [...] Anyhow, Ulrike Meinhof decides to do a TV play and asks Inge to be on the filming staff. [...] A couple of weeks later, early June, right about the time when I ran into Faith at Berkeley, this group issues a statement calling themselves the Rote Armee Fraktion.[9]

This is important given the role that terrorism plays in *Look at Me*, but it is also relevant for the way in which the disgraced character, Moose Metcalf, an academic, is portrayed in that later text. Moose's position in this novel is that of an academic on the absolute fringe; his title of "Adjunct Assistant Adjunct Professor of History" is designed to "capture the vivid tenuousness" of his status within academe.[10] In his early twenties, Moose undergoes some form of claimed incommunicable experience of academic revelation pertaining to the horrors of modernity that he then makes it his life's work to confer. As Kelly points out, however, in keeping with its historicized moment, *Look at Me* is a novel that explicitly explores the discourses of high Theory, with direct reference to Lacan at one stage, and it is in the character of Moose that this is most acutely focused, particularly with reference to various schools of antihumanist histories and his aversion to the reduction of experience to text and metaphor.[11] Moose is presented, however, as a totally dysfunctional character. He finds inter-personal conversation difficult and prefers to avoid it where possible, a stance that sits at odds with his desire to share his supra-linguistic vision.

This correlation of academia, violence, and a renewed questioning of the relationship between 'words and things' is part of a trend that is also on the increase in certain other strands of American contemporary fiction. In the aesthetic realm, it is clear that the process of working towards this final moment, the "point after which there is nothing to say", has been building ever since the limit-modernist prose of Samuel Beckett's *The Unnamable* (1953/1958) and *Worstward Ho*.[12] Of

---

9   Ibid., p. 231.
10 Idem, *Look at Me* (London: Corsair, 2011), p. 134.
11 Kelly, 'Beginning with Postmodernism', p. 410.
12 Georges Bataille, 'Nonknowledge', in *The Unfinished System of Nonknowledge*, ed. by Stuart Kendall, trans. by Michelle Kendall and Stuart Kendall (Minneapolis: University of Minnesota Press, 2001), pp. 196–205 (p. 196).

more relevance for the matter at hand, it has been clear for some time now that the works of many writers, here to be exemplified by Don DeLillo in a brief digression, shift dramatically in their formal aesthetic structure around the millennial break.[13] The aesthetic telos of DeLillo's novels is best described in terms of a formal career-long movement from postmodern play, through to quasi-encyclopaedicism to a contracted minimalism. From his Pynchon-influenced phase in *Ratner's Star* (1976), the texts shift to *Libra* (1988) and *Underworld*'s (1997) grand explorations of history, film and American culture. Around the turn of the new century, in line with a re-politicization of the contemporary through an engagement with real-world terrorism and the Iraq War, DeLillo's fiction contracts. This contraction, most prominent in his recent novels, *Point Omega* (2010) and *Zero K* (2016), reads as a pushing at the limits of representation, a probing into the discursive field that DeLillo, as a non-combatant writer, cannot know, but to which he nonetheless contributes; a contraction that seems headed for extinction, for the omega point after which there is nothing to say. As *Point Omega* puts it through the words of Richard Elster: "[t]he true life is not reducible to words spoken or written".[14]

The Iraq War in *Point Omega* is represented through Richard Elster, the war apologist and academic, and the key, glaring metaphorical fact that he loses his daughter in the desert ("[t]he desert was outside my range, it was an alien being"), never fully understanding why.[15] DeLillo's work moves on, however, to provide information on one of Elster's academic pieces; a study of the etymology of the word "rendition". Rendition and "enhanced interrogation techniques" — which Elster knows to be criminal as he projects a future scenario in which "the administration's crimes" are tried in a Nuremberg/Eichmann-esque fashion with "men and women, in cubicles, wearing headphones" — are always undertaken by "others".[16] Those who "ask pointed questions of flesh-and-blood individuals", "behind closed doors", are not the government but "finally

---

13 Of course, this may be because the generation of novelists who formed the postmodernist canon are now coming to the end of their lives, moving to a 'late style', as Edward Saïd might have it. Edward W. Saïd, *On Late Style* (London: Bloomsbury, 2006).
14 Don DeLillo, *Point Omega* (London: Picador, 2010), p. 17.
15 *Ibid.*, p. 20.
16 *Ibid.*, p. 33.

others, still others".[17] The implications of the government structure is that it constitutes at once an international entity of political standing but contains its own alienated sub-national others. This works, once more, bi-directionally, for this is how the United States is fictionally depicted here and it is also how the invasion of another sovereign power can be justified on the basis of terrorism. Indeed, Elster makes this explicit within his fictional article, mediating between the collective will of a power-structure nation and the sub-national, terrorist component as:

> [t]oward the end of the commentary he wrote about select current meanings of the word *rendition* — interpretation, translation, performance. Within those walls, somewhere in seclusion, a drama is being enacted, old as human memory, he wrote, actors naked, chained, blindfolded, other actors with props of intimidation, the renderers, nameless and masked, dressed in black, an what ensues, he wrote, is a revenge play that reflects the mass will and interprets the shadowy need of an entire nation, ours.[18]

In contrast to Egan's vision of Moose as a dysfunctional but perhaps harmless academic, the vision of linguistic/literary analysis that Elster undertakes in DeLillo's world is linked directly to State violence. In fact, a dark justification for torture emerges through a parallel with drama within an academico-literary context. Once more, the conjunction of aesthetics and politics are here presented, in a work of fiction, through a condemnatory reflection of the academy's complicity with various problematic ethical acts.

However, if Moose is the amiable side of dysfunctional academia, Egan does nonetheless also give a far darker breed in her future academics. While these graduate students are not quite at the same level as DeLillo's Elster, they are in fact, complicit with the very apocalypse that Moose fears. In *Look at Me*, a group of entrepreneurs are establishing a Facebook-like social media space, PersonalSpaces, and are seeking out high-profile individuals to feature as live-streamed content for which people will pay to view. Phillipe, a participant in this project and a "too old and insufficiently sleek" Frenchman working on a PhD in media studies at NYU, represents, in this text, all that is wrong with

---

17   Ibid.
18   *Ibid*, p. 34.

academia.[19] Phillipe is interested in, as Marx would have it, interpreting the world, rather than changing it. Although he shares Moose's social awkwardness to a lesser degree — dropping his pen at a crucial moment — he documents the meeting in which Charlotte consents to the grim project of PersonalSpaces, whose aim is to textualize existence for commercial benefit, but does not intervene with any suggestion that the project might be morally wrong.[20] Even worse, Phillipe's interpretation will clearly be biased; he makes "less of an effort to capture" Charlotte's remarks than those of Thomas and Victoria. This is presumably because, in addition to her non-exceptional post-accident visual appearance, he has pre-decided upon the theoretical content of his work and will shape reality to fit his textual ideal; exactly the same project undertaken by PersonalSpaces who wish to reduce reality to a sampled cross-section of the population.[21] In this light, Look at Me shows two pathological sides to academia: an isolated, nihilistic stagnation from Moose (connected perhaps to apocalypse and terror), who feels powerless to communicate his paralysing horror at post-industrial virtualisation and who feels joy only in the face of his 'disease' spreading, and an unreflexive participation with/complicity in an acceleration of this phenomenon from Phillipe.

If, in Look at Me, then, Egan spins out a vision of academics as either powerless to change, or complicit with, the rise of virtualised commodity forms that reduce reality to text — with many of the same overtures of Foucault's famous retort to Derrida — her presentation of academia changes drastically in the period between 2002 and 2006.[22] Egan's twenty-first-century re-working of Calvino-esque gothic metafiction, *The Keep*, moves away from the juxtaposition of academia with terrorism and political marginality and instead shifts the critical focus to indentured systems of labour, predominantly through the representation of graduate students in that text. Egan's most explicitly metafictional work, the diegetic layering of *The Keep* is ingenious; the protagonist Danny is actually a character in a subsidiary intra-diegetic work of fiction

---

19 Egan, *Look at Me*, pp. 241–42.
20 *Ibid.*, p. 246.
21 *Ibid.*, p. 248.
22 Michel Foucault, 'My Body, This Paper, This Fire', in *History of Madness* (London: Routledge, 2006), pp. 550–74.

created by Ray for a prison writing course. This layering, however, is fluid and there is a metaleptic violation of the discrete layers when it is revealed that Mick is actually an autobiographical representation of Ray (Raymond Michael Dobbs), the character who kills Danny.[23] Meanwhile, the conclusion of *The Keep* leaves readers wondering how it is that the textual object has come to be produced since Holly, Ray's writing teacher, buried the manuscript in her backyard before leaving for Europe to find the, perhaps, real-world instantiation of the keep and its "imagination pool". These metafictional traits, metaleptic violations, and impossible auto-textual objects are important because one would expect, given McCann's and Kelly's respective observations, to see the direct presence of Egan's academics proportionately increase in a work so clearly indebted to the postmodern, Theory-inflected tradition.

This does not, however, seem to be the case; or at least not directly. In contrast to the extensive focus on Moose in *Look at Me*, fewer of the protagonists in *The Keep* are academics, although Holly is an instructor on a creative writing programme, a fact that ties in well with Mark McGurl's observations on the significance of these programmes for post-boomer American fiction.[24] Instead, in this text we are shown a group of graduate students who are present to assist in the construction of Howard's alternative holiday destination.[25] The depiction here is important for its numerous contradictions: Howard's vision for the retreat is overwhelmingly weighted towards that of unquantifiable, un-textualised experience, imagination, and purity, while he meanwhile happily uses the precarious and uncompensated labour of MBA graduate students to achieve his goal.[26] In many ways, this runs exactly in parallel to Moose in *Look at Me*: an attempt to articulate the fundamentally irreducible experience of art (as also seen earlier in relation to *2666*) while also being situated within an exploitative and precarious labour situation. The fact also that the central symbol of this later text is a castle, or, in fact, a tower, a keep, should encourage speculation on the place of the ivory tower. After all, we can surely remember, as can a post-boomer

---

23 Jennifer Egan, *The Keep* (London: Abacus, 2008), p. 217.
24 Kelly, 'Beginning with Postmodernism', p. 396; McGurl.
25 There is also the character Nora, who jokingly claims to have written a PhD on Mary Poppins. Egan, *The Keep*, p. 72.
26 Although one cannot help but feel that Egan's point might have been more sharply made through the use of humanities graduate students.

Theory generation of novelists, Foucault's famous rhetorical question to which we only might add 'universities': "[i]s it surprising that prisons resemble factories, schools, barracks, hospitals, which all resemble prisons?"[27]

The context in which the majority of the graduate students in this text appear — and also their narrative priority — is absolutely clear and is introduced through an innovative three-point list. Point 1 in this list introduces Ann, Howard's wife, while point 3 introduces the eventual narrator, Mick, her ex-lover. Point 2 in this list, hinged between two essential characters for the plot are the graduate students. They are not, however, introduced as students at first but rather as "workers" who are "churned" through swinging doors, as they are churned through their utilitarian postgraduate degrees, studying MBAs at Illinois or hotel management at Cornell.[28] The irony here is that "Howard's renovation was their summer project" meaning that "they were doing this for credit", once more demonstrating the systems of precarity that are intrinsic to the type of utilitarian business activities for which they are being trained (Howard was, after all, a bond trader).[29] If, in this instance, the students of business 'get what they deserve' — by which I mean that in being trained for utilitarian business, they are used in a utilitarian fashion — then there are even graver repercussions, on the academic front, in the representation of Danny in this novel, to which I will return shortly.

Such a critique of labour structures in academia also occurs in other works of contemporary fiction. A particularly striking instance of this is the Arthur C. Clarke Award-winning novel *Station Eleven* (2014) by Emily St. John Mandel. This text, which focalises the familiar post-apocalyptic genre through a series of chance character interactions and an innovative time-hopping structure, uses its temporal distortions to reflect on the precarity of the early twenty-first century. For example, it is common in this novel to read proleptic temporal-locative sentences that ration the present time: "two weeks before the end of commercial

---

27 Michel Foucault, *Discipline and Punish: The Birth of the Prison*, trans. by Alan Sheridan (New York: Vintage, 1997), p. 228.
28 Egan, *The Keep*, p. 21.
29 *Ibid.*

air travel, Miranda flew to Toronto from New York".[30] As with all of the texts dealt with in this book, however, *Station Eleven* does not miss its single opportunity to disparage the academy, here done by a parallel with the corporate world. When Clark is interviewing Dahlia she notes that "it's like the corporate world's full of ghosts". So far, so standard. But the interview continues: "[a]nd actually, let me revise that, my parents are in academia so I've had front-row seats for *that* horror show, I know academia's no different, so maybe a fairer way of putting this would be to say that adulthood's full of ghosts". This is centred around the idea, we are told, that she is referring to "these people who've ended up in one life instead of another and they are just so disappointed. [...] They've done what's expected of them. They want to do something different but it's impossible now, there's a mortgage, kids, whatever, they're trapped".[31] In other words, in *Station Eleven*'s brief critique of academia, working at a university is a form of labour like any other, subject to financial path dependencies that trap workers within "one life" rather than "another". This is all framed within a text that shows how limited our time is in the present through an apocalyptic event.

To return to Egan, although Danny appears as the narrator of the novel until the end, he is, diegetically speaking, a creation of Ray/Mick, whose backstory, thoughts, and feelings are created as part of a creative writing programme. Curiously, though, despite Holly's actual lack of formal training as a writing instructor, Ray's creation (i.e. the intra-diegetic Danny narrative of *The Keep*) spurns a realist mode. Characters' speech is indicated, for instance, in the fashion of scripted drama: "Danny: Nothing happened".[32] Furthermore, the narrative voice that Ray uses owes a great deal to the style and manner of John Fowles, among others. This is most evident in the moments where the text forks in the manner of *The French Lieutenant's Woman* (1969) and elements of narrative indeterminacy are introduced, such as when Danny posits two separate answers to the question of whether his night excursion — including his sexual involvement with the centenarian baroness — was a dream or reality.[33]

---

30 Emily St. John Mandel, *Station Eleven* (London: Picador, 2015), p. 205.
31 *Ibid.*, p. 163.
32 Egan, *The Keep*, p. 156.
33 *Ibid.*

This digression from the attempted realist mode of which one would expect amateur storytellers to partake in the American novelistic tradition — the affected naivety of, say, Willa Cather's Jim Burden in *My Ántonia* (1918) who claims not to "arrange or rearrange" but "simply" to "wr[i]te down" with the supposition (falsely in that case) that it "has n't any form" — might lead the reader to suspect that Ray is simply a further diegetic layer, a fantasy invention of Holly to escape the crystal-meth-infused lifestyle that she shares with her partner.[34] Conversely, however, it may instead open up a space in which to think about different forms of knowledge production. Coupled with the critique of utilitarian higher education implicit in the earlier jibes at the MBA students, the narrator is keen to claim, early in the text, that "all the things Danny had achieved in his life — the alto, the connections, the access to power, the knowing how to get a cab in a rainstorm, and the mechanics of bribing Maître d's, and where to find good shoes in the outer boroughs" amounted to "the equivalent of a PhD, all the stuff Danny knew".[35] This 'university of life' approach, however, appears, in retrospect, as an affected compensation by Ray for his own lack of formal education and, now, incarceration. This is evident in the fact that Ray's character Danny is deliberately infantilised. He is, for instance, "terrified" of the fact that he must be an adult, terrified by "the girls especially, with their black bras and purses stocked with multi-colored condoms and exact ideas of what they liked in bed. It terrified him because if these were adults then he must be, too".[36] Yet, we are also led to believe that this figure, terrified of young adult women, terrified of his own maturation and responsibilities, has (at least in his own egotistic mind, as written by Ray) the "equivalent of a PhD".

The narrative voice here is incredibly difficult to place and, at this depth of layering, it becomes almost impossible to nail down a definitive critique of the represented object; each diegetic layer brings a fresh stance. It is therefore only possible to analyse the function of the layering in relation to the object of representation through a permutation of the stances, many of which are, as with the earlier section on Percival Everett, *sous rature*. In Danny's perspectivized take, the supposed

---

34 Willa Cather, *My Ántonia* (New York: Dover, 1994), p. 3.
35 Egan, *The Keep*, p. 33.
36 *Ibid.*, p. 28.

'street'-equivalence of his knowledge is surely a sign of self-reassurance against his own, Delphic self-knowledge of his true inadequacy. At Ray's level, there is a desire both to infantilise Danny and to cast him as an unsympathetic character (as despite his assurances that he "liked Danny" he did, nonetheless, shoot him).[37] In doing so, a doctoral qualification is denigrated; brought down to Danny's level. In turn, this serves twofold to position Danny as, firstly, an insecure individual who falsely reassures himself and, secondly, to allow Ray to swipe at formal education. On the other hand, if we are to take Holly as a writer of Ray's story — she does, after all, possess the manuscript — then the contrasting inflection between Ray and Danny serves to endear Ray at Danny's expense. Danny is, in this mode, a cleverly crafted creation of Ray, designed to evoke the specific caricature presented in the first mode, thereby showing Ray's ability to thrive and create without higher education. Where Egan's own voice sits here is debatable and probably impossible to place, but it is indisputable that the status of the academy is complex, inflected, and layered within *The Keep*, despite the appearance, at first glance, of a retreat from the subtlety of *Look at Me*.

This type of metafictive diegetic layering, linked to ontological instability and dreams, often forms a surrounding context for novels that deal with the academy, most likely for the historicised reasons posited by McGurl. That said, and with this survey portion now complete, I will now move to consider Egan's most recent work, *A Visit from the Goon Squad*. This text is curiously placed because it is unclear whether it is a series of (extremely) loosely interconnected short stories or a novel, howsoever the historical permutations on that term are taken. In some senses, then, this latest text represents the most extreme form of layering yet encountered in Egan's work. It also, though, represents an extension and modification of her treatment of academia.

Theories From the *Goon Squad*

In terms of its most obvious themes, *A Visit from the Goon Squad* doesn't make much effort to hide its hand. As the text explains its own title in terms of an entropic descent, in combination with its Proustian

---

37 *Ibid.*, p. 209.

epigraph, we are told: "[y]ou don't look good anymore twenty years later, especially when you've had half your guts removed. Time's a goon, right?"[38] As well as spanning a large chronological and geographical range, the text is, however, also extremely formally playful with an entire segment of the narrative conveyed through a series of Powerpoint-style presentation slides, as just one instance.[39] As would be expected by the trajectory that I have been tracing here, though, the text is also one saturated by academia.

Certainly, *Goon Squad* is a novel populated by a disproportionately high number of, often unfulfilled, postgraduate researchers: "I'm in the PhD program at Berkeley", proclaims Mindy;[40] "Joe, who hailed from Kenya [...] was getting his PhD in robotics at Columbia";[41] "Bix, who's black, is spending his nights in the electrical-engineering lab where he's doing his PhD research";[42] while only Rebecca "was an academic star".[43] In this text, academia seems a place of misery, of "harried academic slaving to finish a book while teaching two courses and chairing several committees",[44] and, ultimately, a seeming outcome of "immaturity and disastrous choices".[45]

While these figures are scattered throughout the entire text — and Egan seems deliberately to push them to the margins, continuing the 'approach and avoid' style of *The Invisible Circus* — the most protracted point of focus comes in the fourth section of the novel: 'Safari'. This was not originally the case. In an early draft of the novel, Egan had written in an academic figure to comment on the Rock 'n' Roll pauses section, a fact that she revealed at the Q&A session of the first international conference held on her work.[46] Had this remained, the role of academia in this novel might have been very different. As it is, this did not come to fruition and 'Safari' remains the high point for institutional mimesis.

---

38 Jennifer Egan, *A Visit from the Goon Squad* (London: Corsair, 2011), p. 134.
39 *Ibid.*, pp. 242–316.
40 *Ibid.*, p. 67.
41 *Ibid.*, p. 346.
42 *Ibid.*, p. 194.
43 *Ibid.*, p. 331.
44 *Ibid.*
45 *Ibid.*, p. 86.
46 Organised by Zara Dinnen, this event was held at Birkbeck, University of London in April 2014 and was called *The Invisible Circus*. Egan graciously attended the event, listening to an entire day of academic papers on her own work.

6. *Labour and Theory*   149

This chapter was originally published in *The New Yorker* as a standalone story, thereby demonstrating the discrete nature of *Goon Squad*'s components.[47]

The presentation of academia in this chapter is centred on Mindy, the "twenty-three-year-old girlfriend" of Lou, "a powerful male".[48] Mindy is an anthropology candidate at Berkeley whose disciplinary grounding is founded upon Claude Lévi-Strauss's structuralism, which she hopes to move beyond and refine, rather than simply "rehash". This explains the rationale for her identity presentation in terms of being a girlfriend; despite its anti-feminist connotations, Egan's character inherently thinks in structuralist terms. Mindy's central theorisation rests upon "the link between social structure and emotional response", a thought process that in turn orbits around her claimed concepts of "Structural Resentment", "Structural Affection", "Structural Incompatibility", "Structural Desire", "Structural Fixation", and "Structural Dissatisfaction".[49] These terminological components, in addition to satirising various forms of academic discourse, also form a more complex tapestry that interlinks with other portions of *Goon Squad*'s narrative.

Remaining within 'Safari' for now, however, it is worth extrapolating a few of the remarks that form Mindy's "structural" social phenomena as they reveal the mechanisms through which academic anthropology is here satirised. The first point to note is that "Structural Resentment" and "Structural Affection", as defined by Mindy, are heavily infused with psychoanalytic tropes. In "Structural Resentment", "the adolescent daughter", we are told, "will be unable to tolerate the presence of [her father's] new girlfriend" and will use her "own nascent sexuality" to "distract him from said girlfriend's presence".[50] Several schools of psychoanalytical thought seem to fit this mould. In the first instance, Jung's proposition of an Electra complex springs to mind, although the refinement made here to the age range (three to six years) for the phallic stage in which the complex is supposed to occur makes a direct mapping difficult. This Freudian/Jungian approach is also

---

47 Jennifer Egan, 'Safari', *The New Yorker*, 11 January 2010, http://www.newyorker.com/magazine/2010/01/11/safari-3.
48 Egan, *A Visit from the Goon Squad*, p. 67.
49 *Ibid.*, pp. 67–69, 85.
50 *Ibid.*, p. 68.

present in "Structural Affection" where the "pre-adolescent son" has not "yet learned to separate his father's loves and desires from his own", the complementary Oedipus complex.[51] Perhaps another avenue for exploration, also, is the focus here on the "powerful male" aspect, thus bringing structural anthropology into closer contact with Karen Horney's revisions to Freudian analysis, particularly as it pertains to women and social-structural envy of power, rather than anatomy. Further exploration might find interest in Horney's essay 'The Genesis of the Castration Complex' with the strong "emphasis Horney places in it on the father-daughter [sexual] relationship".[52]

While this could be a reflection upon the interdisciplinary approaches of psychological and psychoanalytic anthropology, it also points to another target site: literary studies. As Peter Osborne notes, fields as diverse the "'textuality' of a general semiotics, the 'discourses' of a Foucauldian historicism or the 'topography' of a Lacanian metapsychology" enjoyed a period of remarkable academic hegemony under the label of 'T/theory' "largely via [their] occupation of the institutional space of literary criticism, in conjunction with an aspiration to social criticism".[53] The conjoined depictions here of psychoanalysis and structuralism with that of anthropology (a discipline of social observation, classification, and criticism) within a work of literary fiction that will, itself, knowingly be subjected to literary-critical reading practices, culminates in a work that has two functions.

The first identifiable function here is to once more situate Egan's work clearly in the realm of metafiction. Although deeply encoded, the mimetic aspiration in 'Safari' is directed towards the highly interdisciplinary area of literary studies itself; a knowing wink to the academic readers of her works who are being satirised while they read (this book and myself included).[54] Even Mindy's remarks on her own structural placement serve a critical-reflexive function, in this

---

51 Ibid., p. 68.
52 Bernard J. Paris, *Karen Horney: A Psychoanalyst's Search for Self-Understanding* (New Haven: Yale University Press, 1994), p. 69.
53 Peter Osborne, 'Philosophy after Theory: Transdisciplinarity and the New', in *Theory after 'Theory'*, ed. by Jane Elliott and Derek Attridge (New York: Routledge, 2011), pp. 19–34 (pp. 19–21).
54 Another good instance of this type of satirical undoing of academico-readerly practices can be found in Robert Coover, *Pinocchio in Venice* (London: Minerva, 1993).

instance undertaken upon a literary character amid the whirl of fields that constitute the dialectical counter-reflex of English's integration of cultural studies against Leavis. The second function of this initial setup is to characterise literary studies in a New Historicist and/or Cultural Materialist vein. This comes about twofold because of the character name, "Chronos", with his emphasis (as per the remainder of *Goon Squad*) on "time" and its interaction with literary texts but also because of the focus that Mindy places upon power-relations through structural inter-connection in her own readings of societal situations.

Observations of this type contribute to the dialectic of metafiction against realism. As has been covered throughout this work, one of the old refrains of material that criticises metafiction is the allegation that the form only looks inward, preferring to focus upon literature and its own tropes and study. This type of thinking, coupled with a counter-ironic reflex, led to David Foster Wallace's manifesto-type documents, including the most well-known 'E Unibus Pluram' (1993), against irony (in turn generating the type of focus upon sincerity that was covered above). It seems, in the case of Egan, however, to have generated a different type of response. As with Moose's longing to communicate his experience of a non-textualised reality in *Look at Me* — a "reality hunger" as Shields might have it in his book of that name — in *A Visit from the Goon Squad* and especially in 'Safari', the inward focus reveals a mode of textual literary studies that carries an "aspiration to social criticism", as Osborne puts it. This bi-directional relationship with reality is the solution that Egan's metafiction poses to the historicised conjunction of Theory's passing and the claim of metafiction's retreat to political inefficacy. Egan here gives a vision that looks inwards so as to avoid a naïve realism (the problematisation to which the first generation of metafiction responded) while ensuring that the mode in which it casts itself is one that looks outwards (New Historicist/Cultural Materialist). This is not, however, without irony and, as might be expected, generates a fresh field of problematization upon which multiple areas of practice collide.

To demonstrate this aspect further, consider a few additional examples that illustrate that the conjunction of multiple theoretical perspectives is an integral part of 'Safari'. For instance, when Chronos leaves the jeep to observe the lion more closely (in a show of competitive bravado that Mindy labels "*Structural Fixation*: A collective, contextually induced obsession that becomes a temporary locus of greed, competition, and envy")[55] it is in the spirit of Adorno and Horkheimer's *Dialectic of Enlightenment* (1944), wherein "[m]yth is already enlightenment, and enlightenment reverts to mythology".[56] This is because, as Chronos comes directly to approach nature, his cocksure positivist attitude results in an abrupt alienation from that very nature. As the lion "vaults at Chronos in an agile, gravity-defying spring" the regression is enacted as Albert kills the lion "with a rifle he'd secreted somewhere".[57] In addition to the innocence of Rolph, who "just [likes] watching" the animals instead of killing them, this assault on positivist assurance also seems to come out in the indictment of colonial practice that is inherent in the safari expedition.[58] Albert, the character who permits the reckless venture and eventually destroys the natural phenomena whose observation he was supposed merely to facilitate, is described as a "surly Englishman" with "longish brown hair and mustache", looking, in the child Rolph's eyes, "like a real explorer",[59] as opposed to the feared "black men" from whom Lou earlier wants to "yank" Charlie away.[60] Moreover, Albert's mother, who comes from "back in Minehead" (implying that this ethnically un-diverse area of rural England is Albert's point of origin, with a 95.8% white population according to the 2011 census)[61] foresees this "latest in a series" of white enlightenment "failures"; she decries his "self-destructive tendencies".[62]

This leads to an entanglement of postcolonial aspects. This is a scenario in which the white man is said to look like a "real explorer" and in which the innocent, but perversely societally conditioned, child holds the view that Africa should be full of white 'explorers'. At the same time,

---

55 Egan, *A Visit from the Goon Squad*, p. 69.
56 Max Horkheimer and Theodor W. Adorno, *Dialectic of Enlightenment*, ed. by Gunzelin Schmid Noerr, trans. by Edmund Jephcott (Stanford: Stanford University Press, 2002), p. xvii.
57 Egan, *A Visit from the Goon Squad*, p. 73.
58 *Ibid.*, p. 81.
59 *Ibid.*, pp. 67, 78.
60 *Ibid.*, p. 64.
61 Office for National Statistics, '2011 Census: Key Statistics for Local Authorities in England and Wales, March 2011', 11 December 2012, http://www.ons.gov.uk/ons/rel/census/2011-census/key-statistics-for-local-authorities-in-england-and-wales/index.html.
62 Egan, *A Visit from the Goon Squad*, p. 74.

the dialectic of enlightenment here leads to a white alienation from nature that is joined by the many feminist critiques that inhere within this section. It is clear that Lou uses Mindy as a competitive mediation between himself and other men, being a "man who cannot tolerate defeat",[63] thereby echoing the sentiments of Pynchon's Lake Traverse in *Against the Day* (2006), who asks Deuce Kindred and Sloat Fresno whether they might "just leave me out of it and do each other for a change", recognising herself in exactly the same role as *Goon Squad*'s Mindy.[64] If, for Lou, women are simply objects of exchange and mediation, used by men, this takes the form of his metonymic objectifying pronouncement that "[w]omen are cunts", a phrase that Rolph finds himself unable to repeat.[65] Although Rolph himself is not exempt from this trafficking economy — in an extremely psychoanalytic move, it becomes clear that he had an affair with his father's girlfriend, Jocelyn, who shared his exact birthday[66] — he is presented as damaged by the patriarchal effects of this setup. In a proleptic temporal distortion similar to Frobischer in David Mitchell's *Cloud Atlas* (2004), who writes in his own diary of how he "[s]hot [him]self through the roof of [his] mouth at [the upcoming] 5 a.m.",[67] it is revealed at the end of 'Safari' that this moment, the two children dancing, will be a memory that Charlie "will return to again and again, for the rest of her life, long after Rolph has shot himself in the head in their father's house at twenty-eight".[68] As noted, Rolph is not excluded from the patriarchal system, but he is described as a "gentle boy"[69] and is, clearly, among the most hurt by it, as made clear from the fact that he kills himself "in their father's house", an aspect that is seemingly accurately mimetic from the figures of the American Foundation for Suicide Prevention, which show that 78.9% of those who died by suicide in 2010 were male.[70]

This proleptic leap at the end of the 'Safari' section brings the subtext back full-circle to its initial anthropological critique. We

---

63 Ibid., p. 83.
64 Thomas Pynchon, *Against the Day* (London: Jonathan Cape, 2006), p. 303.
65 Egan, *A Visit from the Goon Squad*, p. 82.
66 Ibid., pp. 93–94.
67 David Mitchell, *Cloud Atlas* (Sceptre, 2008), p. 487.
68 Egan, *A Visit from the Goon Squad*, p. 87.
69 Ibid., p. 90.
70 American Foundation for Suicide Prevention, 'Facts and Figures', http://www.afsp.org/understanding-suicide/facts-and-figures.

are told, early in the text, that Mindy "hasn't cracked her Boas or Malinowski". Indeed, it would be remiss not to remark upon the fact that she is a terrible anthropologist. Her neglect of these core texts is an ironic joke, since Boas and Malinowski were invested, through such concepts as "participatory observation" in exploring how the presence of the anthropologist — the observer — shapes discourse (participant observation). In 'Safari', Mindy is simplistically overlaying a theoretical framework — structuralism — onto her reality in a way that creates a falsified detachment from that reality. Had she cracked her Boas and Malinowski, she might have seen this. Although this forms another piece of the novel's anti-Theory discourse, once again the ironic joke rebounds upon the reader, for it is only at the moment of dislocation from the main temporal setting of the text that the empathic and affective elements of the work come to the fore. A reader who has been viewing 'Safari' cynically as pure parody can be shocked by distancing; the change of perspective that highlights our own participatory observation of Egan's anthropological story spaces, spaces that are never quite as disconnected and isolated as we might think, reflected in Egan's short-story/novel form crossover.

In this way, *A Visit from the Goon Squad* begins to do something different and notable with the range of theoretical tropes that it deploys within its fictional bounds. It remains the case that Mindy's range of "structural" phenomena are pretentious and are here used to satirise academia. The way in which this satire plays out, though, is not the same as in other parodies, such as Everett's spin on Barthes's *S/Z*. For one, although Egan's character is perhaps obscuring, rather than clarifying, reality with her complex terminologies, her observations do turn out to be fairly accurate. Furthermore, the theoretical paradigms of postcolonialism, psychoanalysis, anthropology, the dialectic of enlightenment, and feminism — which could, in some ways, be said to be touchstones of contemporary (or at least recent/high-Theory era) university English — are hardly subjected to ridicule at all in Egan's novel. In fact, they form the core of the chapter's pathos. Rolph's suicide is directly linked to the patriarchal environment, with its masculine destruction of nature, which feeds back into the episode's eponymous, analeptic episode. Reformulated: yes, of course, Egan's academics are there for readers to laugh at, but that's not all. The text still needs, as does most contemporary fiction with any kind of political mimesis or ethical intent, to legitimate itself against the discourses of the academy. At the same time, though, Egan's text seems more to claim this discourse for itself and demonstrate its superior ability to weave plausible cause and effect — and affect — into theory.

From *Before* to *After*

One of the most striking aspects of *A Visit from the Goon Squad*'s deployment of theoretical tropes, in conjunction with the continued depiction of precarious academic labour that was so prevalent in *The Keep*, is that its (Theory's) moment is past. Given that I have been arguing that the effect of this combination of representations (diverse modes of Theory, academic precarity) within a work of fiction is to legitimate a fictional work against the academic discipline of English itself, and specifically a New Historicism and/or Cultural Materialism of the present, what picture does *Goon Squad* paint for the future of this field of endeavour in the wake of Theory's passing? Firstly, academia and English seem, in some ways, to have met their own squads of goons. The flow of linear time that sits so centrally to what some optimistically call late capitalism has demonstrated the inability of the Leftist, committed stances of Cultural Materialism to effect revolutionary change.[71] *The Invisible Circus*, for this reason, keeps its academics out of sight. As '68 showed potential, the figures of the academy who failed to change the world are marginalised in a retrospective act of textual-economic punishment. As Adorno then puts it, referencing Marx's famous statement on the purpose of philosophy: "philosophy lives on because the moment of its realisation was missed".[72] As Adorno notes, though, "[t]his is why theory is legitimate and why it is hated: without it, there would be no changing the practice that constantly calls for change", a fact that Egan's text also seems to acknowledge.[73] That Egan's academics become ever more prominent as their ability to effect change proportionately decreases, however, says much about

---

71 With apologies to John Berger for borrowing his formulation of "optimistically called late capitalism".
72 Adorno, *Negative Dialectics*, p. 5.
73 *Ibid.*, p. 142.

Egan's indebtedness to postmodern stylistics. Secondly, the depiction of academia in Egan's trajectory is one of a critique of politics in her first novel, through to a critique of precarious labour in *The Keep*, until in *A Visit from the Goon Squad* it becomes possible to see the academics, especially through Mindy in 'Safari', as enmeshed in many of the book's major theoretical themes: feminism, politics, metafiction, and academia itself. This ambivalent attitude towards the academy reflects the fact that, once more, Egan's novels are on the same turf and they must fight for the right to speak alongside the academy, even while needing to denigrate the academy for that legitimation.

PART IV: DISCIPLINE

PART V: DISCIPLINE

7. Genre and Class

In the preceding parts of this book, I have demonstrated several reasons why contemporary fiction may choose to represent the academy, mostly focusing on the fact that in contemporary metafiction, the critical space is shared by the academy and fiction. This results in a struggle for the right to express critique and then a legitimation battle. Beginning with Tom McCarthy's oblique engagement with the academy through his public intellectualism and canny understanding of generic conventions, I suggested that *C*, although not a work that directly depicts academia, is a novel tightly bound to formalist criticism and canon formation and a novel that charts a literary history. Taking McCarthy's extra-novelistic presence as a challenge to the academy, I pointed out how this type of text, with its knowing self-situation in generic histories, competes with university English as a canon-forming agent, a technique that other texts, such as Mark Z. Danielewski's *House of Leaves*, also deploy. In the second chapter, having already broached the formal-aesthetic side of the equation, I then moved to detail how Roberto Bolaño enacts a political critique of the university in *2666*, twinning it with the police department (in an Althusserian vein), but also tying his academics to complicity with racism and, perhaps eventually, the Holocaust. In this way, I opened the discussion to aesthetic and political critiques (conditions of possibility) for the university and the novel, forms of critique to which I contend that metafiction is well suited.

In the next part of this book, I moved to examine the ways in which various fictions can legitimate themselves against the academy when they need to contest a space of authority. In Percival Everett's case, this took the form of a complex layering (including the author's status as a tenured academic himself). In *Erasure*, I contended, a dialectic emerged in which the novel was ironically dependent upon its readers' schooling in literary Theory but seemed, also, to wish its readers to forget this training in order to liberate themselves from the constraint of such thinking. Like Wittgenstein, Everett seems to encourage his readers to discard the ladders of learning once they have been climbed.[1] In demeaning the place of the academy as an authority to speak on issues of race, but also ridiculing literary prize culture and processes of canonisation, Everett's satire is multi-faceted and is more a 'playing with', and destabilization of, the academy's authority in the face of the novel, than a wholesale reconfiguration. To some extent, the same can be said of Jennifer Egan's treatment of academia. On the one hand, across her oeuvre, her texts make a playful mockery of academics. At the same time, though, a far more complex game is played here wherein Egan seems to demonstrate the superiority of the novel at providing plausible demonstrations of a continued viability of Theory, often through a critique of the labour structures of the academy. In this case, then, the parody function that remains in her work legitimates her texts, only so that they can then deploy the very discourses that were demeaned in a serious fashion.

If, then, in the preceding sections I have detailed the 'what?' in the introductory Part One, the 'why'?' in Part Two (critique) and the 'how?' in Part Three (legitimation), this next section could be titled, with tongue firmly in cheek: the 'so what?' (discipline). As a tentative answer to this flippant question and in light of the closing references to Adorno in the preceding chapter, it seems right to make reference to Marx: "philosophy has so far only interpreted the world. The point is to change it".[2] In this final part, I turn to texts that seem to want to change academic practice, texts that want to discipline the academy. In each of these instances, these authors deploy the strategies that have been outlined in the chapters above. The focus here now, though, is to show how this can translate into a feedback loop in which the reading practices and political alignments of the academy can be changed (or at least asked to change)

---

1   Ludwig Wittgenstein, *Tractatus Logico-Philosophicus* (London: Routledge, 2006), sec. 6.54.
2   Karl Marx, 'Theses on Feuerbach', in *Ludwig Feuerbach and the Outcome of Classical German Philosophy*, by Frederick Engels (London: Martin Lawrence, 1934), pp. 73–75.

by the fiction that it studies. This leads to a question of 'determination in the last instance' that is of enduring significance for literary studies and ethics: are the ethical preoccupations of the academy derived from the works they study or are such readings drawn, in the last instance/ at base, from the presuppositions of academics? The answer is not simple and is probably 'a bit of both'. The feedback loops of discipline in contemporary metafiction that I here chart will, by design, fail to resolve this, instead opting to further muddy the waters. I intend to open this discussion with an examination of the continuing practices of historiographic metafiction as they manifest themselves in the works of Sarah Waters. In many ways, the discussion of genre here extends the thinking in Chapter Three on McCarthy's C, but also changes direction to suggest a more active engagement from Waters's work.

Sarah Waters and Historiographic Metafiction

Following in the wake of Linda Hutcheon, those working on the lineage of the ever-nebulously-titled postmodern fiction have become accustomed to thinking about a certain sub-genre of this form as "historiographic metafiction".[3] Indeed, there has been a proliferation of works of fiction that highlight their own fictionality (metafiction) while dealing with the nature of the study/construction of history (historiography), thereby positing the distinctions and overlaps between events, narratives, and discursively encoded facts.[4] With the usual postmodernist suspects mentioned throughout this book acting as the most prominent US representatives of the 'movement', historiographic metafiction is also firmly recognised as the generic descriptor to which much neo-Victorian material was traditionally subordinated, despite the substantial divergences between canonised neo-Victorianists and high postmodernists.[5] A cursory glance at the fiction of Sarah

---

3   Hutcheon, *A Poetics of Postmodernism*.
4   Of course, in most instances historiographic metafiction is presumed to need a verifiable historical context and it might be argued that I am stretching the definition too far here. For *Affinity* is somewhat strange under such a classification, as its setting is a verifiable historical London, but its characters do not and did not ever exist.
5   Elizabeth Ho, *Neo-Victorianism and the Memory of Empire* (New York: Bloomsbury, 2012), p. 7.

Waters — the subject to which this chapter will devote itself — would seem to confirm this. As Ann Heilmann and Mark Llewellyn put it, "[m]uch neo-Victorianism [...] plays on the margins with a self-reflective and metafictional stance".[6] From Margaret Prior's opening line in *Affinity*, for instance, the reader is clearly reminded of Hayden White's theorisation of emplotment, wherein history and fiction exist as though within the axioms of an almost thermodynamic system; although neither may be created or destroyed, their form may be interchangeable. As Margaret reflects, "Pa used to say that any piece of history might be made into a tale", the implication being also that any tale might just as well be history.[7]

More recently, however, there have been signs of the exhaustion of historiographic metafiction as a fictional mode (or, at least, as a generic category). As noted by Shawn Smith, it no longer appears "new or revolutionary" to state that "history is a field of competing rhetorical or narrative strategies", which seems to encompass most of the claims associated with the 'meta' prefix and 'graphic' suffix.[8] In pointing this out, I do not mean to downplay the ethical validity of allowing counter-narratives of alterity to surface, which has been key in many readings of the function of historiographic metafiction alongside the rise of postcolonialism.

Conversely, whatever ill-phrased term we use to refer to that which succeeds postmodernism — 'post-postmodernism?'; a "modernist future?" — there are now signs of a shift in focus.[9] Although history and metafictive practice are both alive and well, the target of these metafictional elements seems more squarely aligned with ideas of genre theory, as I implied through the study of canonisation in Chapter Three, rather than solely with historiography. Consider a return, for example, to Thomas Pynchon's later works. Although initially classed as an out-and-out historiographic metafictionalist — most notably for *V.*, *Gravity's Rainbow* and *Mason & Dixon* — since his 2006 epic *Against the Day*,

---

6   Ann Heilmann and Mark Llewellyn, *Neo-Victorianism: The Victorians in the Twenty-First Century, 1999–2009* (Basingstoke: Palgrave Macmillan, 2010), p. 148.
7   Sarah Waters, *Affinity* (London: Virago, 2000), p. 7.
8   Shawn Smith, *Pynchon and History: Metahistorical Rhetoric and Postmodern Narrative Form in the Novels of Thomas Pynchon* (London: Routledge, 2005), p. 2.
9   Jeffrey T. Nealon, *Post-Postmodernism, Or, The Cultural Logic of Just-in-Time Capitalism* (Stanford: Stanford University Press, 2012); James.

Pynchon's focus seems to have moved (albeit incrementally) to explore the same notions of historiography, but to do so through the history of literary taxonomy in a practice that Brian McHale has called "genre poaching".[10] Similarly, moving across the Atlantic, although his work broadly lacks the standard characteristics of historiographic metafiction, such as explicit textual self-awareness and a focus on the parallels between fiction and history that is found in other British writers, such as John Fowles or even Russell Hoban, the writings of China Miéville have demonstrated the nuance that can be brought to such genre bending, melding science fiction with Lovecraftian 'weird' and even, in the case of *King Rat* (1998), fusing in subcultural narratives of jungle music in a mode that seems to mimic a historiographic function.

Of note for the subject of this chapter, both of the above cited authors have also veered into the territory of 'steampunk', a term denoting the anachronistic transposition of the technologies of the Industrial Revolution to new settings. In the case of Pynchon this takes place through his dime novel balloon boys in *Against the Day*, the temporally disjointed "Chums of Chance", whereas for Miéville steampunk is a dominant aesthetic in *Perdido Street Station* (2000) and *Iron Council* (2004). While recognising that the specific designation of steampunk is not interchangeable with 'neo-Victorian', this re-situation of Victorian motifs, coinciding with the rise of genre-play superseding historical-play, should give us pause for thought: is there something special about the Victorian era and its transcription into contemporary fiction that lends itself to this type of genre play? Is there something in the academic study of literature that privileges this time period in relation to genre studies and historiographic metafiction?

The neo-Victorian fiction of Waters, primarily her 1999 novel *Affinity*, affords an excellent case-study to explore these issues. Although *Affinity* initially looks like historiographic metafiction, it might better be designated under a new label: 'taxonomographic metafiction'. This term is a shorthand I propose for 'fiction about fiction that deals with the study/construction of genre/taxonomy' and constitutes, I contend, a useful alternative means of classifying such works. As a pre-emptive

---

10 Brian McHale, 'Genre as History: Pynchon's Genre-Poaching', in *Pynchon's* Against the Day*: A Corrupted Pilgrim's Guide*, ed. by Jeffrey Severs and Christopher Leise (Newark: University of Delaware Press, 2011), pp. 15–28.

rationale for the selection of *Affinity*, on which much critical work has already been undertaken, it is important to note that there are certainly other novels in which this mode may be observed, not least the aforementioned later fiction of Pynchon, as theorised by McHale, and other outright neo-Victorian works such as A.S. Byatt's *Possession* (1990). One of my core contentions is that many texts could be categorised as taxonomographic metafiction, even if hypothesised here from close reading of a single text. *Affinity*, however, provides an example, *par excellence*, of the fixation upon genre as a disciplining tool that I will be describing, particularly so because the novel's plot twists rely upon readers' conceptions and expectations of genre. Rather than performing its genre play through a multitude of voicings, as has become customary among other contemporary authors working on genre — for instance David Mitchell in *Cloud Atlas* — *Affinity* not only explicitly encodes its generic games within its own narrative statements (as, surely, do many metafictional works) but also, as will be shown, functionally deploys genre for its narrative path. In fact, Waters's novel hinges upon genre for the unfolding interrelation between its narrative and its metanarratorial statements, making it eminently suited for a taxonomographic analysis. While some might argue that the usual suspects of neo-Victorianism (Byatt, Fowles, Atwood, Waters, etc.) seem, on the surface, to be no longer exciting in terms of their genre-play and have been eclipsed by Pynchon, Miéville, and other more 'global' authors, by re-reading and returning to Waters's *Affinity*, we can actually see that even back in 1999 this 'new' form of taxonomography was in gestation and critics have missed an opportunity to look at neo-Victorianism in this way.

The second thrust of this chapter, as one might expect for the subject of this volume, is to suggest that the specific taxonomographic games that Waters plays are directed at the academy. It is my contention that Waters uses the academy's fixation upon alternative histories of sexuality in the Victorian era (via Foucault's argument against the "repressive hypothesis"), the Victorian prison, and Victorian spirituality to mislead the reader until a crucial moment in the novel. In fact, Waters seems to know that readers who have been schooled in the high-Theory period of the academy will be on the lookout for these features. This allows Waters to cloak her antagonist using 'class' (itself, conveniently enough, another term for 'category' or 'genre', as is the novel's title).

Academic readers of the text are often so busy congratulating themselves on feature spotting the tropes of sexuality/the prison/spiritualism that they overlook the servant character, whose class (and gender) situation allows her to remain hidden until the key moment in the novel. In this way, Waters disciplines the academy, asking academic readers not to make the same mistake twice. 'Look out for class', her novels seem to say, 'because you have been neglecting it at your peril'. As such, I will go on to argue here that despite the fact that Waters's novels are saturated with Foucauldian imagery, they are in fact *anti-Foucauldian* in their focus on class, an area that Foucault dismissively consigned to the dustbin of Marxism.

This analysis will now adopt a tripartite structure, moving from an overview of genre theory (including notions of academic disciplinarity), through to an evaluation of Waters's novel, before finally considering the applicability of this terminology beyond the specific contexts set out here. There are many problems of writing about fiction that writes about genre, mostly pertaining to notions of self-awareness and self-perception: for example, how can this article accurately classify when it deals with theorisations that de-stabilise classifications? Yet the re-growing stature of genre studies in twenty-first-century fiction makes this task one that is both needed and, to date, still under-addressed.

Genre Studies and the Process of Systematisation

In order to assess a shift from a mode of historiographic metafiction to one of taxonomographic metafiction, it first becomes necessary to define what is meant by 'genre', 'taxonomy', and 'taxonomography' and also to query whether, in itself, taxonomography can be considered a subcategory, under specific conditions, of historiography. For reasons of economy and also for their long-standing recognition in the critical canon, I will refer readers to Hayden White and Linda Hutcheon for their well-known definitions, respectively, of historiography (through metahistory) and historiographic metafiction.[11] Yet there is far less consensus on the definition and function of genre. At its most basic level, genre derives from the French meaning 'sort' or 'kind', itself

---

11   White; Hutcheon, *A Poetics of Postmodernism*.

descended from the Latin 'genus', a term used most prominently in contemporary biological taxonomies. Genre seems to appear, then, as a kind of sorting, a mode of filing, of classifying. There is, however, a real problem with this way of thinking, which is, counter-intuitively, also analogously found in biology and other rule-following disciplines, such as mathematics (explored most prominently by Ludwig Wittgenstein).[12] Framing genres in this way leads to a linguistic confusion in which the abstract concept of 'a genre' is reified until the belief emerges that genres are 'out there' waiting to be discovered, akin to a mechanistic process of filing into pre-existing boxes. Yet we also know that genres must come from somewhere. Taking this as problematic leads to the further questions of the origin of genres and the power structures behind their configurations.

One of the most incisive (and concise) explanations of the major problems of genre has come from Robert Stam who identifies four key difficulties of generic labels that are worth recapitulating: 1) extension: generic terms can often be too narrow to represent their subjects accurately while they are also, frequently, too broad to capture fully the nuance of individual works; 2) normativism: generic terms can lead to simplistic membership criteria that are then reduced to a crude tick-box exercise in merely existing categories; 3) monolithic definitions: genre can be tyrannous and lead to the false assumption that one generic title will be sufficient to characterise a work or series of works; and 4) biologism: genres are fallaciously believed to evolve in a standardised way over a common 'life cycle'.[13] Each of these problematic aspects begins to build a negative definition of genre wherein it becomes possible to state what genre is not. Genre is not a substitute for the specificities of a work. Genre should not be a tool for re-inscribing pre-existing norms. Genre is not an organism with known phases of development upon which we can rely, but a post-determined unique context in each case.

The assignation of genre is also a process enmeshed in issues of cyclicality and, more importantly, self-knowledge. As Andrew Tudor frames it, to analyse a genre means to identify its principal characteristics,

---

12 Ludwig Wittgenstein, *Remarks on the Foundations of Mathematics*, 3rd edn (Oxford: Blackwell, 1978).

13 Robert Stam, 'Text and Intertext: Introduction', in *Film Theory: An Anthology*, ed. by Robert Stam and Toby Miller (Malden: Blackwell, 2000), pp. 145–56 (pp. 151–52).

which must first involve generating a list of works that fall under the generic term. However, in a fine instance of a chicken-and-egg problem, these works can only be identified as fitting the genre-label through possession of the principle characteristics that they are supposed to embody in the constitution of the generic term.[14] This formulation, often cited in genre studies, has broader repercussions for ideas of academic disciplinarity, not least neo-Victorian studies. Academic disciplines, after all, work on a similar type of category formation for objects or methods of study. But, then, whence do academic disciplines appear? How are academic genres formed? These questions are asked not out of a tangential interest in the formulations that shape our discourse and ability to speak, but rather because they are absolutely central, as shall be seen, to the ideas of taxonomographic metafiction being put forward here. Neo-Victorian metafiction frequently signals its own consciousness of the academic debates surrounding literary 'merit' vs. populism (as just one example). This mode, however, as with historiographic metafiction, is also intensely aware of the paradigms of the academy. As a result, its treatment of literary, historical, and social categories, or genres, cannot be divorced from the genres of the academy, enforced through division of labour and entrenched in a rarely successful, but nonetheless worthwhile, quest for false reconciliation: disciplines.

If, as Stam suggests and I have hinted, this outcome of assigned genre is problematic, then there might be another way of understanding genre that proves more productive and that could form a framework for thinking about taxonomographic metafiction. Re-classifying genre as a 'formation process' can be of help in dissociating ideas of genre from notions of Platonic ideals. As a move towards this dynamic mode of formation, Stephen Neale has framed the issue thus: "genres are not systems: they are processes of systematisation".[15] It may not, at first glance, be obvious what is meant by this statement. After all, who said genre was a system? System is meant here as a collection of objects; as one might say 'solar system'. Thinking of genre as a title for a system leads to the problems outlined above. By contrast, to say that genre is a 'process of systematisation' acknowledges that the formation of such

---

14   Andrew Tudor, *Theories of Film* (London: British Film Institute, 1974), p. 135.
15   Stephen Neale, *Genre* (London: British Film Institute, 1980), p. 51; Neale, 'Questions of Genre', p. 163.

systems is a dynamic or behavioural process, an active undertaking of inclusion/exclusion and categorisation. 'Genre' becomes the name we might give to the drafting of a mutable set of rules for isolation.

Such an approach to genre has several advantages, most clearly that in emphasising the dynamic nature of genre and acknowledging the constant negotiation of terminology within a changing environment it becomes possible also to pre-admit the defeat of our taxonomies to incorporate definitively their subject matter. Genre no longer becomes a substitute for the specificities of a work, a tool for re-inscribing pre-existing norms, or a developmental certainty. Finally, this focus upon process also foregrounds the material conditions of production for cultural artefacts and the market services into which genre is pressed. 'Children's literature', 'young adult fiction', 'romance' and so forth serve as much a wish-fulfilment function for the consumer as they do a marketing tool for those doing the selling. Thinking of genre in this way shows the exact degree to which assigned genre can become constricting, an aspect of commercial systems that serves only to reproduce the extant conditions of reproduction. Thus, as Derrida puts it in his study 'The Law of Genre', in a polemic opening hypothetical statement typical of his style wherein such declarations form the aspect of enquiry and are then undermined and reversed throughout the piece, "as soon as genre announces itself, one must respect a norm, one must not cross a line of demarcation, one must not risk impurity, anomaly, or monstrosity".[16] As shall be seen, Waters's text undertakes a similar reversal from this position, promising a novel of star-crossed romance and supernatural mystery while subtly exploiting, introducing, and proliferating generic impurity.

Certainly, this 'process of systematization' model helps to think about the uses to which genre is put, rather than fixating on the term itself, and this leads on to the theorisation of taxonomographic metafiction to which the remainder of this chapter will be devoted. From this brief incursion into genre theory, there are four key points and suppositions worth reiterating, as they form the crux of the evaluation here: 1) taxonomography is the study of genre, when genre

---

16 Jacques Derrida, 'The Law of Genre', trans. by Avital Ronell, *Critical Inquiry*, 7.1 (1980), 55–81 (p. 57).

is defined as a 'process of systematization'; hence taxonomography is more accurately defined as the study of processes of systematisation; 2) this process of systematisation, by which a text continually forms and then destabilises generic markers as it unfolds, is often performed through the use of intertextual reference as such a marker. As we saw in the case of McCarthy's novel, however, this can also take the form of an implied intertextuality, or an implied archive, even to works that do not exist. Most crucially, though, texts manipulate the behavioural process of systematization; 3) material conditions of production and/or reception are important for a study of these systematising processes; and 4) academic disciplines are types of genre. They are formed as the outcomes of processes of systematisation over which academics are not themselves the masters. Each of these precepts will now be examined in the context of Waters's adjusted mode of metafictive practice.

History, Setting, and Critical Analepsis

Set in 1870s London, Waters's second novel, *Affinity*, is narrated by two alternate female speakers with shared leanings towards same-sex desire: the middle-class spinster Margaret Prior and the working-class convicted felon Selina Dawes. The primary plot in the novel revolves around the philanthropic activities of Margaret, a visitor to Millbank prison where Selina, an imprisoned spiritualist medium, has been sentenced to a five-year term for a never-wholly-explicated charge of fraud and assault. Through Margaret's diary entries, the text continually signals her ongoing grief for the death of her father and also for the loss of her past love, Helen, who is now her brother's wife. Over the course of the novel, Margaret's visits to Millbank become more and more frequent as she becomes at first curiously interested in and then romantically infatuated with Selina. Selina's diary entries, on the other hand, detail her life as an infamous London spiritualist prior to her imprisonment. The novel concludes with an episode wherein Selina claims that she will be able to escape from prison by using her supposed supernatural abilities and that she will then appear before Margaret. In actual fact, the reader is cruelly deflated when it turns out that Selina is involved in a conspiracy with Margaret's servant, Ruth Vigers, and has successfully defrauded the woman who has fallen in love with her.

This spiritualist setting, in addition to chiming with the late-twentieth and early-twenty-first-century popular resurgence of interest in supernatural mediation as entertainment, allows Waters to project an environment that is at once historically accurate and exotic, but also one that is highly sexually charged. The intersection of spiritualism, sexual danger, and criminality are continually at the forefront of the text, an aspect that is clearly evidenced in the slim portions of the novel that recall Selina's trial: "'She asked you to remove your gown? Why do you think she did that?' — 'She said that I must do it for the development to work properly'".[17]

If, however, *Affinity* can be said to be a novel concerned with spiritualism and its possible links to illicit sexuality, the text itself, as with the later *Fingersmith* (2002), is more specifically centred around notions of confinement and, as Rosario Arias argues, two rather than one imprisoned individual/s.[18] After her suicide attempt, Margaret is only infrequently allowed to leave her home, kept suitably subdued by her mother-'jailor'. As a result, to some extent, Waters mirrors Selina's imprisonment in this character. In a deliberately ironic inversion, however, the only time that Margaret is free is when she visits Selina in the prison. Conversely, it is only owing to the visits of one prisoner (Margaret) to another (Selina) that the latter eventually achieves her freedom, with the novel's surprise conclusion bringing the supernatural very much down to earth in a traditional escape narrative with the aforementioned cruel twist: Margaret's servant, Vigers, turns out to be Selina's lover, having connived with the medium to secure her release and deprive Margaret of her inheritance.

Thinking hypothetically for a moment under a mode of assigned genre, it would seem clear from critical work to date that the primary thematic (if not formal) characteristics that define the genres of this novel are: a Victorian setting (although written in the late-twentieth century, hence neo-Victorian), lesbian gothic romance, spiritualism, and the prison. Perhaps the ultimate intersection of these aspects, brought

---

17 Waters, *Affinity*, p. 140.
18 Rosario Arias, 'Epilogue: Female Confinement in Sarah Waters' Neo-Victorian Fiction', in *Stones of Law, Bricks of Shame: Narrating Imprisonment in the Victorian Age*, ed. by Frank Lauterbach and Jan Alber (Toronto: University of Toronto Press, 2009), pp. 256–77 (p. 259).

about through a sexualised sadomasochistic context, comes from the description of the prison's disciplinary apparatus:

> "Here we have handcuffs — some for girls, look — look how dainty these are, like a lady's bracelets! Here we have gags," — these are strips of leather, with holes punched in them to let the prisoner breathe "but not cry out" — "and here, hobbles".[19]

In this mapping out of assigned genres, though, things are not quite so straightforward.

In order to begin to appraise each of these aspects under what I will term a process-genre model, it is worth first assessing the Victorian setting of the text, an element that also involves thinking more broadly about the status of historical and historiographic fiction. In this latter area, M.-L. Kohlke has persuasively argued that Waters's brand of historiographic metafiction is substantially different from its traditional antecedents on the premise that "historiographic metafiction may have exhausted its transgressive possibilities and become problematic rather than liberating to writers such as Waters".[20] While Kohlke argues that "[h]istorical fiction offers women writers and their female protagonists a way into history through the back door", she also asserts that Waters's fiction is queerly orientated for traditional thinking on historiographic metafiction.[21] Rather than the more explicit practice of Fowles's *The French Lieutenant's Woman*, for instance, in which the narrative forks into three alternative, parallel endings in order to signpost mimetically the constructed nature of history as narrative, Kohlke makes a good case that Waters's novel "mimics history's obscuration of its own narrativity, not merely critiquing but re-enacting it", a mode she dubs "new(meta)realism".[22] This is an aspect that is reinforced by the intertextual reference to Henry James's *The Turn of the Screw* (1898) that is surely implied by Waters's Peter Quick (Ruth Vigers's impersonation of Selina's spirit-guide) re-enacting the sexualised, ghostly Peter Quint.

While I will return to these broader questions of historiography, it is worth, at this point, delving more specifically into the re-mediation

---

19 Waters, *Affinity*, p. 179.
20 Kohlke, p. 156.
21 *Ibid.*, p. 153.
22 *Ibid.*, p. 156.

of the historical setting of the novel and to examine the lenses through which *Affinity* re-presents its Victorian timeframe. This is important because, as will be seen, the frames of reference used have a strong bearing upon academic disciplinarity and taxonomography in relation to the text. As at least five critics have noted, it is clear that Waters's text deploys Jeremy Bentham's Panopticon as a deliberate model for the prison setup (even if Millbank was not, ultimately, to be Bentham's ideal instantiation) alongside Henry Mayhew's *The Criminal Prisons of London and Scenes of Prison Life* (1862).[23] Yet the Victorian is even more strongly represented through the 'Foucauldian' element that carries particular implications for academic readings — in spite of the triteness of employing 'Foucauldian' as a broad catch-all adjective. I want to suggest that the specific reading practices that Waters encourages (and which therefore shape the processes of systematisation for the text) are heavily inflected by this high-Theory reference point through Foucault. To demonstrate briefly the Foucauldian inscriptions that have already been ably explored, one need look no further than Foucault's famous explanation in *Discipline and Punish* (1975) that, in Bentham's prison design, the "annular building" frames a tower "pierced with wide windows that open onto the inner side of the ring" such that the cells situated within the "peripheric building" may be backlit and overseen by a single supervisor. In other words, "[t]he Panoptic mechanism arranges spatial unities that make it possible to see constantly and to recognize immediately", thus transforming visibility into a trap.[24] When this description is compared to that in *Affinity*, the direct modelling upon the Panopticon is clear. As the prison governor Mr Shillitoe leads Margaret along the "spiral staircase that wound upwards through a tower", they arrive at "a bright, white, circular room, filled with windows" that houses Mrs Haxby, "the Argus of the gaol". From this description and the direct reference to Argos 'Panoptes', it is as clear

---

23 Kohlke; Mark Llewellyn, '"Queer? I Should Say It Is Criminal!": Sarah Waters' *Affinity* (1999)', *Journal of Gender Studies*, 13.3 (2004), 203–14, http://dx.doi.org/10.1080/0958923042000287821; J. Millbank, 'It's about This: Lesbians, Prison, Desire', *Social & Legal Studies*, 13.2 (2004), 155–90; Arias; Barbara Braid, 'Victorian Panopticon: Confined Spaces and Imprisonment in Chosen Neo-Victorian Novels', in *Exploring Space: Spatial Notions in Cultural, Literary and Language Studies*, ed. by Andrzej Ciuk and Katarzyna Molek-Kozakowska (Cambridge: Cambridge Scholars, 2010), pp. 74–82.

24 Foucault, *Discipline and Punish*, p. 200.

to the informed reader as to Miss Prior how the prison functions as a Victorian intertext: "you will see the logic of the design of this", as the novel knowingly remarks.[25]

Alongside Waters's 1995 doctoral thesis on lesbian and gay historical fictions that necessitated reference to Foucault, there are other clues throughout the text of *Affinity* that strengthen the assertion that it is Foucault whose image is supposed to most clearly materialise in the mind of the academic reader.[26] We are told, for example, of "how the world might gaze at [Selina]", of how "it was a part of her punishment", with Jacobs, the prisoner in the "darks", screaming "damn you for gazing at me", the objectifying gaze forming a core part of Foucault's early institutional histories.[27] Furthermore, Waters does not miss the opportunity to pun on the name of her warder, Ellen Power, using the surname-only homonym to flag up the second of Foucault's core axes: knowledge, power and ethics. For example, early in the text, Margaret recalls that "[w]hen I gazed at Power, I found her smiling", while later we are given the blunt query: "Power gone?".[28]

In addition to highlighting the aspects of class, power, and the gaze that I will later contend are the key elements in this novel, these clear allusions to Foucault are important for thinking about *Affinity*'s taxonomographic aspects for two reasons. Firstly, in sowing Foucault's genealogies throughout her text, Waters appears not only to be staking her position as a writer of literary fiction through the processes of canonisation outlined in Chapter One, but also seems to be writing under the genre of what we might term a *critical* historiography. This is made clear through the way in which *Affinity*, alongside her earliest neo-Victorian novel *Tipping the Velvet* (1998), both overturns the repressive hypothesis and also makes sexuality a part of identity formation in the Victorian era. Notably for Waters, these two aspects are used to reflect a feminist, lesbian critique of the present in the same way that utopian and dystopian texts deploy temporal and spatial differentiation and repetition in order to enact critiques upon their own origins. Writing

---

25 Waters, *Affinity*, pp. 10–11.
26 Sarah Waters, 'Wolfskins and Togas: Lesbian and Gay Historical Fictions, 1870 to Present' (unpublished doctoral thesis, Queen Mary University of London, 1995).
27 Waters, *Affinity*, pp. 64, 181.
28 *Ibid.*, pp. 39, 278.

of Waters's exploration of "how women in the nineteenth century were ostracised, criminalised and placed outside society", Llewellyn fittingly remarks that "[t]he use of an historical period can imply that there is a parallel or affinity between the age about which an author is writing and the one in which she writes".[29]

While Llewellyn warns of the dangers of attributing a direct correlation between the source history and contemporary target era in a mode of trans-historical critical affinity, he also notes that "there is an inescapable desire to categorise the kind of novel Waters wants to write".[30] This brings me to my second point, under which it becomes possible to re-join genre (a process of systematisation) with Waters's novel: the intended discourse community for such Foucauldian references appears to be those readers with an academic background and an interest in the (neo-)Victorian, the foreknowledge of which means that, at this level, Waters can play some elaborate generic games.

Affinity (Noun): "A Similarity of Characteristics"

This notion of an "inescapable desire to categorise the kind of novel Waters wants to write" brings the argument back full circle to issues of genre and classification, which seem to be central to this novel, if admittedly locked in a further classificatory desire. On multiple fronts, this initial attempt to thwart generic placement can be seen with ease: the text is the lesbian novel that isn't a 'lesbian' novel (as this identity formation did not exist at the time of its setting); it is a historical fiction that is about the present; it looks to be a work of historiographic metafiction that has exhausted its transgressive potential; it is a supernatural thriller that is wholly natural; it is a prison novel in which confinement is ultimately removed to a panoptic society; and it is two diary accounts told through impossible, already-destroyed diary objects (perhaps evoking the paradigms of erasure that were remarked upon in Chapter Five). There is also a process at work here that caters specifically for an informed academic discourse community. This is one of decoding Waters's encoded text and re-reading the deliberate

---

29   Llewellyn, p. 213.
30   Ibid.

Foucauldian inscriptions that she makes, thereby systematising the Foucauldian text through this reading process.

Following the logical regress, the consequence of this mode of thinking, which asks why a certain discourse community goes through a specific process of systematisation, is to ask how that discourse community was systematised in the first place. As with the discussion in Chapter Six of Jennifer Egan, this means that we should treat academic disciplines in exactly the same way that we think about genre: as problematic and cyclical when assigned — which accounts for some of the problems of why, as Stanley Fish put it, "interdisciplinarity is so very hard to do" — but better understood as a process of systematisation.[31] Even at a broad level, the study of literature, of mathematics, of physics and so forth each requires a definition based upon a systematisation of the objects of study that does not exist independently of humans, but is entwined in processes of practice and ideology. For reasons of labour scarcity, disciplinary boundaries are defined that dictate (and are, paradoxically, defined by) not only the 'object' studied, often, but also the behavioural patterns that form a conservative sanity check for the practice of the study of those objects. Self-situation and identification also plays a core role here. Within each 'discipline' there are sub-disciplinary practices constrained by the typed hierarchy in which they are situated.

In recent days, perhaps the best example of the difficulties of thinking about 'discipline' have emerged surrounding the multiple strangely aligned denizens of the 'digital humanities' arena. If this can even be thought of as a 'discipline', it is unified neither by object of study nor methodology. In fact, in this particular instance, self-identification is the strongest factor: if your work uses computation in any way and you would call yourself a digital humanist, then you most likely are. In this light, what is the purpose of disciplinarity? Some have argued that this naming function is a crucial act of legitimation that parallels the demarcation of expertise that I have claimed, in this work, that many novels also undertake. To some degree, the isolation of the academy is a historical function of professional specialisation and is inherent in notions of expertise and authority. For instance, Samuel

---

31 Stanley Fish, 'Being Interdisciplinary Is so Very Hard to Do', *Profession*, 89 (1989), 15–22, http://dx.doi.org/10.2307/25595433.

Weber states that "[i]n order for the authority of the professional to be recognized as autonomous, the 'field' of his 'competence' had to be defined as essentially self-contained [...] In general, the professional sought to *isolate* in order to control".[32] As Weber goes on to note, "[t]he university, as it developed in the latter half of the nineteenth century, became the institutional expression and articulation of the culture of professionalism. [...] The 'insulation' or 'isolation' of the American academic community from other segments of society is the negative prerequisite of that demarcation that marks the professional perspective, above all that of the university professor".[33]

This thinking around disciplinarity is important for readings of *Affinity*, because this text plays a game of taxonomography, knowingly luring different discourse communities with aspects of their vocabularies, but also seems to attempt to re-systematise academic disciplines themselves. For an instance of how others have begun to hint at this structure, consider that Sarah A. Smith, in a take also reframed by Rosario Arias, suggests that *Affinity* is a text that shows that "[t]he conclusions that Margaret's story prompts — that gender is a form of prison and a kind of madness — are predictable commonplaces of feminist studies of the Victorian period".[34] Firstly, this meta-situation reflects back on the novel, rather than on any external politics: it becomes "more about the politics of the novel than sexual politics".[35] This is because Arias's claim is not that *Affinity* reflects anything about the society it depicts at the moment of its setting, it rather depicts the obsessions of the academy when thinking about this era. Secondly, though, it would be foolhardy to say that sexual politics are not aspects that the text covers; Margaret *is* trapped by the status that society affords her gender within the novel and also believes in notions of her own hysteria. Such statements simultaneously acknowledge that this *is* what the text does, while calling it trivial and obvious, eventually arguing

---

32 Samuel Weber, *Institution and Interpretation* (Stanford: Stanford University Press, 2001), p. 27; part of this argument on disciplinarity was first advanced in Martin Paul Eve, *Open Access and the Humanities: Contexts, Controversies and the Future* (Cambridge: Cambridge University Press, 2014), http://dx.doi.org/10.1017/CBO9781316161012.
33 Weber, pp. 32–33.
34 Sarah A. Smith, 'Love's Prisoner [Review of Sarah Waters' *Affinity*]', *The Times Literary Supplement*, 28 May 1999, p. 24; Arias, p. 256.
35 Sarah A. Smith, p. 24.

that *Affinity*'s final aim is to expose the commonplaceness of these traits. What such a reading misses, however, is that the text's surprise ending would not be possible were it not for the foregrounding of all aspects except for class, the single element that allows the antagonist Ruth Vigers to go unnoticed for the majority of the work. As Heilmann and Llewellyn put it: "we don't really 'see' what is presented to us because we displace our belief onto another part of the narrative [...] we fail to realize that the servant in the household carries the key".[36] Although such an accusation of neglecting class in favour of exoticised deviance could here be being levelled at Foucault, it is more clearly aimed at the reader who is ensnared in the generic game.

To elaborate, a taxonomographic approach allows us to see the way in which class is elided in readings of Waters's work: through genre. The novel rests upon a notion of class that is buried by the study of gender, homo-normativity, the prison, and the gaze. In this instance, the traditional objects of study for the sub-disciplines of gender studies and others derived from Foucauldian genealogical methods serve to mask other understandings of the work. This is a game of pre-empting and guessing, a game that the text metafictionally replicates in the relationship between Margaret and the aptly named Miss Riddley, of which Margaret notes, "I guessed what she guessed".[37] More specifically on notions of class, the reader should recall that, when Margaret finally realises how she has been manipulated and defrauded, she casts her mind back to Vigers and says: "[w]hat was she, to me? I could not even recall the details of her face, her look, her manners. I could not say, cannot say now, what shade her hair is, what colour her eye, how her lip curves" — and neither can the reader.[38] Vigers is furthermore described as having "lumpish servant's limbs", but, despite this description of bulk and substance, she thrives on invisibility. Early on in the text, Margaret writes of how she hopes that the warders might "see the weakness in me and send me home", only to lament that "they did not see it".[39] This aspect of unseeing, of invisibility, is the only way that the novel's twist can come about. The text makes a specific type of academic

---

36   Heilmann and Llewellyn, p. 149.
37   Waters, *Affinity*, p. 250.
38   *Ibid.*, p. 340.
39   *Ibid.*, p. 13.

reader complicit with a wish-fulfilling pleasure in which many of the expected aspects of neo-Victorianism — sexuality, female confinement, and the prison — are amplified and thrust into sight, so that it can underplay notions of class, embodied in Vigers, in order to keep the key antagonist hidden. Margaret is advised to "keep [her] rings and trinkets hidden [as she would] from the eyes of a servant", but keeping the servant hidden from the eyes of the reader, through a distraction technique that will appeal to specific disciplinary environments, is part of the taxonomographic game that the novel plays.[40]

While the authorial game-playing is clear in retrospect, Waters does sow a few clues throughout that indicate that class might be an underpinning factor, thus adding the metafictional element that interweaves narrative and metanarratorial discourse. When talking about the penalties for suicide, Margaret asks, in a pun that also diverts us through the use of the term "queer": "[d]on't you think that queer? That a common coarse-featured woman might drink morphia and be sent to gaol for it, while I am saved and sent to visit her — and all because I am a *lady*?".[41] Of course, the actual affinity between the characters here lies in societal penalty for lesbian desire, but there is a secondary, ironic meaning to the novel's title. In the varying treatment afforded to Selina and Margaret for their respective crimes of fraud and attempted suicide and shared 'crime' of same sex desire, which are handled entirely differently on the grounds of their different class backgrounds, we are shown the basis of the plot twist: societal groupings and treatment of those groups. In this reading, 'affinity' and also 'class' become terms for genre, for ways in which things are grouped on the basis of their characteristics, as part of an ongoing process of systematisation.

The novel affords further clues to the discerning reader of a staged inter-class difference between Vigers and Margaret. For instance, although at one point Vigers's "gaze seemed dark", Prior describes her face as being as "pale *as my own*".[42] Conversely, inter-class delineation through surname-only appellation also proves key to the plot. Consider that, were class structures not present, the reader would have been alerted far earlier to the fact that "Ruth" and "Vigers" are the same

---

40 Ibid., p. 16.
41 Ibid., p. 256.
42 Ibid., p. 241, emphasis mine.

person; one of Selina's entries clearly alludes to her interaction with an individual called "Ruth".[43] Even the fact that Vigers is never referred to as "Miss Vigers" encourages us to think of her surname as her sole identity and dissuades the reader, through the downplaying of class, in the genre process, from forging the connection between the two.

It is worth noting that this focus on genre and classificatory desire in Waters's novels is not confined to *Affinity*, but is nonetheless most strongly concentrated within this text. The trajectory of genre within an economy of game-playing as a focus in Waters's works, to which *Affinity* contributes, was one that was kick-started in her first novel, *Tipping the Velvet*, wherein the lead character remarks that she "had believed [herself] to be playing in one kind of story, when all the time, the plot had been a different one".[44] Many aspects of this antecedent book foreshadow elements of *Affinity*. When, for example, that novel's protagonist, Nancy Astley, first becomes fascinated by Diana Lethaby's servant, Zena Blake, she suddenly realises that she has been using her surname-only address: "I had grown used to calling her only 'Blake'". Perhaps even more importantly, Nancy also remarks that "I had grown used to not *looking* at her, not *seeing* her at all".[45] This earlier work is notable for its situation in the picaresque tradition — with more than a hint of roaring Moll Cutpurse — but also for the way in which each of its parts takes on particular genre functions: the rags-to-stardom first section, the down-and-out rescue segment, and the socialist-to-love redemption phase. The second is perhaps the most important (and would merit further investigation) with its twofold inscription of a consenting sadomasochistic relationship atop a deliberate reference to Angela Carter's reworking of the Bluebeard myth in *The Bloody Chamber*: "[t]here might be a heap of girls in suits — their pomaded heads neat, their necks all bloody".[46]

Continuing the genre-play, *Fingersmith*, Waters's next neo-Victorian work after *Affinity*, also adopts this theme. In many ways closely replicating *Affinity*'s structure of two mirrored female protagonists who narrate in alternation, *Fingersmith* encodes the bait-and-switch

---

43 *Ibid.*, p. 191–195, *passim*.
44 Sarah Waters, *Tipping the Velvet* (London: Virago, 1999), p. 398.
45 *Ibid.*, pp. 300–301.
46 *Ibid.*, p. 238.

distraction that *Affinity* attempts within its own narrative. Waters casts the mis-reader into the role of the stooge within the text, identifying with Susan 'Sue' Trinder. In *Fingersmith* this distraction is achieved through a perspectivised pre-emption wherein the reader empathically identifies with the narratorial figure and projects his or her desires upon the text in this light. *Affinity*, on the other hand, is primarily concerned with pre-empting the reader's expectations of the conventions of the neo-Victorian novel and using them to form its own distraction fraud. In both *Affinity* and *Fingersmith*, Waters is her own form of con artist.

To unpack this statement a little further with relation to *Fingersmith*, consider that it is a prerequisite of the text that the narration begins from the perspective of Sue. This is necessary because it allows a subtextual prejudice of class morality to emerge: Maud Lilly, the lady of social standing, is portrayed as a "poor girl" in need of defending (even by one of her supposed con artists) and naïve.[47] The reality is that Maud is herself the co-participant in a reversed (and therefore mutual) female betrayal of Sue and is hardly innocent: her uncle has brought her up from a young age to transcribe and index his pornographic library and she is more than happy to purchase her freedom through Sue's lifelong incarceration (as Sue was, likewise, happy to liberate herself financially through Maud's). The reader is, however, misled (despite the ominous proleptic hints) into believing that, because Sue's class position puts her in a position of seemingly greater material need, she will be more inclined to lie, to cheat and to steal. *Fingersmith*, however, is a text that works to unsettle this: "'I am not what you think', I will say. 'You think me good. I am not good'".[48] As Gentleman asks, knowingly, of Maud, but really in a pointed jibe at the reader: "who wouldn't, in her place, believe you innocent?".[49]

This is the generic play of *Fingersmith*, which is similar to *Affinity*: to inculcate presuppositions in the reader, once again, that the novel's focus is upon: 1) female confinement; 2) hysteria and madness; and 3) a re-inscription of 'lesbianism' into the Victorian period (overturning the repressive hypothesis). All these are the fascinations of the same aforementioned academic disciplines. The signs are clear, though,

---

47 Sarah Waters, *Fingersmith* (London: Virago, 2003), pp. 82, 131.
48 *Ibid.*, p. 284.
49 *Ibid.*, p. 227.

that the text is actually one that is, like each of Waters's neo-Victorian texts, a taxonomographic distraction con. As Waters is to the con artist Gentleman, so Sue is to the reader: she "will be distracted by the plot into which I shall draw her. She will be like everyone, putting on the things she sees the constructions she expects to find there".[50]

To return to *Affinity*, however, which is the novel that demonstrates these taxonomographic aspects with the greatest clarity, the way in which we can most easily discern the text's attempt to pre-empt the pre-emption of all readers (rather than just academic readers) is in the false trail that it lays to suggest an imminent death at the end of the novel. There are strong hints that statements such as those surrounding the prison garment boxes ("[i]t was as if the boxes were coffins") are proleptic, especially given that much of the text concerns the supernatural and an ability to communicate with the dead; why not also an ability to see into the future?[51] This false foreshadowing is also echoed in Selina's diary, which is presented to the reader as potentially supernatural at this stage, wherein Peter Quick (whose surname, ironically, carries the Biblical contrast to the 'the dead') refers to a *"fatal gift"*, thus strengthening these notions.[52] In reality, it is unclear whether Margaret kills herself at the end of the text. She speaks of the "final thread of [her] heart" growing "slack", but she cleans her wounds and tidies the house as if to carry on living, a way in which the novel then both frustrates expectations of stereotypes while also clearly dodging the earlier proleptic hints.[53] While this is certainly an unorthodox take on the strong implications of suicide presented at the end of the novel, the taxonomographic aspects that I am suggesting here teach us to be wary of textual insinuation.

The final twist of the knife that *Affinity* sticks into historiographic, as opposed to taxonomographic, metafiction comes from the impossible objects upon which the text's history rests. While the historical study of life-writing remains dependent upon the continued existence of the material artefact, whether through narrative necessity or in a deliberate amplification of the counter-factual history contained in the text, *Affinity* destroys the intra-textual objects that would support its assertions.

---

50   Ibid., p. 227.
51   Waters, *Affinity*, p. 237.
52   Ibid., p. 261.
53   Ibid., p. 351.

"How queer", the text finally puns, "to write for chimney smoke" as Margaret burns her diary.[54]

Others, such as Heilmann and Llewellyn, alongside Kohlke, have done a great service to the field in re-situating *Affinity* as a text that moves away from an exhausted postmodern historiography, despite its potential characterisation as such a text; and also as a work that links Victorian class-blindness to a contemporary parallel. What I have argued is that these twofold shifts are achieved in Waters's novel through the mechanism of a move to taxonomography, a metafictive focus upon the nature and play of genre (meaning: a process of systematisation) in relation to both reader and critical expectations. Waters is acutely aware of different discourse communities and plays the academic reader like putty with sown allusions to Foucault, imprisonment, spirituality, and Victorian lesbianism — knowing that these will excite members of this discourse community — so that she can cloak aspects of class and the novel can achieve its pay-off (this is not to understate the fact that part of Waters's immense skill is to play this game without lessening her novels' commercial appeal). These stereotypes — the lonely, and in the case of Margaret, suicidal, tragic homosexual (consider also that Selina Anne Dawes has the initials 'SAD'); the pitfalls of gender and its constructed nature; the Victorian setting encouraging Foucauldian readings; the prison; aspects of madness and suicide; the life-writing/diary form; even the signposting of the text as historiographic metafiction in Margaret's opening line — are all aspects that *Affinity* bowls at an academic discourse community, putting them into a competitive economy of genres with one another, so that the true aspect that it wishes to explore, namely class, remains undiscovered. In multiple ways this seems to mirror the critiques made by proponents of, say, intersectional feminism, namely that certain forms of feminist discourse pay inadequate attention to race. It could certainly be said here that Waters's novel implies that there are academic readers entrenched within discourses of queer and gender theory who are, analogously, under-representing class within their areas.

In many ways, this is an undoing of a stance that has been building since around 1978, when Foucault asked whether we were facing the

---

54   *Ibid.*, p. 348.

end of the era of revolution. Certainly, as Daniel Zamora charts it, for Foucault, "this transformation parallels the decline of Marxism and the contemporary problems to which it led".[55] In this narrative, Foucault's project becomes in part about abandoning Marxist class conceptions as the substructure of struggle and instead redistributes it across a historically contingent matrix of forms: sexuality, prisons, lepers, and the insane. Importantly, for a book so saturated with these forms, Waters's text is actually anti-Foucauldian. Waters uses her attention to genre to focus upon class, even through the multiplied lenses of excluded bodies.

This taxonomographic focus is an advanced technique that is aware of the shifting nature of genre, of the fact that it is a process driven by behavioural patterns, for as the text temporally unfolds, it must anticipate the process through which its target discourse communities — whether academic or popular — will systematise its contents; it must guess what the reader will guess. This, in turn, involves an awareness of the constructed nature of disciplines — of those very discourse communities — by the same processes. *Affinity* is a novel that, in its metafictive practice, reflects back, not just on itself — the constant accusation levelled by detractors of the form — but on the academy, on commercial processes of genre, on conditions of production, and, through these socio-cultural contexts, on class, in what may be described as a new ethical act that attempts to systematise the academy and its discourses through a mutual shaping process.[56] *Affinity* is an example of a neo-Victorian novel that attempts to discipline the reading practices to which it is subject, asking the academy to return to class as a fundamental issue in reshaping cultural narratives. In its pre-emptions of the processes to which it is subject, *Affinity* is a text that always seems to have one up on its academic readership, attempting to reshape our forms and ways of thinking about forms. One should always remember, academic reader, the text seems to say, whose girl you are.

---

55 Daniel Zamora, 'Foucault, the Excluded, and the Neoliberal Erosion of the State', in *Foucault and Neoliberalism*, ed. by Daniel Zamora and Michael C. Behrent (Cambridge: Polity, 2015), p. 63.
56 James, p. 10.

8. Discipline and Publish

As mentioned in the opening to the final part of this book, succinct critiques of teleology find their apex in Theodor Adorno's well-known opening to *Negative Dialectics* where he writes that philosophy lives on because the moment of its realisation was missed.[1] This statement — a clear reference to Marx's proclamation in the *Theses on Feuerbach* (1845/1888) that philosophers have so far only interpreted the world, but that the point is to change it — came at a time when it seemed that the potential for revolutionary action was past. In his perpetual pessimism, Adorno advocates for a return to philosophy (Theory) in the wake of the seeming failure of the predictions of the future expressed in Marx's historical materialism.

Likewise, throughout this book a spectre that stands against a proposed teleology has been haunting the fictional landscape: postmodernism. Detractors have proclaimed its death but often with no new terminology to describe a present literary moment beyond additional prefixes to 'modernism'. Robert Eaglestone even notes that the term post-postmodernism is, in fact, "silly".[2] Metafiction and postmodernism live on, then, because the problems of representation that they address were never overcome. The interaction with the academy and the melding of criticism and fiction are aspects that remain, even in the wake of detractors' continued assaults. This is none so clear than in the work of Ishmael Reed, to which this final literary chapter will be addressed.

---

1   I am, of course, aware that there is no small irony in heralding Adorno as a standard bearer of concision.
2   Eaglestone, p. 1099.

Ishmael Reed and Anti-Enlightenment Values

It is no secret that Reed has made a career out of grotesque and unconventional satires of American life, but also from his frequent spats with feminist movements.[3] Most commonly compared to a generation of postmodern writers including Kathy Acker, William Burroughs, and Norman Mailer, Reed's novels are also often strangely aligned (for crass grouping by skin colour) with Toni Morrison and Alice Walker.[4] Stylistically, it is easy to see the postmodern aspects of Reed's work but it is also possible to trace them within a history of a "Black aesthetic", as does Reginald Martin.[5] Usually extremely playful, Reed's metafictive creations also mount critique of both their conditions of production and the environments depicted. For instance, the plot of Reed's 1972 novel, *Mumbo Jumbo*, revolves around the advocacy of a counter-Western trickster spirit known as Jes Grew (a homophonic reference to spontaneity: 'just grew') that manifests in dance and jazz. Some have argued that this fixation on folk magic — or 'hoodoo' — that pervades much of Reed's writing has broader social implications. Kathryn Hume, for example, traces Reed's hoodoo influence to a desire for presentness, a form of eluding the coercive structures of control that decree an obligatory preparedness against the future,[6] an aspect that then chimes well with the core line of the (then unwritten) Pynchon novel: "to fetch them through the night and prepare them against the day".[7]

Part of Reed's antagonism, however, has certainly been directed at the academy. As Hume points out of *Mumbo Jumbo*:

---

3   Ishmael Reed and Bruce Dick, 'Ishmael Reed: An Interview with Bruce Dick', in *Conversations with Ishmael Reed*, ed. by Bruce Dick and Amritjit Singh (Jackson: University Press of Mississippi, 1995), pp. 344–56 (pp. 345, 348–49); see also Womack, p. 124.
4   Madelyn Jablon, *Black Metafiction: Self-Consciousness in African American Literature* (Iowa City: University of Iowa Press, 1997).
5   Reginald Martin, *Ishmael Reed and the New Black Aesthetic Critics* (Basingstoke: Macmillan, 1988).
6   Kathryn Hume, 'Ishmael Reed and the Problematics of Control', *PMLA*, 108.3 (1993), 506–18 (p. 509), http://dx.doi.org/10.2307/462618.
7   Pynchon, *Against the Day*, p. 805; Reed was quite clearly an influence on Pynchon who suggested that the reader should 'Check out Ishmael Reed. He knows more about it [Masonic mythopoesis] than you'll ever find here'. Pynchon, *Gravity's Rainbow*, p. 588.

> [i]ndustrialism and capitalism reduce the already narrow Western values to a yet narrower materialism, and efficiency becomes the primary virtue. In the 1920s of *Mumbo Jumbo*, these values are promulgated by the Wallflower Order, a coterie representing the Ivy League, the Social Register, and other wealthy upper-class white institutions. This Wallflower Order rules America. Its members are wallflowers because they cannot dance.[8]

That such Ivy League universities are referenced as members of the elite, prejudiced Wallflower Order in this text is significant for this study and, indeed, demonstrates the lineage within which the critique of the university, via sly side-swipes, is rooted within postmodern fiction. Harking back to the reading of Bolaño's critique of the university that I undertook in Chapter Four, the university structure here is not one of universal enlightenment, but is rather entwined with repression and regression.

In *Mumbo Jumbo*, there is one passage in particular that lends itself to a reading as a critique of the university. While the plot of *Mumbo Jumbo* defies clear synopsis, the passage in question to which I will refer relates the autobiography of Abdul Sufi Hamid, a Muslim convert previously known as "Johnny James", born on the "Chicago South Side". Hamid goes on in the novel to destroy the Book of Thoth, the presumed sacred Text of Jes Grew, after growing disgusted with the supposedly lewd content therein. However, the passage that I am about to discuss is important because, as Steven Weisenburger has noted, Abdul appears "to be the sole character exempted from Reed's satiric ridicule".[9] The passage also throws ridicule on institutions of learning.

Indeed, Hamid claims to have "always wondered why the teachers just threw the knowledge at us when we were in school, why they didn't care whether we learned or not". Furthermore, he observes that "the knowledge which they had made into a cabala, stripped of its terms and private codes, its slang, you could learn in a few weeks" and it certainly "didn't take 4 years". In fact, Hamid claims, "the 4 years of university were set up so that they could have a process by which they

---

8   Hume, p. 509.
9   Steven Weisenburger, *Fables of Subversion: Satire and the American Novel, 1930-1980* (Athens: University of Georgia Press, 1995), p. 167.

would remove the rebels and the dissidents". In this text, the university becomes an enforcer of social norms, a space in which students are expected to internalise the value structures of broader society and to leave rigorous social critique behind. As the passage continues:

> [b]y their studies and the ritual of academics the Man has made sure that they are people who will serve him. Not 1 of them has equaled the monumental work of J.A. Rogers, a 1-time Pullman porter. Some of these people with degrees going around here shouting that they are New Negroes are really serving the Man who awarded them their degrees, who has initiated them into his slang and found them to "qualified", which means loyal.[10]

This is, as with the entirety of Reed's novel, a confusing passage that merges several different strands of critique into one. First of all, the religious terminology of the setup must be noted. The esoteric jargons of the university become "cabala". While this also chimes, etymologically, with 'cabal', the term for a secret grouping that must include the novel's Wallflower Order, it also clearly links in to Jewish mysticism and textual interpretation. At the same time, however, Hamid is a convert to Islam whose holistic system of learning incorporates aspects of religion, alongside other disciplinary practices. Certainly, he was not born into the faith: "I wasn't born with a caul on my face, PaPa LaBas", he notes, "[n]or was my coming predicted by a soothsayer as yours was, Black Herman".[11] Furthermore, we are told that Hamid's new education is one in which he "was borrowing from all of these systems: Religion, Philosophy, Music, Science and even Painting", which perhaps yields an intertextual link to the eponymous subject of Herman Hesse's *The Glass Bead Game* (1943).[12]

The questions that could arise here are multiple: why is the academy affiliated to Jewish mysticism in Hamid's tale? (A hypothetical answer: because the claimed theological role of university English, apparent in Robert Alter's discussions of the 'sacred'/theological nature of canons, can appear to be to produce meaning from arcane texts through recodings, decodings, and permutations of language, which are all, in

---

10 Ishmael Reed, *Mumbo Jumbo* (New York: Atheneum, 1989), p. 37.
11 *Ibid.*, p. 36.
12 *Ibid.*, p. 37.

Kabbalistic frameworks, permutations on the name of God.)[13] Why does this particular religious take lead to hegemony? Is this an anti-Semitic trope? While I do not propose specifically to address the last of these questions, Weisenburger does propose a way to approach these issues. In Weisenburger's take, the contradictions that centre around Hamid position him as "a potential threat to the opposition between Atonism [part of the Wallflower Order's conspiracy] and Jes Grew that is driving Reed's satire".[14] By featuring Hamid as a mass of contradictions, the character can represent the "synthesis" of the "primary opposition" against the "normative center" of *Mumbo Jumbo*; at once a character who embraces plurality while also espousing monotheistic dogmatism.[15]

The position of the university and formal higher education within this synthesis is clear: it represents the dogmatic, unified past against the spontaneous freedom and plurality of the future Jes Grew. The association of the university's knowledge systems with Jewish mysticism is, therefore, not necessarily a congruent juxtaposition. It is rather meant to signal the esotericism, privileged exclusionary, and hidden nature of the doctrinal teachings of higher education, even if this cloaking is an aspect that Hamid himself later propounds in various ways. If this critique of the university is not necessarily coherent, it does not mean that it lacks force. The place of the university within an evolving dialectic towards plurality is cemented, but the side on which it is placed is not the forward-thinking, supposed liberal humanist, critical-centric institution. It is, rather, the tool of the past and authority.

This criticism of the academy as authoritarian was most explicit in Reed's 1993 novel, *Japanese by Spring*. This text, clearly a campus novel, revolves around the changing fortunes of its unloveable protagonist, Benjamin 'Chappie' Puttbutt. The son of a US military general, Puttbutt is a black academic at Jack London College, where, in the hope of achieving tenure and finding acceptance with his white colleagues, he writes screeds against affirmative action that blame the black population for its own social inequality. This seems to be a manifestation of an older Black aesthetic into the plot, in Martin's terms, which involves "hating a society which loathes one's self, while at the same time doing

---

13 Alter, *Canon and Creativity*.
14 Weisenburger, p. 168.
15 Reed, *Mumbo Jumbo*, p. 168.

everything possible to become a symbiotic part of that society".[16] Predictably, this backfires and Puttbutt is denied tenure. As Audre Lorde once put it: "the master's tools will never dismantle the master's house".[17] Unpredictably, however, the university is, at this precise moment in the novel, purchased by a Japanese corporate entity that turns the Anglo/Euro-centrism of the current US university curriculum on its head and attempts to universalise elements of Japanese culture (as well as, apparently, being part of a larger plot to overthrow the Japanese government). The novel takes its title from the supposed timeframe of Puttbutt's Japanese language course, into which he has thrown himself in the belief that Japan will be the dominant economic, military, and political force of the twenty-first century. As with all of Reed's novels, the satire of monoculturalism is outrageous, contentious, and biting.

More specifically, *Japanese by Spring* is of note for this book because it straddles firstly (but loosely) the literary genre of the campus novel, and secondly the legitimation against the academy that I have been outlining in this work. Most of the texts that I have focused on in this book could not be described as 'campus novels'. In fact, as noted, the works on which I have chosen to focus tangentially assault the university amid their focus elsewhere. There are a subset of books, however, that can be called the 'postmodern campus novel', and *Japanese by Spring* sits among these (others include DeLillo's *White Noise* and John Barth's *Gilles Goat-Boy*). These types of novel function differently from other works of contemporary fiction that bash the academy. While, I have contended, the passing jibes at the expense of the academy usually fulfil a legitimating role, in which the author proclaims his or her superiority over the critics that read such works, this usually serves to validate the literary representation of something else. Postmodern campus novels sprawl and can rarely be said to concern one singular topic. The fact that their geographical settings are universities, however, means that once a critique is made, the environment in which the remainder of the novel's action will occur is contaminated. *Il n'y a pas de hors universitaire.* The academy is all that is the case.

---

16 Martin, p. 11.
17 Audre Lorde, 'The Master's Tools Will Never Dismantle the Master's House', in *Sister Outsider: Essays and Speeches* (Trumansburg: Crossing, 1984), pp. 111–13.

In Reed's case, the critique is particularly bitter and the environment especially toxic: "you fucking intellectuals make me sick. All you can think to do is criticize", notes one character.[18] Reed's academics are shown as purely self-interested narcissists, ethically and socially lacking in almost every sense. In many cases, Reed attributes this malaise to the stagnation of high Theory in which, it is claimed, "all you had to do was string together some quotes from Benjamin, Barthes, Foucault, and Lacan and you were in business. Even a New Critic like himself could make some cash".[19]

Yet, as usual, all is not so straightforward in Reed's fictional worlds. There is a section in *Japanese by Spring* where Puttbutt ruminates on the beliefs of the universalists and American exceptionalists. These 'Back to Basics' conservative characters, as presented through Puttbutt, cannot conceive of "a time when the domination of the United States by people of the same background would come to an end". "These people", it is claimed, also said that "rock and roll was the music of the devil" and believe that "English would always be the official language of the United States". Most importantly, though, in a view that Reed clearly rejects, "they said that postmodernist literature was just a passing fad and that people were returning to the ordinary".[20]

Japanese by Spring also demonstrates other features that merit the designation of 'postmodern campus novel'. Among the references to its own generic classification, it also directly features the author himself, as a character. This is a well-known trope of postmodern metafiction. As Timothy Aubry puts it in his discussion of David Foster Wallace, when "the author actually appears as a named character within the fiction" this "seems to straddle the boundary between the real and the fictional world".[21] In fact, Reed's character in the novel comes head-to-head with the critique of high Theory that I have just discussed. When 'Ishmael Reed' is contemplating the rationale for his attraction to the

---

18 Ishmael Reed, *Japanese by Spring* (New York: Atheneum, 1993), p. 181.
19 *Ibid.*, p. 49.
20 *Ibid.*, pp. 47–48.
21 Timothy Aubry, *Reading As Therapy: What Contemporary Fiction Does for Middle-Class Americans* (Iowa City: University of Iowa Press, 2011), p. 125; see also Marshall Boswell, 'Author Here: The Legal Fiction of David Foster Wallace's *The Pale King*', *English Studies*, 95.1 (2014), 25–39, http://dx.doi.org/10.1080/0013838X.2013.857850.

language Yoruba, he poses a series of hypothetical questions.[22] Was he, he asks, drawn to Yoruba because he liked the idea that "West Africa would eventually become a world leader"? Or, after many other such questions, "[m]aybe it was because of Derrida's 1968 message about the age of the death of the author. There was no perceivable role for the critic in Yoruba art".[23]

This sneaky self-insertion into the text (which, as we must remember from Everett's work, is *not* the same as the author) has two critical facets. Firstly, it draws attention to the role of voice; the difficulty of extracting a communicated 'message' from fiction (as per the Adorno/Sartre debate in my earlier discussion of Roberto Bolaño) is compounded by the uncertain placement of authorial figures. Secondly, it highlights the role that the academy ascribes to the author in the process of interpretation. The novel therefore demonstrates the importance of considering who is speaking (and the impossibility, often, of definitively knowing this) through such polyvalent authorial self-representation. This has an important knock-on effect for the above consideration of the critique of the university environment. Specifically, the character who observes that intellectuals "make him sick", is none other than Puttbutt Sr., the military general who has wiretapped his own son's communications and deliberately written to the university to block Chappie's tenure application, believing that it would have been better for his son to have continued the family's military heritage.

The dilemma posed by this particular challenge is complex. In a way, it is similar to the questions of double negation that I earlier posed of Everett's *Erasure*.[24] In another way, though, it is somewhat more political because of the connotations of militarism and Western imperialism that Reed packs behind the statement.

The point that emerges from these considerations of voicing is that, in actual fact, it does not always matter whence the enunciation. In *Japanese by Spring*, for instance, the fact that General Puttbutt criticizes the university does not undermine the critique, despite his militaristic

---

22 As has become a convention, I here place the author's name in quotation marks when referring to the intra-diegetic representation of the author, rather than the author himself.
23 Reed, *Japanese by Spring*, p. 122.
24 When a parody is effected within a novel by a character that is, itself, a parody, is the result a parody or is the effect of parody thereby lessened?

placement, but instead acts only to intensify it. As, perhaps, with James English's analysis of scandal in the literary prize scene, it often seems that critique, whatever the intra-diegetic source of its utterance, adds to the credence of the critique, rather than to detract from it (furthering my earlier work on *Erasure*). This is not universally the case. If the critique were only to come from the general — and if it were purely a critique against critical thinking in which the army disliked academia for its own criticisms — the matter might be very different. In Reed's worlds, though, the university comes under assault from a large number of locations and the words of a war hawk do not, in this case, undermine the critique. Rather, it seems to signify alignment across the political spectrum.

Juice!, the Media, and Disciplining Academic Publishing

In 2011, after an eighteen-year hiatus from writing novels, Reed published *Juice!* with the Dalkey Archive Press, the book towards which the remainder of this chapter will turn in its demonstration of Reed's disciplinary technique. The novel is narrated from the perspective of Paul ('Bear') Blessings, a cartoonist who is obsessed with the OJ Simpson trials and who rigorously protests the innocence of the former NFL star and actor. At every instance possible, Bear reads OJ's troubles as enhanced, or more frequently entirely produced, by structural racism; after all, "the men who run the networks prefer blondes".[25] Were this simply a tool of communication, though, a polemic rant on the continued deplorable state of US race-relations, *Juice!* could hardly be said to merit its sub-title: "*A novel*". Instead, as with Everett's *Erasure*, Reed seeks to complicate his protagonist's distorted narrator in order to extend the traditional postmodernist deconstruction of binaries, again centred around supposed post-raciality. Bear alternates between poles of paranoia and viable critique, the one continually undercutting the plausibility of the other in order to show, at one remove, how it is that cultural reading practices of paranoia and truth degrade the efficacy of radical critique.

---

25   Ishmael Reed, *Juice!: A Novel* (Champaign: Dalkey Archive, 2011), p. 75.

The book is also one that states its own metafictionality through a critique of metafiction, thus clearly demonstrating Currie's assertion that no point in the regress of self-awareness is ever totally sufficient. For instance, the novel contains many striking passages that are concerned with flagging up the relationship between the diegetic environment, the author, and the history of the realist novel. At one point, for instance, the narrator states that:

> somebody had to strike a blow for the return to common sense in the arts. You have these self-reflexive novels where the novelist interjects himself as a character. Novels like those written by that Ishmael Reed. He's probably out in some obscure hole in California right now, thinking of another way by which he can badger himself into his work having been criticized for introducing himself as a character in his novel *Japanese by Spring*.[26]

Yet this is not all. As with all the texts studied in this book, Reed's novel is one that subtly, but persistently, situates the academy at its margins and as the subject of its ridicule. The most prominent of these references is to an article in *"Critical Inquiry"*. At this moment, Bear describes how this journal will "fill an entire issue" with his cartoon of OJ Simpson "pretending to stab a white woman with a banana", which "sends out a whole bunch of signs".[27] The critique here is one of triviality and over-reading (in-accessibility), alongside an inefficacy compared to the domineering power of the media (un-accessible). The implication is that the unpacking of the obvious semiotics of this cartoon — with its phallic and racial registers — is trivial and yet those authors publishing in *Critical Inquiry* will be more than happy to waste their breath with verbose commentary on a straightforward matter.

This is a strategy that is frequently deployed by other writers and, given the postmodern heritage here, it is an aspect that I will turn to in the works of Thomas Pynchon, for the final time, before returning to Reed. Although there are other prominent instances of the university in Pynchon's oeuvre — famously, Oedipa Maas in *The Crying of Lot 49* (1966) walks through the campus at Berkeley — Pynchon's latest novel, *Bleeding Edge* (2013), becomes the foremost satirical representation

---

26 Ibid., p. 321.
27 Ibid., p. 193.

of the academic humanities in his work. In *Bleeding Edge* the reader is introduced to the academic research of Heidi, a character who is working on an article for the *"Journal of Memespace Cartography"*.[28] Clearly supposed to be humorous, the passage ridicules the academic debates over irony and sincerity that have raged in recent years as a result, again, of Wallace's 'E Unibus Pluram', a piece that itself targets Pynchon.[29]

Despite its parodic nature, however, this section of *Bleeding Edge* that deals with Heidi and the *Journal of Memespace Cartography* is symptomatic of a broader trend in Pynchon's later writing: direct engagement with and representation of academic communities. In fact, *Bleeding Edge* parodies Otto Rank and Jacques Lacan throughout and mocks the academic who uses the terms "post-postmodern" and "neo-Brechtian subversion of the diegesis".[30] Likewise, Pynchon's preceding novel, *Inherent Vice* (2011), connected the supposedly innocent academics working on the ARPAnet to the sinister histories of the ICBM traced in his earlier work, *Gravity's Rainbow*.

Consider Pynchon's reference to a fusion of Rank and Lacan. On page two of *Bleeding Edge*, we are told that:

> [t]he Otto Kugelblitz School occupies three adjoining brownstones between Amsterdam and Columbus…the school is named for an early psychoanalyst who was expelled from Freud's inner circle… It seemed to him obvious that the human life span runs through the varieties of mental disorder as understood in his day — the solipsism of infancy, the sexual hysterics of adolescence and entry-level adulthood, the paranoia of middle age, the dementia of late life… all working up to death.[31]

At a first evaluative glance, we might think of this as a straightforward reference to Rank. After all, Rank shares a first name with Pynchon's ball-lightning-surnamed character. Rank was also prominently cast out of favour in Freud's inner circle for his near-heretical take on the Oedipal complex in *The Trauma of Birth* (1924/1929). However, Rank's theories do not seem to fit that closely with Pynchon's description of

---

28 Thomas Pynchon, *Bleeding Edge* (London: Jonathan Cape, 2013), pp. 334–35.
29 David Foster Wallace, 'E Unibus Pluram: Television and U.S. Fiction', *Review of Contemporary Fiction*, 13.2 (1993), 151–98.
30 Pynchon, *Bleeding Edge*, pp. 2, 9, 245.
31 *Ibid.*, p. 2.

Kugelblitz. Rank proposed that there was a phase before the Oedipal (the pre-Oedipal) in which a human life is spent attempting to recover from the trauma of birth. By contrast, Lacan is a figure we might more closely associate with "the solipsism of infancy", given his focus on the mirror phase and the moment of self recognition. Lacan is explicitly mentioned later in the novel, ironically having been put out of business by supposed "neoliberal meddling", even though Lacan's 'variable-length sessions' have been decried as a mere exercise in money-spinning and may be the reason that Leopoldo has such a "decent practice".[32]

Lacan sits at the heart of at least one psychoanalytic school of literary criticism and much contemporary Theory owes some form of debt to his thinking, particularly in the works of Slovoj Žižek. It is also the case that a great deal of contemporary fiction makes side-swipes at dense literary theoretical approaches for the aforementioned reasons of inaccessibility. But this seems to be particularly acute in *Bleeding Edge*. Furthermore, the reference to a character that speaks of the "neo-Brechtian subversion of the diegesis" in *Bleeding Edge* is a particular attack on an aesthetic application of social theories and/or philosophy.

The term itself ("neo-Brechtian subversion of the diegesis") is, in fact, an accurate rendition of the particular act at this moment in the text. It refers to the moment when Reg Despard first discovers that he can zoom on his video camera and begins doing so, totally unnecessarily, while recording a movie to sell on the bootleg market. The diegesis refers to the narrative inside the frame. Reg's zooming disrupts the realist certainty of what is being seen and forces the viewer's attention onto the framing device itself; Brechtian alienation subverting the diegesis. At the same time, though, there is a parody underway of the complex terminology used, in this case, by an "NYU film professor", perhaps pointing to Robert Stam.[33] Tracing the specificity of this hostility is not straightforward, however, and, as above, it would be a mistake simply to consider extra-textual referents as true one-to-one mappings. So far as I know, however, Tom LeClair was the first to suggest a connection between Brechtian alienation techniques and Pynchon's writing in his 1989, *The Art of Excess*, an aspect to which Stefano Ercolino has recently

---

32 Ibid., p. 244.
33 Ibid., pp. 8–9.

returned in his writing on *The Maximalist Novel*, so there are a range of possible targets at which this parody might point.[34]

The other aspect to note is that the only reason that the NYU professor is able, at this point, to comment upon the "neo-Brechtian subversion of the diegesis" is because "Reg managed to sell one of his cassettes" to this professor. In other words, the shady underworld of the 1990s pirate video scene that Pynchon uses as a parallel to the contemporary online piracy space and the Deep Web sits beneath this parodied academic pronouncement. There are a range of interpretative paths that we might follow from this point. Firstly, it appears that academia is complicit with the system of piracy that precedes the hashslingerz project of Gabriel Ice in Pynchon's unsummarizable text, an aspect that might be radical but that is also entwined with the recuperation of alternative hidden underspaces by venture capital. "Someday there'll be a Napster for videos, it'll be routine to post anything and share it with anybody", Reg remarks.[35] Secondly, though, academia is making pretentious statements about elements in Reg's filming that don't exist or were not intentional, even though the text, like many of Pynchon's novels, is concerned with hidden digital spaces of plausible deniability; projected worlds.

The other moment on which we might briefly dwell is the use of the phrase "post-postmodern" in proximate connection to the aforementioned neo-Brechtian spiel. This ties in with a theme pertaining to irony and literature that runs throughout the entire novel and, particularly, the deliberate reference to the debates around New Sincerity and the works of David Foster Wallace, as classified by Adam Kelly. In one sense, this is a continuation of the discourse parody that recurs throughout Pynchon's novel. Furthermore, as mentioned above, the mere proliferation of -modernist suffixes and accumulating post- prefixes is now becoming an almost-silly way in which we seek to classify any new literary movement (i.e. base any new taxonomy of literature on a named paradigm that, in its canonical high form, ostensibly has 'newness' as its guiding principle). Perhaps what we actually need is a manifesto for 'No More Modernisms'. On the other hand, once more, the debate around irony and sincerity that is at least

---

34 Tom LeClair, *The Art of Excess: Mastery in Contemporary American Fiction* (Urbana: University of Illinois Press, 1989); Ercolino.

35 Pynchon, *Bleeding Edge*, p. 348.

part of the characterisation of post-postmodern literature is one that has broader political ramifications for society. While Pynchon's caustic remark through Maxine casts the debate as overstated — that it seems, in this quarrel, as though irony "actually brought on the events of 11 September" — there is surely an attempt at a deeper societal diagnosis than this acknowledges.[36]

There is a final element of Pynchon's treatment of the academy to which I here wish to turn: those elements to do with societal isolation (un-accessibility). If Pynchon depicts academic arguments as overstating their influence on world events he also depicts the denizens of the university as insular individuals, communicating obscurely among themselves and powerless against the larger forces, inefficacious except to lament the current state. In *Bleeding Edge*, for instance, Professor Lavoof is the "generally acknowledged godfather of Disgruntlement Theory" and develops the "Disgruntled Employee Simulation Program for Audit Information and Review, aka DESPAIR".[37]

The main jab, perhaps, at academic insularity, though, comes through a critique of dissemination and reach of scholarly communications. Even before we get to academia, *Bleeding Edge* has several moments that deal with information dissemination. For instance, Maxine says to Gabriel Ice, "come on, it's only a Weblog, how many people even read it?", to which he responds, "one is too many, if it's the wrong one".[38] On the other end of the scale, Reg Despard speaks of a future age of information overload, in which there is "way too much to look at" and in which, as a consequence, "nothing will mean shit".[39] This all comes to a head in the parody of Heidi writing the article for the *"Journal of Memespace Cartography"* entitled "Heteronormative Rising Star, Homophobic Dark Companion" that makes the aforementioned argument that irony has supposedly taken the fall for 9/11.

Remarkably, and to return to Reed, these mentions of academic publications and their in- and un- accessibilities can be read as far more than a simple signpost to highlight the academic community. Although, as a reference to academic journals, it fulfils the role of a pointer to the

---

36 Ibid., pp. 334–35.
37 Ibid., p. 87.
38 Ibid., p. 137.
39 Ibid., p. 143.

academy, the fact that such devices are rarely used in respectful contexts in contemporary academic fictions brings to the fore a new angle. If the humanities disciplines in particular — those that would be signalled by "*Critical Inquiry*" — are supposed to promote critical thinking, in the tradition of critique — that is, thought that attempts to comprehend the structural limits of its own possibility — then what might be signalled by the particular mention of journal serials as a signalling mechanism for the academy?

As I have written elsewhere on many occasions, the sphere of journal publications in the academy is one of abject a-criticality.[40] This is not to say that material that is expert within its own subject domain does not appear in academic journals. Far from it: research work that thinks rigorously and critically about its subject matter is far more likely than not to be published in these venues than elsewhere. What I mean instead is that academics often do not think critically about their own publication practices and the serials (journal) environment is a clear indicator of this.

For instance, the cost of subscribing to all the journals that an institution needs rose by approximately 300% between 1986 to 2012.[41] Even Harvard University has cancelled subscriptions on the basis of price.[42] Researchers, though, are usually unaware of the material price of the journals in which they publish: they have no price sensitivity. Instead, researchers work within a symbolic economy of prestige whereby their publications, in addition to fulfilling a dissemination function, act as currency for accreditation based on the brand of the journal. This symbolic capital is then re-converted into material capital through hiring, tenure, and promotion procedures. At the same time, some commercial publishers are making hundreds of millions of dollars' worth of profit per year out of academic publishing, without remuneration to academics who give them the material for nothing and are also not usually compensated for peer review labour (this system is beneficial in many ways: it frees academics from market populism

---

40 See Eve, *Open Access and the Humanities*.
41 Association of Research Libraries, 'Expenditure Trends in ARL Libraries, 1986-2012', http://www.arl.org/storage/documents/expenditure-trends.pdf.
42 Ian Sample, 'Harvard University Says It Can't Afford Journal Publishers' Prices', *The Guardian*, 24 April 2012, http://www.theguardian.com/science/2012/apr/24/harvard-university-journal-publishers-prices.

in the object of their research inquiries but the benefits are financially obviated if publishers are beholden to that same market). Only 20% of researchers feel that it is acceptable for academic publishers to make a shareholder-driven profit and to do with such proceeds what they wish.[43] That said, far more than 20% of researchers publish in venues that work on exactly this model and thereby deny access to their colleagues at other institutions who often cannot purchase the work.

This is a matter of critique. Publication, as the driver of contemporary systems of accreditation in the academy, forms the conditions that structure the everyday practices of most academics. This is, in many ways an awful way to proceed and to evaluate, but it is what exists. However, researchers usually have to think in terms of self-gain in order to play the system to their advantage. Publishing outside of recognised venues on the basis of principle is usually not an option unless one feels suicidally inclined with respect to an academic job. This means that it is usually easier not to consider the economic consequences and to ignore the ways in which we continually, communally fuel the bizarre economic cycles that constitute the serials crisis.

The specific target of Reed's satire, *Critical Inquiry*, though, is owned by the University of Chicago Press. This is hardly the most exploitative of journal venues. In fact, in contrast to many subscription venues, *Critical Inquiry* is positively good value for money with an individual subscription costing $58 per year. This is still enough to pose a financial burden upon some (especially if they may have to subscribe to dozens of such publications and do not have institutional access), thereby limiting the circulation (un-accessibility). The primary focus here, though, is upon the petty nature of the critique that is mounted within the venue and probably also upon a limitation of circulation. Specifically, this is a co-joined focus on *over*-interpretation and under-circulation, the twin critiques that I contended were enacted by Reed's novel.

On the first front, the accusation of 'over-interpretation' has been levelled at the hermeneutic/critical front of literary studies since the discipline began. The recent swing towards archival and historical practices, away from the formalist and philosophical pole, is not a new phenomenon. The blow aimed at criticism has long been that it

---

43 OAPEN-UK, 'Researcher Survey', 2012, http://oapen-uk.jiscebooks.org/research-findings/researchersurvey.

is "an affair of subjective impressions", a selective activity that merely collects "anecdotes or isolated facts" without reference to a socio-cultural whole.[44] Yet, criticism was legitimated as a valid paradigm most strongly in the twentieth century, usually alongside a historicist approach. The question was: how much historical context did one need to ground an interpretation? New Critical approaches, usually framed through I.A. Richards's *Practical Criticism* (1929), tended to answer 'none' or 'little' while later twentieth-century thinking on historiography and discontinuous history reversed the relationship through the New Historicism, reading history out of textual culture.[45]

The degree to which an interpretation can be deemed an 'over-interpretation' depends upon one's perspective. To cite Gerald Graff one last time, from outside of literary studies departments, *all* activities that scholars and critics undertake can appear arcane and obscure: "it is hard to think of any field from Chaucer to Pynchon studies that is not ingrown and esoteric if viewed from the lay point of view".[46] For most 'lay' or 'common' readers, the research, hermeneutic, and scholarly approaches of the academy can all be seen as jargonistically over-interpreting a body of work that speaks for itself; an in-accessibility. In turn, this leads to the age-old debate over whether literature can be taught at all or whether it is an area whereof we cannot speak and thereof literary studies should remain silent.

The moment in Reed's text containing *Critical Inquiry* emphasises the over-interpreting nature of university English through both the presentation of an incommensurate volume ("a whole issue") of critical writing on a single cartoon and the low cultural status of the object of study. In the first instance, Reed signals that the critical material is reading more than the object contains. Like Adorno's critique of applied philosophy, criticism here "reads out of works that it has invested with an air of concretion nothing but its own theses".[47] Such signalling then

---

44 Graff, p. 137; André Morize, *Problems and Methods of Literary History, with Special Reference to Modern French Literature: A Guide for Graduate Students* (Boston: Ginn, 1922), p. 130, http://archive.org/details/problemsmethodso00moriiala.
45 Ivor Armstrong Richards, *Practical Criticism: A Study of Literary Judgment* (London: Transaction, 2008).
46 Graff, p. 251.
47 Theodor W. Adorno, *Aesthetic Theory*, ed. by Gretel Adorno and Rolf Tiedemann, trans. by Robert Hullot-Kentor (London: Continuum, 2004), p. 447.

hinges on an assumption (on the part of the creator) that the cartoon cannot be an object that "sends out a whole bunch of signs". Finally, this assumption rests upon a notion of intentionality; over-interpretation implies a kind of critical perpetual-motion machine in which more is taken out of the system by the critic than was ever put in by the author.

That Reed's critique is of over-interpretation can be deduced with reference to the criteria that Umberto Eco sets out in *Interpretation and Overinterpretation* (1992). For Eco, a non-paranoiac interpretation is one that "cannot be explained more economically; that [...] points to a single cause (or a limited class of possible causes) and not to an indeterminate number of dissimilar cases; and that it fits in with the other evidence".[48] In this case, it is primarily the first of these that Reed sets upon: there is a clear proliferation of discourse that Reed's character feels could be explained more economically and, indeed, may be entirely obvious.

The problem is that Reed's novel and tradition are steeped in postmodern irony, a tradition that complicates this high/low binary. Furthermore, a critical work such as this book becomes trapped by the metatextual paradigm. As the cartoon within the text becomes a metonym for the novel, critical discourse on the text is pre-invalidated by the work it studies. When Reed's character, Bear, criticises academics for reading more into his trivial work than was invested by the author or is present in the text (an imbalance towards the latter in the conflict between the "rights of texts and the rights of their interpreters", as Eco might put it), it is impossible for the same not to apply to work written about the novel itself.[49] This is certainly a disciplinary technique, designed to silence academic writing about the novel by destroying its legitimation claims, in advance, so that the critical space is left wholly to the novel.

The second point of discipline that we can infer from Reed's swipe at academic publishing is linked to the above comments on the economics of scholarly communications. For *Juice!* is a novel that is saturated by the mass media. The hysteria over the OJ Simpson trial can only be

---

48 Eco, 'Overinterpreting Texts', p. 49.
49 Umberto Eco, 'Interpretation and History', in *Interpretation and Overinterpretation*, ed. by Stefan Collini (Cambridge: Cambridge University Press, 1992), pp. 23–43 (p. 23).

described as a 'media circus' in which the forces of mass technology were harnessed to achieve mass dissemination. In which case, what are we to make of *Critical Inquiry*? A recent (contentious) analysis in the discipline of physics claimed that "as many as 50% of [academic] papers are never read by anyone other than their authors, referees and journal editors", a figure justified by looking at citation analysis.[50] Certainly a survey of article counters on toll-access/subscription journals reveals a similar anecdotal picture for English studies. In addition, therefore, to a disparity of input/output ('over-reading'), there is a disjunct in circulation. A book that deals with the mass media and its multi-million-viewer coverage of a racially charged US murder trial that also mentions an academic journal with comparatively trivial circulation cannot but be making a critique of triviality and readership. At the same time we might ask what the circulation of Reed's obscure novel is likely to be and from where his primary audience demographic might be drawn. We might conclude that the academy is one such site.

In this way, Reed's novel is a good case study to show the unification of the structure that I have explored over this book. It disciplines the academy by pre-invalidating the critical discourse that Reed knows will be brought to bear on his work. In a cunning double-move, this legitimates his text as an originary art-object above the critical voice. Finally, by claiming the legitimate right to speak and silencing the academic commentary that might run alongside it, *Juice!* is left alone to speak in the critical space. Discipline, legitimation, and critique.

As a closing remark, we might note that while I have here claimed that discipline is a silencing technique, English studies does not remain quiet. Its discourses continue to proliferate. Some, like this book, write at the meta-level, describing how such texts create feedback circuits with the academy that trouble and disrupt our normal practices (except that this then becomes one such set of normal critical practices). Others simply ignore such injunctions and proceed in the usual vein. The question then becomes one of whether English studies adapts to its object of scholarship or whether this relationship is actually one-way. We see fictions emerging that critique the academy. Do we see the academy

---

50 Lokman I. Meho, 'The Rise and Rise of Citation Analysis', *Physics World*, 20:1 (2007), 32–36.

responding to the injunctions of such fiction? I would answer positively to the former and, for the most part, more negatively to the latter. In this case, strangely, given the course that I have charted through this book, it seems that the anxiety of academia is most strongly held by fiction, and not by critics fearing their target fictions.

PART V: THE END

PART V: THE END

9. Conclusion

Throughout this book I have demonstrated a variety of ways in which the university — and specifically university English — is used and abused in works of contemporary fiction. While far from a conclusive study, the representative range of texts here examined leads to several conclusions about the interaction between the novel and the academy. Roughly speaking, these findings can be schematised into aesthetic and political critique, legitimation, and disciplinary feedback loops.

My argument has been, to reverse the order in which this book initially progressed, that the 'writing back' to the academy that Judith Ryan has previously identified has a triple interlinked function. Texts discipline the academy in order to legitimate their own voices so that they can speak in the same critical space as academic discourse. This makes for an increasingly competitive space in which fiction and university English vie with each other for the cultural authority to speak. We can trace this paradigm back a fairly long way, such as when Saul Bellow pronounced his disdain for the academy, noting that although he felt that the university helped to discard "bad thought", he "preferred to read poetry on [his] own without the benefit of lectures" and believed that his novel, *Herzog* (1964), demonstrated "how little strength 'higher education' had to offer a troubled man", associating the institution with "pedantry".[1]

In much contemporary fiction, we can see the traces of university English engrained more subtly within narrative paths. When Sarah

---

1   Saul Bellow, 'Foreword', in *The Closing of the American Mind*, by Allan Bloom (New York: Simon & Schuster, 1988), pp. 11–18.

Waters distracts academics with Foucauldian tropes to be unpacked, it is no longer simply a ludic exercise in occupying the professors, but is instead crucial to the textual pleasure of the narrative that we derive from her diversion cons. When Ishmael Reed or Thomas Pynchon now satirise the venues in which academics publish, it is not simply a blustering critique of a fusty institution, but is rather about the authority of institutional voices and claiming a right to speak in public. When Tom McCarthy places his own works in a canon, it is not just about marketing and sales, but about working in the same labour space as formalist, aesthetic critique.

None of this would be possible, I have argued, without the metafictional paradigm that runs throughout much contemporary fiction, albeit perhaps more gently than it did in its postmodern heyday. Metafiction is, in the way I have described it here, an overlapping of creative and critical practices; a way of operating that pitches university English and its objects of study into the same discursive space. When we conceive of fiction and criticism as operating in the same discursive field, the reasons for 'writing back' become clearer but should be seen as more aggressive and competitive.

Objections to the argument that I have made here might begin with a hostility to the idea that fiction and the academy might 'compete' or be in conflict. Some will probably not accept Robert Scholes's and Mark Currie's arguments about the definition of metafiction. Still others will say that the interaction between the university and fiction is more complicated and comprised of many more historical factors than have been covered here. These are all fair criticisms that can freely be made. However, without an understanding of the ways in which discursive spaces overlap and the modes by which narratological approaches can countenance the presence of the academy in fiction, even these broader arguments will remain partial. This is what I have sought to argue in this book: that one of the paradigms under which university English appears in contemporary fiction is a space of competitive discipline, legitimation, and critique. I call this type of presence, an 'incursion', fed off an economy of anxiety. An anxiety of academia that pitches literature against criticism.

Bibliography

Adorno, Theodor W., *Aesthetic Theory*, ed. by Gretel Adorno and Rolf Tiedemann, trans. by Robert Hullot-Kentor (London: Continuum, 2004)

—, 'Commitment', in *Aesthetics and Politics*, trans. by Francis McDonagh (London: Verso, 2007), pp. 177–95

—, *Negative Dialectics*, trans. by E.B. Ashton (London: Routledge, 1973)

—, *The Jargon of Authenticity*, trans. by Knut Tarnowski and Frederic Will (London: Routledge and Kegan Paul, 1986)

Aira, César, *The Literary Conference*, trans. by Katherine Silver (New York: New Directions, 2010)

Algee-Hewitt, Mark, and Mark McGurl, *Between Canon and Corpus: Six Perspectives on 2-Century Novels*, Pamphlets of the Stanford Literary Lab (Stanford: Stanford Literary Lab, 2015), https://litlab.stanford.edu/LiteraryLabPamphlet8.pdf

Alter, Robert, *Canon and Creativity: Modern Writing and the Authority of Scripture* (New Haven: Yale University Press, 2000)

—, *Partial Magic: The Novel as a Self-Conscious Genre* (Berkeley: University of California Press, 1975)

Althusser, Louis, 'Ideology and Ideological State Apparatuses (Notes towards an Investigation)', in *Lenin and Philosophy and Other Essays*, trans. by Ben Brewster (London: NLB, 1971), pp. 121–73

Altieri, Charles, *Postmodernisms Now: Essays on Contemporaneity in the Arts, Literature and Philosophy* (University Park: Pennsylvania State University Press, 1998)

American Foundation for Suicide Prevention, 'Facts and Figures', http://www.afsp.org/understanding-suicide/facts-and-figures

American Library Association, 'Frequently Challenged Books', http://www.ala.org/bbooks/frequentlychallengedbooks

Ameriks, Karl, 'Introduction: Interpreting German Idealism', in *The Cambridge Companion to German Idealism*, ed. by Karl Ameriks (Cambridge: Cambridge University Press, 2000), pp. 1–17

Amis, Kingsley, *Lucky Jim* (New York: Penguin, 1992)

Arias, Rosario, 'Epilogue: Female Confinement in Sarah Waters' Neo-Victorian Fiction', in *Stones of Law, Bricks of Shame: Narrating Imprisonment in the Victorian Age*, ed. by Frank Lauterbach and Jan Alber (Toronto: University of Toronto Press, 2009), pp. 256–77

Aristotle, *The Nicomachean Ethics*, trans. by David Ross (Oxford: Oxford University Press, 2009)

Association of Research Libraries, 'Expenditure Trends in ARL Libraries, 1986–2012', http://www.arl.org/storage/documents/expenditure-trends.pdf

Aubry, Timothy, *Reading As Therapy: What Contemporary Fiction Does for Middle-Class Americans* (Iowa City: University of Iowa Press, 2011)

Ballard, J.G., *The Atrocity Exhibition* (San Francisco: RE/Search, 1990)

Barthes, Roland, 'An Introduction to the Structural Analysis of Narrative', trans. by Lionel Duisit, *New Literary History*, 6 (1975), 237–72, http://dx.doi.org/10.2307/468419

Bataille, Georges, 'Nonknowledge', in *The Unfinished System of Nonknowledge*, ed. by Stuart Kendall, trans. by Michelle Kendall and Stuart Kendall (Minneapolis: University of Minnesota Press, 2001), pp. 196–205

Bauer, Heike, 'Vital Lines Drawn From Books: Difficult Feelings in Alison Bechdel's *Fun Home* and *Are You My Mother?*', *Journal of Lesbian Studies*, 18 (2014), 266–81, http://dx.doi.org/10.1080/10894160.2014.896614

Bechdel, Alison, *Fun Home: A Family Tragicomic* (London: Jonathan Cape, 2006)

Becker, Howard, *Tricks of the Trade: How to Think About Your Research While You're Doing It* (Chicago: Chicago University Press, 1998)

Beckett, Samuel, *Three Novels: Molloy, Malone Dies, The Unnamable*, trans. by Samuel Beckett and Patrick Bowles (New York: Grove, 1958)

—, *Worstward Ho* (London: John Calder, 1983)

Belfiore, Eleonora, and Anna Upchurch, eds., *Humanities in the Twenty-First Century Beyond Utility and Markets* (London: Palgrave Macmillan, 2013)

Bellow, Saul, 'Foreword', in *The Closing of the American Mind*, by Allan Bloom (New York: Simon & Schuster, 1988), pp. 11–18

Belsey, Catherine, *Critical Practice* (London: Routledge, 2002)

Bennett, Tony, *Formalism and Marxism* (London: Routledge, 1979)

Berthoff, Warner, 'Ambitious Scheme', *Commentary*, 44 (1967), 110–14

Bérubé, Michael, 'Value and Values', in *The Humanities, Higher Education, and Academic Freedom: Three Necessary Arguments*, by Michael Bérubé and Jennifer Ruth (New York: Palgrave Macmillan, 2015), pp. 27–56

Billett, Stephen, *Vocational Education: Purposes, Traditions and Prospects* (London: Springer, 2011)

Bloom, Harold, *Poetry and Repression* (New Haven: Yale University Press, 1976)

—, *The Anxiety of Influence: A Theory of Poetry* (Oxford: Oxford University Press, 1979)

Bolaño, Roberto, *2666*, trans. by Natasha Wimmer (London: Picador, 2009)

—, *Amulet*, trans. by Chris Andrews (New York: New Directions, 2008)

Boswell, Marshall, 'Author Here: The Legal Fiction of David Foster Wallace's *The Pale King*', *English Studies*, 95 (2014), 25–39, http://dx.doi.org/10.1080/0013838X.2013.857850

Bourdieu, Pierre, *Outline of a Theory of Practice* (Cambridge: Cambridge University Press, 1977)

—, 'Social Space and Symbolic Power', *Sociological Theory*, 7 (1989), 14–25, http://dx.doi.org/10.2307/202060

Bowen, Elizabeth, 'Notes on Writing a Novel', in *The Mulberry Tree: Writings of Elizabeth Bowen*, ed. by Hermione Lee (London: Virago, 1986), pp. 35–48

Boxall, Peter, *The Value of the Novel* (Cambridge: Cambridge University Press, 2015)

—, *Twenty-First-Century Fiction: A Critical Introduction* (Cambridge: Cambridge University Press, 2013)

Braid, Barbara, 'Victorian Panopticon: Confined Spaces and Imprisonment in Chosen Neo-Victorian Novels', in *Exploring Space: Spatial Notions in Cultural, Literary and Language Studies*, ed. by Andrzej Ciuk and Katarzyna Molek-Kozakowska (Cambridge: Cambridge Scholars, 2010), pp. 74–82

Britton, Celia, 'Structuralist and Poststructuralist Psychoanalytic and Marxist Theories', in *The Cambridge History of Literary Criticism*, ed. by Ramsey Selden (Cambridge: Cambridge University Press, 1993), 197–252

Broich, Ulrich, 'Intertextuality', in *International Postmodernism: Theory and Literary Practice*, ed. by Hans Bertens and Douwe Fokkema (Amsterdam: John Benjamins, 1997), pp. 249–55

Brown, Wendy, *Undoing the Demos: Neoliberalism's Stealth Revolution* (New York: Zone, 2015)

de Bruyn, Ben, '"You Should Be Teaching": Creative Writing and Extramural Academics in *Perdido Street Station* and *Embassytown*', in *China Miéville: Critical Essays*, ed. by Caroline Edwards and Tony Venezia (London: Gylphi, 2015), pp. 159–83

Byatt, A.S., *Possession: A Romance* (London: Vintage, 1991)

Byatt, Jim, 'Being Dead?: Trauma and the Liminal Narrative in J.G. Ballard's *Crash* and Tom McCarthy's *Remainder*', *Forum for Modern Language Studies*, 48 (2012), 245–59, http://dx.doi.org/10.1093/fmls/cqs017

Carter, Ian, *Ancient Cultures of Conceit: British University Fiction in the Post-War Years* (London: Routledge, 1990)

Carty, Peter, 'C, By Tom McCarthy', *The Independent*, 14 August 2010, http://www.independent.co.uk/arts-entertainment/books/reviews/c-by-tom-mccarthy-2049878.html

Cather, Willa, *My Ántonia* (New York: Dover, 1994)

Coover, Robert, *Pinocchio in Venice* (London: Minerva, 1993)

Court, Franklin E., *Institutionalizing English Literature: Culture and Politics of Literary Study, 1750–1900* (Stanford: Stanford University Press, 1992)

Currie, Mark, 'Introduction', in *Metafiction*, ed. by Mark Currie (London: Longman, 1995)

Dames, Nicholas, 'The Theory Generation', *n+1*, 14 (2012), https://nplusonemag.com/issue-14/reviews/the-theory-generation

Danielewski, Mark Z., *House of Leaves* (London: Anchor, 2000)

Danius, Sara, Stefan Jonsson, and Gayatri Chakravorty Spivak, 'An Interview with Gayatri Chakravorty Spivak', *boundary 2*, 20 (1993), 24–50, http://dx.doi.org/10.2307/303357

Davidson, Cathy N., and David Theo Goldberg, 'Engaging the Humanities', *Profession* (2004), 42–62

Davies, William, *The Limits of Neoliberalism: Authority, Sovereignty and the Logic of Competition* (Thousand Oaks: SAGE, 2014)

Dean, C.J., 'Empathy, Pornography, and Suffering', *Differences*, 14 (2003), 88–124

Dean, Michelle, 'Campus Novels: Six of the Best Books about University Life', *The Guardian*, 29 August 2016, https://www.theguardian.com/books/2016/aug/29/campus-novels-best-books-university-life

Deckard, Sharae, 'Peripheral Realism, Millennial Capitalism, and Roberto Bolaño's *2666*', *Modern Language Quarterly*, 73 (2012), 351–72, http://dx.doi.org/10.1215/00267929-1631433

Deleuze, Gilles, 'Postscript on the Societies of Control', *October*, 59 (1992), 3–7

DeLillo, Don, *Libra* (New York: Penguin, 1989)

—, *Point Omega* (London: Picador, 2010)

—, *Underworld* (London: Picador, 1998)

—, *White Noise* (London: Picador, 2011)

—, *Zero K* (New York: Picador, 2016)

Derrida, Jacques, *Of Grammatology*, trans. by Gayatri Chakravorty Spivak (Baltimore: Johns Hopkins University Press, 1998)

—, *Positions*, trans. by Alan Bass (Chicago: Chicago University Press, 1981)

—, 'The Law of Genre', trans. by Avital Ronell, *Critical Inquiry*, 7 (1980), 55–81

Dick, Alexander, and Christina Lupton, 'On Lecturing and Being Beautiful: Zadie Smith, Elaine Scarry, and the Liberal Aesthetic', *ESC: English Studies in Canada*, 39 (2013), 115–37, http://dx.doi.org/10.1353/esc.2013.0032

Docherty, Thomas, *For the University: Democracy and the Future of the Institution* (London: Bloomsbury, 2011)

'Doctoral Degrees: The Disposable Academic', *The Economist*, 18 December 2010, http://www.economist.com/node/17723223

Doležel, Lubomír, 'Structuralism of the Prague School', in *The Cambridge History of Literary Criticism*, ed. by Ramsey Selden (Cambridge: Cambridge University Press, 1993), 33–57

Dove, Patrick, 'Literature and the Secret of the World: *2666*, Globalization, and Global War', *CR: The New Centennial Review*, 14 (2014), 139–61, http://dx.doi.org/10.14321/crnewcentrevi.14.3.0139

Eaglestone, Robert, 'Contemporary Fiction in the Academy: Towards a Manifesto', *Textual Practice*, 27 (2013), 1089–101, http://dx.doi.org/10.1080/0950236X.2013.840113

Eagleton, Terry, *Criticism and Ideology: A Study in Marxist Literary Theory* (London: Verso, 1976)

—, 'The Silences of David Lodge', *New Left Review*, 1.172 (1988), 93–102

Eco, Umberto, 'Interpretation and History', in *Interpretation and Overinterpretation*, ed. by Stefan Collini (Cambridge: Cambridge University Press, 1992), pp. 23–43

—, 'Overinterpreting Texts', in *Interpretation and Overinterpretation*, ed. by Stefan Collini (Cambridge: Cambridge University Press, 1992), pp. 45–66

—, 'Reply', in *Interpretation and Overinterpretation*, ed. by Stefan Collini (Cambridge: Cambridge University Press, 1992), pp. 139–51

—, *The Role of the Reader: Explorations in the Semiotics of Texts* (Bloomington: Indiana University Press, 1997)

Egan, Jennifer, *A Visit from the Goon Squad* (London: Corsair, 2011)

—, *Look at Me* (London: Corsair, 2011)

—, 'Safari', *The New Yorker*, 11 January 2010, http://www.newyorker.com/magazine/2010/01/11/safari-3

—, *The Invisible Circus* (London: Corsair, 2012)

—, *The Keep* (London: Abacus, 2008)

English, James F., *The Economy of Prestige Prizes, Awards, and the Circulation of Cultural Value* (Cambridge, MA: Harvard University Press, 2005)

—, 'Winning the Culture Game: Prizes, Awards, and the Rules of Art', *New Literary History*, 33 (2002), 109–35

Ercolino, Stefano, *The Maximalist Novel: From Thomas Pynchon's* Gravity's Rainbow *to Roberto Bolaño's* 2666, trans. by Albert Sbragia (London: Bloomsbury, 2014)

Eve, Martin Paul, 'Keep Writing: The Critique of the University in Roberto Bolaño's *2666*', *Textual Practice*, 30 (2015), 949–64, http://dx.doi.org/10.1080/0950236X.2015.1084363

—, *Open Access and the Humanities: Contexts, Controversies and the Future* (Cambridge: Cambridge University Press, 2014), http://dx.doi.org/10.1017/CBO9781316161012

—, *Pynchon and Philosophy: Wittgenstein, Foucault and Adorno* (London: Palgrave Macmillan, 2014)

—, '"Structural Dissatisfaction": Academics on Safari in the Novels of Jennifer Egan', *Open Library of Humanities*, 1 (2015), http://dx.doi.org/10.16995/olh.29

—, '"Too Many Goddamn Echoes": Historicizing the Iraq War in Don DeLillo's *Point Omega*', *Journal of American Studies*, 49 (2015), 575–92, http://dx.doi.org/10.1017/S0021875814001303

—, '"You Will See the Logic of the Design of This": From Historiography to Taxonomography in the Contemporary Metafiction of Sarah Waters's *Affinity*', *Neo-Victorian Studies*, 6 (2013), 105–25

Everett, Percival, *Erasure* (London: Faber, 2003)

—, *I Am Not Sidney Poitier: A Novel* (Saint Paul: Graywolf, 2009)

Farred, Grant, 'The Impossible Closing: Death, Neoliberalism, and the Postcolonial in Bolaño's *2666*', *MFS: Modern Fiction Studies*, 56 (2010), 689–708

Felski, Rita, *The Limits of Critique* (Chicago: University of Chicago Press, 2015)

Fish, Stanley, 'Being Interdisciplinary Is So Very Hard to Do', *Profession*, 89 (1989), 15–22, http://dx.doi.org/10.2307/25595433

—, 'Literature in the Reader: Affective Stylistics', in *Is There a Text in This Class?: The Authority of Interpretive Communities* (Cambridge, MA: Harvard University Press, 1990), pp. 21–67

Flax, Jane, 'Soul Service: Foucault's "Care of the Self" as Politics and Ethics', in *The Mourning After: Attending the Wake of Postmodernism*, ed. by Neil Brooks and Josh Toth (Amsterdam: Rodopi, 2007), pp. 79–98

Flood, Alison, 'Lecturer's Campus Novel Gets Black Marks from College Employer', *The Guardian*, 21 November 2014, http://www.theguardian.com/books/2014/nov/21/lecturer-novel-college-employer-stephen-grant-richmond-on-thames

Foucault, Michel, *Discipline and Punish: The Birth of the Prison*, trans. by Alan Sheridan (New York: Vintage, 1997)

—, 'My Body, This Paper, This Fire', in *History of Madness* (London: Routledge, 2006), pp. 550–74

—, 'Pastoral Power and Political Reason', in *Religion and Culture*, ed. by Jeremy R. Carrette (Manchester: Manchester University Press, 1999), pp. 135–52

—, *The Order of Things: An Archaeology of the Human Sciences* (London: Routledge, 2007)

Fowles, John, *The French Lieutenant's Woman* (London: Vintage, 2007)

Franks, Norman L.R., Frank W. Bailey, and Rick Duiven, *The Jasta Pilots* (London: Grub Street, 1996)

Franzen, Jonathan, *Freedom* (London: Fourth Estate, 2010)

Genette, Gérard, *Palimpsests: Literature in the Second Degree*, trans. by Channa Newman and Claude Doubinsky (Lincoln: University of Nebraska Press, 1997)

Golder, Ben, *Foucault and the Politics of Rights* (Stanford: Stanford University Press, 2015)

Gordon, Jill, 'Against Vlastos on Complex Irony', *The Classical Quarterly*, 46 (1996), 131–37

Graff, Gerald, *Professing Literature: An Institutional History* (Chicago: University of Chicago Press, 1989)

Grafton, Anthony, *The Footnote: A Curious History* (Cambridge, MA: Harvard University Press, 1999)

Gray, Jeffrey, 'Roberto Bolaño, Ciudad Juárez, and the Future of Nativism', *Pacific Coast Philology*, 49 (2014), 166–76

de Groot, Jerome, 'Walter Scott Prize for Historical Fiction: The New Time-Travellers', *The Scotsman*, 18 June 2010, http://www.scotsman.com/lifestyle/books/walter-scott-prize-for-historical-fiction-the-new-time-travellers-1-813580

Gunning, Dave, 'Concentric and Centripetal Narratives of Race: Caryl Phillips's *Dancing in the Dark* and Percival Everett's *Erasure*', in *Caryl Phillips: Writing in the Key of Life*, ed. by Bénédicte Ledent and Daria Tunca (Amsterdam: Rodopi, 2012), pp. 359–74

Guyer, Paul, 'Absolute Idealism and the Rejection of Kantian Dualism', in *The Cambridge Companion to German Idealism*, ed. by Karl Ameriks (Cambridge: Cambridge University Press, 2000), pp. 37–56

Habermas, Jürgen, *Moral Consciousness and Communicative Action* (Cambridge, MA: MIT Press, 1990)

Haraway, Donna J., *Simians, Cyborgs and Women: The Reinvention of Nature* (London: Routledge, 1991)

Hartley, John, *A Short History of Cultural Studies* (London: SAGE, 2003)

Hay, Louis, 'Does "Text" Exist?', *Studies in Bibliography*, 41 (1988), 64–76

—, 'Genetic Criticism: Origins and Perspective', in *Genetic Criticism: Texts and Avant-Textes*, ed. by Jed Deppman, Daniel Ferrer, and Michael Groden (Philadelphia: University of Pennsylvania Press, 2004), pp. 17–27

Hayles, N. Katherine, *How We Think: Digital Media and Contemporary Technogenesis* (Chicago: University of Chicago Press, 2012)

Heaney, Seamus, 'Anniversary Verse' (1982), *The Harvard Advocate*, http://theharvardadvocate.com/article/376/tribute-to-seamus-heaney

Heilmann, Ann, and Mark Llewellyn, *Neo-Victorianism: The Victorians in the Twenty-First Century, 1999–2009* (Basingstoke: Palgrave Macmillan, 2010)

Hitchens, Henry, 'The Mystery Man', *The Financial Times*, 8 December 2008, http://www.ft.com/cms/s/0/7c4c7cd2-c264-11dd-a350-000077b07658.html

Ho, Elizabeth, *Neo-Victorianism and the Memory of Empire* (New York: Bloomsbury, 2012)

Holmwood, John, *A Manifesto for the Public University* (London: Bloomsbury, 2011), http://dx.doi.org/10.5040/9781849666459

Horkheimer, Max, and Theodor W. Adorno, *Dialectic of Enlightenment*, ed. by Gunzelin Schmid Noerr, trans. by Edmund Jephcott (Stanford: Stanford University Press, 2002)

Hume, Kathryn, 'Ishmael Reed and the Problematics of Control', *PMLA*, 108 (1993), 506–18, http://dx.doi.org/10.2307/462618

Huneven, Michelle, 'Hilary Mantel's Short-Story Collection Long on Controversy', *Los Angeles Times*, 3 October 2014, http://www.latimes.com/books/jacketcopy/la-ca-jc-hilary-mantel-20141005-story.html

Hungerford, Amy, *Making Literature Now* (Stanford: Stanford University Press, 2016)

—, *Postmodern Belief: American Literature and Religion since 1960* (Princeton: Princeton University Press, 2010)

Hunter, Ian, 'The Time of Theory', *Postcolonial Studies*, 10 (2007), 5–22, http://dx.doi.org/10.1080/13688790601153123

Hutcheon, Linda, *A Poetics of Postmodernism: History, Theory, Fiction* (New York: Routledge, 1988)

—, *A Theory of Parody: The Teachings of Twentieth-Century Art Forms* (New York: Methuen, 1985)

—, *Narcissistic Narrative: The Metafictional Paradox* (Waterloo: Wilfrid Laurier University Press, 2013)

Iser, Wolfgang, 'The Reality of Fiction: A Functionalist Approach to Literature', *New Literary History*, 7 (1975), 7–38, http://dx.doi.org/10.2307/468276

Ishiguro, Kazuo, *The Buried Giant* (London: Faber, 2015)

Jablon, Madelyn, *Black Metafiction: Self-Consciousness in African American Literature* (Iowa City: University of Iowa Press, 1997)

Jakobson, Roman, and Krystyna Pomorska, *Dialogues* (Cambridge: Cambridge University Press, 1983)

James, David, *Modernist Futures: Innovation and Inheritance in the Contemporary Novel* (New York: Cambridge University Press, 2012)

Jockers, Matthew L., *Macroanalysis: Digital Methods and Literary History* (Urbana: University of Illinois Press, 2013)

Johnson, Sarah L., 'Historical Fiction — Masters of the Past', *Bookmarks Magazine*, 2006, http://www.bookmarksmagazine.com/historical-fiction-masters-past/sarah-l-johnson

Kane, Sarah, 'Cleansed', in *Complete Plays* (London: Methuen, 2001), pp. 105–51

Karaganis, Joe, David McClure, Dennis Tenen, Jonathan Stray, Alex Gil, and Ted Byfield, 'The Open Syllabus Project', 2016, http://explorer.opensyllabusproject.org

Kelly, Adam, 'Beginning with Postmodernism', *Twentieth Century Literature*, 57 (2011), 391–422

—, 'David Foster Wallace and the New Sincerity in American Fiction', in *Consider David Foster Wallace*, ed. by David Hering, Amazon Kindle edition (Los Angeles: Sideshow Media Group, 2010), pp. 131–46

—, '"Who Is Responsible?": Revisiting the Radical Years in Dana Spiotta's *Eat the Document*', in *'Forever Young'?: The Changing Images of America*, ed. by Philip Coleman and Stephen Matterson (Heidelberg: Universitatsverlag Winter, 2012), pp. 219–30

Kerr, Norbert L., 'HARKing: Hypothesizing After the Results Are Known', *Personality and Social Psychology Review*, 2 (1998), 196–217, http://dx.doi.org/10.1207/s15327957pspr0203_4

Keucheyan, Razmig, *The Left Hemisphere: Mapping Critical Theory Today* (New York: Verso, 2013)

Kohlke, M.-L., 'Into History through the Back Door: The "Past Historic" in *Nights at the Circus* and *Affinity*', *Women: A Cultural Review*, 15 (2004), 153–66, http://dx.doi.org/10.1080/0957404042000234015

Koopman, Colin, *Genealogy as Critique: Foucault and the Problems of Modernity* (Bloomington: Indiana University Press, 2013)

Kristeva, Julia, *Semeiotike. Recherches pour une sémanalyse* (Paris: Seuil, 1969)

Lamont, Michèle, *How Professors Think: Inside the Curious World of Academic Judgment* (Cambridge, MA: Harvard University Press, 2009)

Latour, Bruno, 'Why Has Critique Run out of Steam?: From Matters of Fact to Matters of Concern', *Critical Inquiry*, 30 (2004), 225–48

LeClair, Tom, *The Art of Excess: Mastery in Contemporary American Fiction* (Urbana: University of Illinois Press, 1989)

Lee, Richard, 'Defining the Genre', *Historical Novel Society*, 2014, http://historicalnovelsociety.org/guides/defining-the-genre

Leitch, Vincent B., *Literary Criticism in the 21st Century: Theory Renaissance* (London: Bloomsbury, 2014)

Levine, Caroline, *Forms: Whole, Rhythm, Hierarchy, Network* (Princeton: Princeton University Press, 2015)

Leypoldt, Günter, 'Singularity and the Literary Market', *New Literary History*, 45 (2014), 71–88, http://dx.doi.org/10.1353/nlh.2014.0000

Liu, Alan, *The Laws of Cool: Knowledge Work and the Culture of Information* (Chicago: University of Chicago Press, 2004)

Llewellyn, Mark, '"Queer? I Should Say It Is Criminal!": Sarah Waters' *Affinity* (1999)', *Journal of Gender Studies*, 13 (2004), 203–14, http://dx.doi.org/10.1080/0958923042000287821

Lorde, Audre, 'The Master's Tools Will Never Dismantle the Master's House', in *Sister Outsider: Essays and Speeches* (Trumansburg: Crossing, 1984), pp. 111–13

Lyons, John, *The College Novel in America* (Carbondale: Southern Illinois University Press, 1962)

de Man, Paul, *Allegories of Reading: Figural Language in Rousseau, Nietzsche, Rilke, and Proust* (New Haven: Yale University Press, 1979)

Mandel, Emily St. John, *Station Eleven* (London: Picador, 2015)

Marin, Louis, *Utopics: The Semiological Play of Textual Spaces* (Atlantic Highlands: Humanities Press International, 1990)

Marinescu, Andreea, '"I Can't Go On, I'll Go On": The Avant-Garde in the Works of Roberto Bolaño and Raúl Ruiz', *Romance Notes*, 54 (2014), 391–98, http://dx.doi.org/10.1353/rmc.2014.0071

Markovits, Elizabeth, *The Politics of Sincerity: Plato, Frank Speech, and Democratic Judgment* (University Park: Pennsylvania State University Press, 2008)

Martin, Reginald, *Ishmael Reed and The New Black Aesthetic Critics* (Basingstoke: Macmillan, 1988)

Marx, Karl, 'Theses on Feuerbach', in *Ludwig Feuerbach and the Outcome of Classical German Philosophy*, by Frederick Engels (London: Martin Lawrence, 1934), pp. 73–75

McBride, Eimear, *A Girl Is a Half-Formed Thing: A Novel* (New York: Hogarth, 2015)

McCann, Sean, 'Training and Vision: Roth, DeLillo, Banks, Peck, and the Postmodern Aesthetics of Vocation', *Twentieth Century Literature*, 53 (2007), 298–326, http://dx.doi.org/10.1215/0041462X-2007-4006

McCarthy, Tom, *C* (London: Jonathan Cape, 2010)

—, '*Gravity's Rainbow*, Read by George Guidall', *The New York Times*, 21 November 2014, http://www.nytimes.com/2014/11/23/books/review/gravitys-rainbow-read-by-george-guidall.html

—, *Remainder* (London: Alma, 2015)

—, *Satin Island* (London: Jonathan Cape, 2015)

—, 'Stabbing the Olive', *London Review of Books*, 11 February 2010, pp. 26–28

—, 'Straight to the Multiplex', *London Review of Books*, 1 November 2007, pp. 33–34

—, 'The Death of Writing — If James Joyce Were Alive Today He'd Be Working for Google', *The Guardian*, 7 March 2015, http://www.theguardian.com/books/2015/mar/07/tom-mccarthy-death-writing-james-joyce-working-google

—, '"*Ulysses*" and Its Wake', *London Review of Books*, 19 June 2014, pp. 39–41

—, 'Writing Machines', *London Review of Books*, 18 December 2014, pp. 21–22

McDonald, Ronan, *The Death of the Critic* (London: Continuum, 2007)

McGettigan, Andrew, *The Great University Gamble: Money, Markets and the Future of Higher Education* (London: Pluto, 2013)

McGurl, Mark, *The Program Era: Postwar Fiction and the Rise of Creative Writing* (Cambridge, MA: Harvard University Press, 2009)

McHale, Brian, 'Change of Dominant from Modernist to Postmodernist Writing', in *Approaching Postmodernism: Papers Presented at a Workshop on Postmodernism, 21–23 September 1984, University of Utrecht*, ed. by Douwe W. Fokkema and Hans Bertens (Amsterdam: John Benjamins, 1986), pp. 53–79

—, 'Genre as History: Pynchon's Genre-Poaching', in *Pynchon's Against the Day: A Corrupted Pilgrim's Guide*, ed. by Jeffrey Severs and Christopher Leise (Newark: University of Delaware Press, 2011), pp. 15–28

—, 'Modernist Reading, Post-Modern Text: The Case of *Gravity's Rainbow*', *Poetics Today*, 1 (1979), 85–110

Meho, Lokman I., 'The Rise and Rise of Citation Analysis', *Physics World*, 20:1 (2007), 32–36

Mendelson, Edward, 'Encyclopedic Narrative: From Dante to Pynchon', *MLN*, 91 (1976), 1267–75

Merritt, Stephanie, 'She's Young, Black, British — and the First Publishing Sensation of the Millennium', *The Guardian*, 16 January 2000, http://www.theguardian.com/books/2000/jan/16/fiction.zadiesmith

Miéville, China, *Iron Council* (London: Pan, 2011)

—, *King Rat*, Kindle Edition (London: Pan, 2000)

—, *Perdido Street Station* (London: Pan, 2011)

Millbank, J., 'It's about This: Lesbians, Prison, Desire', *Social & Legal Studies*, 13 (2004), 155–90

Mitchell, David, *Cloud Atlas* (London: Sceptre, 2008)

—, *The Bone Clocks* (London: Sceptre, 2014)

Moretti, Franco, *Distant Reading* (London: Verso, 2013)

—, *Graphs, Maps, Trees: Abstract Models for Literary History* (London: Verso, 2007)

—, 'The Slaughterhouse of Literature', *MLQ: Modern Language Quarterly*, 61 (2000), 207–27

Morize, André, *Problems and Methods of Literary History, with Special Reference to Modern French Literature: A Guide for Graduate Students* (Boston: Ginn, 1922), http://archive.org/details/problemsmethodso00moriiala

Moseley, Merritt, 'Introductory: Definitions and Justifications', in *The Academic Novel: New and Classic Essays*, ed. by Merritt Moseley (Chester: Chester Academic Press, 2007), pp. 3–19

Moylan, Tom, *Demand the Impossible: Science Fiction and the Utopian Imagination* (New York: Methuen, 1986)

Neale, Stephen, *Genre* (London: British Film Institute, 1980)

—, 'Questions of Genre', in *Film Theory: An Anthology*, ed. by Robert Stam and Toby Miller (Malden: Blackwell, 2000), pp. 157–78

Nealon, Jeffrey T., *Post-Postmodernism, Or, The Cultural Logic of Just-in-Time Capitalism* (Stanford: Stanford University Press, 2012)

Nieland, Justus, 'Dirty Media: Tom McCarthy and the Afterlife of Modernism', *MFS: Modern Fiction Studies*, 58 (2012), 569–99, http://dx.doi.org/10.1353/mfs.2012.0058

OAPEN-UK, 'Researcher Survey', 2012, http://oapen-uk.jiscebooks.org/research-findings/researchersurvey

Office for National Statistics, '2011 Census: Key Statistics for Local Authorities in England and Wales, March 2011', 11 December 2012, http://www.ons.gov.uk/ons/rel/census/2011-census/key-statistics-for-local-authorities-in-england-and-wales/index.html

O'Leary, Timothy, *Foucault and Fiction: The Experience Book* (London: Continuum, 2009)

Omlor, Daniela, 'Mirroring Borges: The Spaces of Literature in Roberto Bolaño's 2666', *Bulletin of Hispanic Studies*, 91 (2014), 659–70, http://dx.doi.org/10.3828/bhs.2014.40

Osborne, Peter, 'Philosophy after Theory: Transdisciplinarity and the New', in *Theory after 'Theory'*, ed. by Jane Elliott and Derek Attridge (New York: Routledge, 2011), pp. 19–34

Packham, Catherine, 'Cicero's Ears, or Eloquence in the Age of Politeness: Oratory, Moderation, and the Sublime in Enlightenment Scotland', *Eighteenth-Century Studies*, 46 (2013), 499–512, http://dx.doi.org/10.1353/ecs.2013.0043

Paris, Bernard J., *Karen Horney: A Psychoanalyst's Search for Self-Understanding* (New Haven: Yale University Press, 1994)

Patterson, Orlando, 'Our Overrated Inner Self', *The New York Times*, 26 December 2006, http://www.nytimes.com/2006/12/26/opinion/26patterson.html

Pelaez, Sol, 'Counting Violence: Roberto Bolano and *2666*', *Chasqui*, 43 (2014), 30–47

Pollack, Sarah, 'After Bolaño: Rethinking the Politics of Latin American Literature in Translation', *PMLA*, 128 (2013), 660–67

Proctor, Mortimer R., *The English University Novel* (Berkeley: University of California Press, 1957)

Pynchon, Thomas, *Against the Day* (London: Jonathan Cape, 2006)

—, *Bleeding Edge* (London: Jonathan Cape, 2013)

—, *Gravity's Rainbow* (London: Vintage, 1995)

—, *Mason & Dixon* (London: Jonathan Cape, 1997)

—, *The Crying of Lot 49* (London: Vintage, 1996)

—, *V.* (London: Vintage, 1995)

Raghinaru, Camelia, 'Biopolitics in Roberto Bolaño's *2666*, "The Part About the Crimes"', *Altre Modernità*, 15 (2016), 146–62, http://dx.doi.org/10.13130/2035-7680/7182

Ramsay, Stephen, *Reading Machines: Toward an Algorithmic Criticism* (Urbana: University of Illinois Press, 2011)

Reballato, Dan, 'Cleansed', 2016, http://www.danrebellato.co.uk/spilledink/2016/2/24/cleansed

Reed, Ishmael, *Japanese by Spring* (New York: Atheneum, 1993)

—, *Juice!: A Novel* (Champaign: Dalkey Archive, 2011)

—, *Mumbo Jumbo* (New York: Atheneum, 1989)

Reed, Ishmael, and Bruce Dick, 'Ishmael Reed: An Interview with Bruce Dick', in *Conversations with Ishmael Reed*, ed. by Bruce Dick and Amritjit Singh (Jackson: University Press of Mississippi, 1995), pp. 344–56

Reilly, Charlie, 'An Interview with Jennifer Egan', *Contemporary Literature*, 50 (2009), 439–60, http://dx.doi.org/10.1353/cli.0.0074

Reinares, Laura Barberán, 'Globalized Philomels: State Patriarchy, Transnational Capital, and the Fermicides on the US-Mexican Border in Roberto Bolaño's *2666*', *South Atlantic Review*, 75 (2010), 51–72

Richards, Ivor Armstrong, *Practical Criticism: A Study of Literary Judgment* (London: Transaction, 2008)

Riffaterre, Michael, *Semiotics of Poetry* (Bloomington: Indiana University Press, 1978)

Rodríguez, Fermín A., 'Fear, Subjectivity, and Capital: Sergio Chejfec's *The Dark* and Roberto Bolaño's *2666'*, *Parallax*, 20 (2014), 345–59, http://dx.doi.org/10.1080/13534645.2014.957550

Roof, Judith, 'Everett's Hypernarrator', *Canadian Review of American Studies*, 43 (2013), 202–15

Rossen, Janice, *The University on Modern Fiction: When Power Is Academic* (London: Macmillan, 1993)

Ryan, Camille L., and Julie Siebens, 'Educational Attainment in the United States: 2009. Population Characteristics', *US Census Bureau*, February 2012, http://files.eric.ed.gov/fulltext/ED529755.pdf

Ryan, Judith, *The Novel After Theory* (New York: Columbia University Press, 2011)

Saïd, Edward W., *On Late Style* (London: Bloomsbury, 2006)

Saldívar, Ramón, 'Speculative Realism and the Postrace Aesthetic in Contemporary American Fiction', in *A Companion to American Literary Studies*, ed. by Caroline F. Levander and Robert S. Levine (Hoboken: Wiley, 2011), pp. 517–31, http://dx.doi.org/10.1002/9781444343809.ch32

Sample, Ian, 'Harvard University Says It Can't Afford Journal Publishers' Prices', *The Guardian*, 24 April 2012, http://www.theguardian.com/science/2012/apr/24/harvard-university-journal-publishers-prices

Sapphire, *Push* (London: Minerva, 1998)

Sartre, Jean-Paul, *What Is Literature?*, trans. by Bernard Frechtman (New York: Philosophical Library, 1949)

Scarry, Elaine, 'On Beauty and Being Just' (presented at the Tanner Lectures on Human Values, Yale University, 1998), http://tannerlectures.utah.edu/_documents/a-to-z/s/scarry00.pdf

Scholes, Robert E., 'Metafiction', *Iowa Review*, 1 (1970), 100–15

—, *The Fabulators* (Oxford: Oxford University Press, 1967)

Selden, Ramsey, 'Introduction', in *The Cambridge History of Literary Criticism*, ed. by Ramsey Selden (Cambridge: Cambridge University Press, 1993), 1–10

Shephard, Alex, 'The Hunt for a Possible Pynchon Novel Leads to a Name', *The New Republic*, 12 September 2015, http://www.newrepublic.com/article/122802/thomas-pynchon-didnt-write-cow-country-aj-perry-probably-did

Shields, David, *Reality Hunger: A Manifesto* (London: Hamish Hamilton, 2011)

Showalter, Elaine, *Faculty Towers: The Academic Novel and Its Discontents* (Philadelphia: University of Pennsylvania Press, 2009)

Slaughter, Sheila, and Gary Rhoades, 'The Neo-Liberal University', *New Labor Forum*, 6 (2000), 73–79

Small, Helen, *The Value of the Humanities* (Oxford: Oxford University Press, 2013)

Smith, Barbara Herrnstein, *Belief and Resistance: Dynamics of Contemporary Intellectual Controversy* (Cambridge, MA: Harvard University Press, 1997)

Smith, Sarah A., 'Love's Prisoner [Review of Sarah Waters's *Affinity*]', *The Times Literary Supplement*, 28 May 1999, p. 24

Smith, Shawn, *Pynchon and History: Metahistorical Rhetoric and Postmodern Narrative Form in the Novels of Thomas Pynchon* (London: Routledge, 2005)

Smith, Zadie, *NW* (London: Penguin, 2013)

—, *On Beauty* (London: Penguin, 2006)

Spiotta, Dana, *Eat the Document: A Novel* (London: Picador, 2007)

Stam, Robert, 'Text and Intertext: Introduction', in *Film Theory: An Anthology*, ed. by Robert Stam and Toby Miller (Malden: Blackwell, 2000), pp. 145–56

Steiner, Peter, 'Russian Formalism', in *The Cambridge History of Literary Criticism*, ed. by Ramsey Selden (Cambridge: Cambridge University Press, 1993), 11–29

Sterne, Laurence, *Tristram Shandy* (Ware: Wordsworth Editions, 1996)

Sterry, David Henry, 'Self-Publishing Literary Fiction: The Good, the Bad and the Ugly: Cari Noga Reveals All to the Book Doctors', *The Huffington Post*, 20 August 2014, http://www.huffingtonpost.com/david-henry-sterry/selfpublishing-literary-f_b_5695364.html

Sutherland, John, Laura Frost, Emma Rees, Sarah Churchwell, and Valerie Sanders, 'This Is Your Life', *Times Higher Education*, 20 November 2014, pp. 34–40

Székely, Péter, 'The Academic Novel in the Age of Postmodernity: The Anglo-American Metafictional Academic Novel' (unpublished doctoral thesis, Eötvös Loránd University, 2009), http://doktori.btk.elte.hu/lit/szekelypeter/thesis.pdf

Trachtenberg, Alan, *The Incorporation of America: Culture and Society in the Gilded Age* (New York: Hill and Wang, 2007)

Trilling, Lionel, *Sincerity and Authenticity* (Cambridge, MA: Harvard University Press, 1972)

Tudor, Andrew, *Theories of Film* (London: British Film Institute, 1974)

UCU, 'Over Half of Universities and Colleges Use Lecturers on Zero-Hour Contracts', 4 September 2013, http://www.ucu.org.uk/6749

Underwood, Ted, '@martin_eve Playing Devil's Advocate, obviously. But I think the skepticism is perhaps best understood as an aesthetic problem. One of the +', *@Ted_Underwood*, 2016, https://twitter.com/Ted_Underwood/status/756135378742943744

—, '@martin_eve that isn't "experienced," I think ppl feel that as an *aesthetic* loss. It's not what they *say,* but I think it's felt.', *@Ted_Underwood*, 2016, https://twitter.com/Ted_Underwood/status/756136113115242496

—, '@martin_eve things lit crit does well is make fragments of individual experience work to illuminate a big picture. When we use evidence +', *@Ted_Underwood*, 2016, https://twitter.com/Ted_Underwood/status/756135767806648320

—, *Why Literary Periods Mattered: Historical Contrast and the Prestige of English Studies* (Stanford: Stanford University Press, 2013)

VanWyngarden, Greg, *Jagdstaffel 2 Boelcke: Von Richthofen's Mentor* (Oxford: Osprey, 2007)

Wallace, David Foster, 'E Unibus Pluram: Television and U.S. Fiction', *Review of Contemporary Fiction*, 13 (1993), 151–98

—, *Infinite Jest* (Boston: Little, Brown and Company, 1996)

—, 'Westward the Course of Empire Takes Its Way', in *Girl with Curious Hair* (London: Abacus, 1997), pp. 231–373

Waters, Sarah, *Affinity* (London: Virago, 2000)

—, *Fingersmith* (London: Virago, 2003)

—, *Tipping the Velvet* (London: Virago, 1999)

—, 'Wolfskins and Togas: Lesbian and Gay Historical Fictions, 1870 to Present' (unpublished doctoral thesis, Queen Mary University of London, 1995)

Watts, Philip, 'Rewriting History: Céline and Kurt Vonnegut', *The South Atlantic Quarterly*, 93.2 (1994), 265–78

Waugh, Patricia, *Metafiction: The Theory and Practice of Self-Conscious Fiction* (London: Methuen, 1984)

Weber, Samuel, *Institution and Interpretation* (Stanford: Stanford University Press, 2001)

Weisenburger, Steven, *Fables of Subversion: Satire and the American Novel, 1930–1980* (Athens: University of Georgia Press, 1995)

White, Hayden, *Metahistory: Historical Imagination in Nineteenth Century Europe* (Baltimore: Johns Hopkins University Press, 1975)

Williams, J.J., 'The Rise of the Academic Novel', *American Literary History*, 24 (2012), 561–89, http://dx.doi.org/10.1093/alh/ajs038

Wittgenstein, Ludwig, *Philosophical Investigations: The German Text, with a Revised English Translation* (Oxford: Blackwell, 2001)

—, *Remarks on the Foundations of Mathematics*, 3rd edn (Oxford: Blackwell, 1978)

—, *Tractatus Logico-Philosophicus* (London: Routledge, 2006)

Womack, Kenneth, *Postwar Academic Fiction: Satire, Ethics, Community* (Basingstoke: Palgrave Macmillan, 2002)

Wright, Richard, *Native Son* (London: Vintage, 2000)

Zamora, Daniel, 'Foucault, the Excluded, and the Neoliberal Erosion of the State', in *Foucault and Neoliberalism*, ed. by Daniel Zamora and Michael C. Behrent (Cambridge: Polity, 2015)

Index

2666 52, 87, 88, 89, 90, 91, 92, 93, 94, 95, 96, 97, 98, 99, 100, 101, 102, 103, 105, 106, 107, 109, 110, 143, 159
  ethical readings of 94

academic readers 14, 15, 20, 41, 133, 150, 165, 181, 182
  practices of 15, 37, 42, 133
academic unconscious 46
Academy Award in Literature from The American Academy of Arts and Letters 132
Acker, Kathy 186
Adorno, Theodor W. 52, 93, 97, 98, 99, 101, 111, 152, 155, 160, 185, 192, 201
  Commitment. *See* Commitment
  Dialectic of Enlightenment. *See Dialectic of Enlightenment*
  Jargon of Authenticity, The. *See Jargon of Authenticity, The*
  Negative Dialectics. *See Negative Dialectics*
Affinity 53, 162, 163, 164, 169, 170, 172, 173, 174, 176, 177, 179, 180, 181, 182, 183
Against the Day 153, 162
Algee-Hewitt, Mark 21, 22
Alter, Robert 29, 188
  Partial Magic: The Novel as a Self-Conscious Genre. *See Partial Magic: The Novel as a Self-Conscious Genre*
Althusser, Louis 30, 103, 129, 159
Altieri, Charles 28

American Fiction at the Millennium: Neoliberalism and the New 125
American Foundation for Suicide Prevention 153
Amis, Kingsley 18
  Lucky Jim. *See Lucky Jim*
Amulet 109, 110
anxiety of academia 16, 46, 50, 204, 208
Anxiety of Influence, The 84
Arias, Rosario 170, 176
Aristotle 121
  Nicomachean Ethics. *See Nicomachean Ethics*
Arnold, Matthew 115
ARPAnet 195
Art of Excess, The 196
Atrocity Exhibition, The 75, 76, 77
Aubry, Timothy 191
authenticity 62, 63, 66, 84, 120, 121, 122, 123, 124, 125, 126, 127

Baader-Meinhof gang 138
Badiou, Alain 61
Balibar, Etienne 30
Ballard, J.G. 60, 61, 73, 75, 76, 77
  Atrocity Exhibition, The. *See Atrocity Exhibition, The*
  Crash. *See Crash*
Balzac, Honoré de 118
  Sarrasine. *See Sarrasine*
Barthelme, Donald 124
Barthes, Roland 118, 126
  S/Z. *See S/Z*

Barth, John 48, 124, 190
  Gilles Goat-Boy. See Gilles Goat-Boy
Baudrillard, Jean 77
Bauer, Heike 82
Bechdel, Alison 82
  Fun Home. See Fun Home
Becker, Harold 42
Beckett, Samuel 51, 73, 139
  Unnamable, The. See Unnamable, The
  Waiting for Godot. See Waiting for Godot
  Worstward Ho. See Worstward Ho
Believer Book Award 132
Bellow, Saul 207
  Herzog. See Herzog
Belsey, Catherine 111
Bennett, Tony 30, 31, 115
Bentham, Jeremy 172
Bible, the 34
Bilder, Geoffrey 24
  reading-avoidance techniques. See reading-avoidance techniques
Billet, Stephen 106
Black aesthetic 186
Bleeding Edge 194, 195, 196, 198
Bloody Chamber, The 179
Bloom, Harold 16, 84, 85
  Anxiety of Influence, The. See Anxiety of Influence, The
  Western Canon: The Books and School of the Ages, The. See Western Canon: The Books and School of the Ages, The
Boas, Franz 154
Bolaño, Roberto 28, 52, 87, 89, 90, 91, 92, 94, 95, 96, 97, 99, 100, 101, 102, 103, 104, 105, 106, 107, 108, 109, 110, 111, 128, 134, 159, 187, 192
  2666. See 2666
  Amulet. See Amulet
Bone Clocks, The 19
Borges, Jorge Luis 101, 124
Bourdieu, Pierre 52, 93, 108, 132
  strategies of condescension. See strategies of condescension

Boxall, Peter 15, 30, 94, 101
Brecht, Bertolt 98, 99, 195, 196, 197
  Resistible Rise of Arturo Ui, The. See Resistible Rise of Arturo Ui, The
British Museum, the 11, 12
Brontë, Charlotte 127
  Jane Eyre. See Jane Eyre
Buried Giant, The 96
Burroughs, William 186
Byatt, A.S. 164
  Possession. See Possession

C 51, 58, 59, 60, 61, 63, 64, 65, 66, 68, 70, 71, 72, 73, 74, 75, 76, 77, 78, 79, 80, 81, 82, 85, 87, 159, 161
  anagrams 78
  as literary-historical fiction 66
  implied archive 68, 70
  structure of 80
Calling all Agents 61
campus novel 17, 18, 46, 48, 52, 136, 189, 190, 191
  as complex 48
canon 12, 20, 21, 22, 23, 24, 39, 42, 57, 58, 60, 62, 72, 73, 74, 82, 83, 84, 85, 86, 115, 159, 165, 208
  Canon Wars. See Canon Wars
  gender bias 21
  racial bias 21
canon wars 21, 57, 84
Carter, Angela 34, 179
  Bloody Chamber, The. See Bloody Chamber, The
Carter, Ian 17
Cather, Willa 146
  My Ántonia. See My Ántonia
Chaucer, Geoffrey 201
Cicero 13
class 165, 177, 178, 180, 182, 183
Cleansed 51
Cloud Atlas 153, 164
College of Santa Fe 132
Columbia University 58, 148
Coming from Behind 49

Commitment 98
Coover, Robert 124
Cornell University 144
Cow Country 49
Crash 61, 80
creative writing programmes 18, 21, 38, 116, 145
Criminal Prisons of London and Scenes of Prison Life, The 172
Critchley, Simon 60
  Necronautical Society. *See* Necronautical Society
critical disability studies 21, 32
Critical Inquiry 53, 194, 199, 200, 201, 203
critique 16, 20, 28, 32, 34, 35, 36, 37, 40, 41, 42, 45, 51, 52, 53, 72, 78, 86, 87, 91, 92, 94, 99, 100, 102, 103, 104, 105, 106, 107, 111, 116, 132, 133, 134, 136, 144, 146, 153, 156, 159, 160, 173, 186, 187, 188, 189, 190, 191, 192, 193, 194, 198, 199, 200, 201, 202, 203, 207, 208
  criticisms of 36, 37
Critique of Pure Reason 35
Cronin, Sheila M. 49
  Gift Counselor: A Novel, The. *See Gift Counselor: A Novel, The*
Crying of Lot 49, The 194
crypto-didacticism 52, 90, 91, 92, 93, 94, 95, 97, 100, 103, 107, 116
Culler, Jonathan 16
Cultural Materialism 151, 155
cultural studies 85, 115, 151
Currie, Mark 29, 194, 208
  Metafiction. *See Metafiction*
Cyborg Manifesto 129

Dalkey Archive Press 193
Dames, Nicholas 41
Danielewski, Mark Z. 58, 68, 69, 70, 83, 84, 85, 159
  House of Leaves. *See House of Leaves*
Davidson, Cathy N. 36

Dean, Carolyn J. 99, 100
Dear Committee Members 49
de Bruyn, Ben 46
Deckard, Sharae 91, 96
deconstruction 30, 32, 33
de Groot, Jerome 66
de Kooning, Willem 83
Deleuze, Gilles 61
DeLillo, Don 60, 73, 77, 78, 124, 140, 141, 190
  Libra. *See Libra*
  Point Omega. *See Point Omega*
  Underworld. *See Underworld*
  White Noise. *See White Noise*
  Zero K. *See Zero K*
de Man, Paul 33
Derrida, Jacques 29, 30, 60, 83, 84, 119, 133, 142, 168, 192
  Law of Genre, The. *See Law of Genre, The*
determination in the last instance 161
Dialectic of Enlightenment 152
Dick, Alexander 40
digital humanities 25, 26, 27, 28, 37, 175
  distant reading. *See* distant reading
  stylometry. *See* stylometry
discipline 15, 20, 30, 36, 37, 42, 44, 50, 51, 53, 57, 58, 59, 106, 110, 115, 116, 150, 155, 160, 175, 183, 200, 202, 203, 207, 208
Discipline and Punish 172
distant reading 25, 26
Doctorow, E.L. 124
Don Quixote 29
Dos Passos Prize 132
double negation 131
Dove, Patrick 94

Eaglestone, Robert 22, 23, 24, 185
Eagleton, Terry 17, 30
Eat the Document 47, 48
ecocriticism 87
Economist, The 136, 137

Eco, Umberto 18, 30, 41, 72, 105, 124, 202
  Interpretation and Overinterpretation. See Interpretation and Overinterpretation
  model reader. *See* model reader
  Name of the Rose, The. See Name of the Rose, The
Egan, Jennifer 46, 52, 135, 136, 137, 138, 141, 142, 143, 145, 147, 148, 149, 150, 151, 154, 155, 156, 160, 175
  Invisible Circus, The. See Invisible Circus, The
  Keep, The. See Keep, The
  Look at Me. See Look at Me
  Visit from the Goon Squad, A. See Visit from the Goon Squad, A
Eichmann, Adolf 96, 140
Electra complex 149
Eliot, T.S. 31, 58
Ellison, Ralph Waldo 117
eloquence 11, 12, 13, 14, 129
English, James F. 22, 132, 193
English studies. *See* university English
Epic of Gilgamesh 12
Erasure 49, 52, 116, 117, 118, 120, 127, 128, 129, 130, 131, 132, 133, 134, 160, 192, 193
Ercolino, Stefano 196
  Maximalist Novel, The. See Maximalist Novel, The
E Unibus Pluram 151, 195
Everett, Percival 34, 49, 52, 75, 116, 118, 119, 120, 122, 125, 128, 129, 131, 133, 134, 136, 146, 154, 159, 160, 192, 193
  Erasure. See Erasure
  I Am Not Sidney Poitier. See I Am Not Sidney Poitier
Exodus 110

Fabulators, The 29
Farred, Grant 94, 102, 104
Felski, Rita 15, 23, 36, 39, 95

feminist criticism 21, 32, 57, 84, 85, 108, 149, 153, 173, 176, 182, 186
Feminist Press 22
fictions of process 91, 119
Fingersmith 3, 170, 179, 180
Fish, Stanley 14, 175
Flax, Jane 32
footnotes, fictional 69, 70
formalism 32, 89, 107, 200
Foucault, Michel 19, 29, 35, 106, 129, 134, 142, 144, 150, 164, 165, 172, 173, 174, 175, 177, 182, 183, 191, 208
  Discipline and Punish. See Discipline and Punish
Fowles, John 124, 145, 163, 171
  French Lieutenant's Woman, The. See French Lieutenant's Woman, The
Franzen, Jonathan 82
  Freedom. See Freedom
Freedom 82
French Lieutenant's Woman, The 145, 171
Freud, Sigmund 60, 149, 195
Frost, Laura 50
Fuck 117, 119, 133
Fun Home 82

Gaddis, William 124
Gass, William 29, 124
Genesis of the Castration Complex, The 150
genetic criticism 31
genre 12, 20, 22, 23, 44, 49, 51, 53, 59, 64, 65, 66, 68, 72, 136, 144, 161, 162, 163, 164, 165, 166, 167, 168, 170, 171, 173, 174, 175, 177, 178, 179, 182, 183, 190
  as process of systematisation 167, 168, 169, 175
Gift Counselor: A Novel, The 49
Gilles Goat-Boy 48, 190
Girl is a Half-Formed Thing, A 73, 132
Glass Bead Game, The 188
Goldberg, David Theo 36
Graff, Gerald 57, 201

Grafton, Anthony 69
Grant, Linda 49
　Upstairs at the Party. See *Upstairs at the Party*
Grant, Stephen 49
　Moment More Sublime, A. See *Moment More Sublime, A*
Gravity's Rainbow 19, 72, 74, 118, 162, 195
Groundhog Day 123
Guardian, The 61
Gulliver's Travels 100

Habermas, Jürgen 123
Hall, Steven 61
Hall, Stuart 115
Haraway, Donna 129
　Cyborg Manifesto. See *Cyborg Manifesto*
Hartley, John 115
Harvard University 199
Hayles, N. Katherine 36
Hay, Louis 31
Heidegger, Martin 119
Heilmann, Ann 162, 177, 182
hermeneutic cycle 18
Herzog 207
Hesse, Herman 188
historical fiction 63, 65, 66, 67, 71, 72, 174
　accuracy of 67
　definition of 65, 66
Historical Novel Society, the 65
historiographic metafiction 161, 162, 165, 167, 171
historiography 68, 70, 81, 161, 162, 165, 171, 173, 182, 201
Hitchens, Henry 110
Hofstadter, Douglas R. 84
Hoggart, Richard 115
Holocaust, the 96, 99, 127, 159
Hoodoo 186
Horkheimer, Max 152
　Dialectic of Enlightenment. See *Dialectic of Enlightenment*

Horney, Karen 150
　Genesis of the Castration Complex, The. See Genesis of the Castration Complex, The
House of Leaves 58, 59, 60, 68, 69, 70, 85, 118, 159
　imprint page 84
Hughes, Thomas 49
　Tom Brown at Oxford 49
Human Stain, The 48
Hume, David 13
Hume, Kathryn 186
Hungerford, Amy 20, 25
　critical not-reading 25
Hunter, Ian 16
Hurston/Wright Legacy Award for Fiction 132
Hutcheon, Linda 29, 70, 71, 161, 165
　historiographic metafiction. See historiographic metafiction
　Narcissistic Narrative: The Metafictional Paradox. See *Narcissistic Narrative: The Metafictional Paradox*
Hypothesizing After Results are Known 44, 45

I Am Not Sidney Poitier 116
idealism 43, 48
incursion 31, 47, 51, 72, 168, 208
Infinite Jest 69
Inherent Vice 195
Interpretation and Overinterpretation 202
Invisible Circus, The 135, 137, 138, 148, 155
Ionesco, Eugène 83
Iowa Review 29
irony 50, 52, 64, 74, 124, 125, 129, 144, 151, 195, 197, 198, 202
Irving, David 127
Ishiguro, Kazuo 96
　The Buried Giant. See *Buried Giant, The*
Ivy League universities 187

Iyer, Lars 3
  Spurious. See Spurious

Jackson, Melanie 75
Jacobson, Howard 49
  Coming from Behind. See Coming from Behind
James, Henry 171
  Turn of the Screw, The. See Turn of the Screw, The
Jane Eyre 127
Japanese by Spring 189, 190, 191, 192, 194
Jargon of Authenticity, The 98
Johnson, Sarah 65
Journal of Memespace Cartography 195, 198
Joyce, James 58, 61
  Ulysses. See Ulysses
Juice! 53, 193, 202, 203
Jung, Carl 149

Kane, Sarah 51
  Cleansed. See Cleansed
Kant, Immanuel 35, 36
  Critique of Pure Reason. See Critique of Pure Reason
Keep, The 137, 142, 143, 145, 147, 155, 156
Kelly, Adam 38, 48, 125, 126, 139, 143, 197
  American Fiction at the Millennium: Neoliberalism and the New. See American Fiction at the Millennium: Neoliberalism and the New
  New Sincerity. *See* New Sincerity
Kempf, Paul Friedrich 'Fritz' 66, 67, 68
Keucheyan, Razmig 130
King Rat 163
King's College, Cambridge 40
King, Stephen 84
Kohlke, M.-L. 53, 171, 182
Kubrick, Stanley 84

Lacan, Jacques 139, 150, 191, 195, 196
Lamont, Michelle 39
Latour, Bruno 36
Law of Genre, The 168
Lawrence, D.H. 31
Leavis, F.R. 39, 115, 151
LeClair, Tom 196
  Art of Excess, The. See Art of Excess, The
legitimation 13, 15, 16, 17, 19, 20, 21, 35, 39, 40, 42, 50, 51, 52, 86, 116, 120, 132, 134, 135, 136, 156, 159, 160, 175, 190, 202, 203, 207, 208
Leitch, Vincent 42
Levine, Caroline 89
Lévi-Strauss, Claude 149
Leypoldt, Günter 39
Libra 140
literary criticism. *See* university English
literary fiction 15, 18, 19, 20, 21, 22, 23, 25, 28, 39, 51, 59, 60, 61, 116, 124, 134, 150, 173
  and politics 88
literary markets 20, 21, 22, 24, 35, 44, 105, 168
literary prizes 25, 118, 132, 160, 193
literary realism 53, 60, 63, 64, 118, 124, 151, 171
  as psychopathy 63
literary studies. *See* university English
Liu, Alan 16
Llewellyn, Mark 162, 174, 177, 182
logos 12
London Review of Books 61
Look at Me 137, 138, 139, 141, 142, 143, 147
Lorde, Audre 190
Lovecraft, H.P. 163
Lucky Jim 18, 48
Lupton, Christina 40
Lyons, John 17

MacDowell, Andie 123
Machery, Pierre 30
Mailer, Norman 186
Malinowski, Bronisław Kasper 154
Man Booker Prize 22, 60
Mandel, Emily St. John 144
   Station Eleven. See Station Eleven
Mantel, Hilary 88
Marinescu, Andreea 92
Marin, Louis 96, 97, 101, 102, 106
Markovits, Elizabeth 120, 123, 125
Martin, Reginald 186, 189
Marxist criticism 21, 30, 32, 57, 85, 115, 129, 165, 183, 213
Marx, Karl 155, 160, 185
   Theses on Feuerbach. See Theses on Feuerbach
Mason & Dixon 162
Maximalist Novel, The 197
May 1968 48, 102, 103, 138, 155
Mayhew, Henry 172
   Criminal Prisons of London and Scenes of Prison Life, The. See Criminal Prisons of London and Scenes of Prison Life, The
McBride, Eimar 73, 132
   Girl is a Half-Formed Thing, A. See Girl is a Half-Formed Thing, A
McCann, Sean 135, 143
McCarthy, Tom 28, 51, 58, 59, 60, 61, 62, 63, 64, 66, 68, 70, 71, 72, 73, 74, 75, 77, 78, 79, 80, 81, 82, 107, 159, 161, 169, 208
   C. See C
   Calling all Agents. See Calling all Agents
   Men in Space. See Men in Space
   Navigation Was Always a Difficult Art. See Navigation Was Always a Difficult Art
   Necronautical Society. *See* Necronautical Society
   Remainder. See Remainder
   Satin Island. See Satin Island
   Tintin and the Secret of Literature. See Tintin and the Secret of Literature

McGurl, Mark 21, 22, 38, 143, 147
McHale, Brian 81, 163, 164
MELUS. *See* Multi Ethnic Literature of the United States
Men in Space 60, 61
metafiction 12, 15, 20, 28, 29, 31, 32, 33, 34, 35, 36, 37, 38, 41, 42, 47, 48, 49, 52, 53, 70, 78, 79, 87, 88, 90, 91, 93, 107, 110, 116, 124, 126, 134, 136, 142, 143, 150, 151, 156, 159, 161, 162, 163, 164, 165, 167, 168, 171, 174, 178, 181, 182, 191, 194, 202, 208
   as critique 28, 30, 31, 35, 37
   as politically abortive 31, 32, 34, 35
   history of 29
   inadequecy of self knowledge 29
   incompatibility with postmodernism 29
Metafiction 29, 35, 37, 161, 185, 208
Metafiction: The Theory and Practice of Self-Conscious Fiction 29
MFA programmes. *See* creative writing programmes
Miéville, China 46, 163, 164
   King Rat. See King Rat
Mitchell, David 19, 153, 164
   Bone Clocks, The. See Bone Clocks, The
   Cloud Atlas. See Cloud Atlas
model reader 18, 41
modernism 31, 39, 58, 59, 60, 61, 64, 66, 68, 73, 74, 75, 78, 80, 81, 82, 96, 124, 139, 162, 185, 197
Moment More Sublime, A 49
Monk, Thelonius Sphere 117
Moore, Lorrie 75
More, Thomas 90, 100
   Utopia. See Utopia
Moretti, Franco 23, 58
   Slaughterhouse of Literature, The. *See* Slaughterhouse of Literature, The
Morrison, Toni 186
Morse code 79
Multi Ethnic Literature of the United States 22

Mumbo Jumbo 186, 187, 189
Murray, Bill 123
My Ántonia 146

Nabokov, Vladimir 49
  Pale Fire. See Pale Fire
  Pnin. See Pnin
Name of the Rose, The 105
Narcissistic Narrative: The Metafictional Paradox 29
Native Son 117
Navidson Record, The 69, 83, 85
Navigation Was Always a Difficult Art 61
Neale, Stephen 167
Necronautical Society 60
Negative Dialectics 93, 185
neoliberalism 52, 94, 102, 104, 105, 106, 111, 196
New American Writing Award 132
New Criticism 27, 37, 126, 191, 201
New Historicism 151, 155
New Sincerity 125, 197
New Yorker, The 149
New York Times 74
New York University 141, 196
Nicomachean Ethics 121
Nieland, Justus 64
Nietzsche, Friedrich 129
No More Modernisms 197
NW 19

Octet 125
Oedipus complex 150
O'Leary, Timothy 91
Omlor, Daniela 94
On Beauty 39, 40, 41, 43, 108, 109
On Beauty and Being Just 40
Orwell, George 134
Osborne, Peter 150
Osiris 71
Oxford, University of 71, 79

Packham, Catherine 13
Paglia, Camille 84

Pale Fire 49
paranoid reading 68
parody 21, 40, 48, 69, 76, 84, 85, 116, 117, 119, 129, 130, 131, 133, 154, 160, 196, 197, 198
Partial Magic: The Novel as a Self-Conscious Genre 29
pastiche 21
Patterson, Orlando 122
Pearson, Adrian Jones 49
  Cow Country. See Cow Country
Pelaez, Sol 94
PEN Center USA Award for Fiction 131
PEN Oakland/Josephine Miles Literary Award 132
phonos 12
Pnin 49
poetry 88, 98, 124, 207
Point Omega 140
police 52, 91, 92, 93, 101, 103, 106, 107, 159
Pollack, Sarah 101
pornography 92, 99, 180
Possession 164
postcolonial criticism 21, 32, 57, 85, 87, 94, 104, 127, 130, 152
Postcolonial Studies Association 22
postmodernism 12, 15, 28, 29, 31, 32, 33, 48, 51, 52, 58, 59, 60, 61, 64, 66, 68, 70, 71, 73, 74, 75, 77, 78, 79, 80, 81, 86, 90, 118, 119, 120, 123, 124, 125, 133, 135, 137, 140, 143, 156, 161, 162, 182, 185, 186, 187, 190, 191, 193, 194, 195, 197, 198, 202, 208
post-postmodernism 162, 185
poststructuralism 27, 32, 33, 37, 83, 85, 96, 119, 139
Pound, Ezra 31
Powers, Richard 124
Practical Criticism 201
Proctor, Mortimer R. 17
Proust, Marcel 147
psychoanalysis 121, 149, 150, 153, 154

publishers 21, 22, 23, 24, 25, 28, 58, 117, 132, 199
  financial risk 24
  labour 23
Push 117
p-value 45
Pynchon, Thomas 19, 49, 58, 60, 72, 73, 74, 75, 77, 82, 83, 102, 118, 124, 133, 140, 153, 162, 163, 164, 186, 194, 195, 196, 197, 198, 201, 208
  Against the Day. See Against the Day
  Bleeding Edge. See Bleeding Edge
  Gravity's Rainbow. See Gravity's Rainbow
  Inherent Vice. See Inherent Vice
  The Crying of Lot 49. See The Crying of Lot 49
  V. See V.

queer criticism 57

Raghinaru, Camelia 90
Rank, Otto 195
  Trauma of Birth, The. See Trauma of Birth, The
reading-avoidance techniques 25, 48
Reality Hunger: A Manifesto 126
Recalcitrance, Faulkner, and the Professors: A Critical Fiction 49
Reed, Ishmael 53, 185, 186, 187, 188, 189, 190, 191, 192, 193, 194, 198, 200, 201, 202, 203, 208
  Japanese by Spring. See Japanese by Spring
  Juice!. See Juice!
  Mumbo Jumbo. See Mumbo Jumbo
Reinares, Laura Barberán 95
Remainder 60, 62, 63, 64, 74, 87
Resistible Rise of Arturo Ui, The 99
Rhoades, Gary 105
Rice, Anne 84
Richards, I.A. 39, 201
  Practical Criticism. See Practical Criticism
Ricœur, Paul 15
Rodríguez, Fermín A. 94

romanticism 12, 58
Roof, Judith 117
Rossen, Janice 17
Roth, Philip 48, 135
  Human Stain, The. See Human Stain, The
Russian Formalism 33, 39
Ryan, Judith 19, 88, 207
  writing back. *See* writing back

sadomasochism 171
Saldívar, Ramón 119, 129
Sapphire 117
  Push. See Push
Sarrasine 118
Sartre, Jean-Paul 98
Satin Island 60, 61
satire 19, 21, 116, 135, 154, 160, 189, 190, 200
Scarry, Elaine 40, 41
  On Beauty and Being Just. See On Beauty and Being Just
scholarly communications 53, 198, 202
Scholes, Robert 29, 136, 208
  Fabulators, The. See Fabulators, The
  Metafiction 29
Schumacher, Julie 49
  Dear Committee Members. See Dear Committee Members
Scott, Walter 65
  Waverley. See Waverley
Selden, Raman 30
self-publishing 23
Self, Will 62
serials crisis 199
Shields, David 126, 151
  Reality Hunger: A Manifesto. See Reality Hunger: A Manifesto
Shklovsky, Viktor 33
Showalter, Elaine 17
Simpson, O.J. 193, 194, 202
sincerity 52, 119, 120, 121, 122, 123, 124, 125, 126, 127, 128, 129, 132, 133, 151, 195, 197

Slaughterhouse-Five 127
Slaughterhouse of Literature, The 23
Slaughter, Sheila 105
Smith, Barbara Herrnstein 73, 93
Smith, Sarah A. 176
Smith, Shawn 162
Smith, Zadie 19, 39, 40, 41, 62, 108
   NW. See *NW*
   On Beauty. See *On Beauty*
Soyinka, Wole 75
Spiotta, Dana 47
   Eat the Document. See *Eat the Document*
Spivak, Gayatri Chakravorti 130
Springer, Jerry 117
Spurious 3
Stam, Robert 166, 167, 196
Stanford University 21
Station Eleven 144, 145
statistical significance. See p-value
strategic essentialism 129, 130
strategies of condescension 92, 108, 110
structuralism 37, 149, 150, 154
stylometry 25, 26, 27, 44, 45
   as not-like-reading 26, 27
Swift, Graham 80
   Waterland. See *Waterland*
Swift, Jonathan 100, 128
   Gulliver's Travels. See *Gulliver's Travels*
symptomatic reading 19, 36, 43, 95
S/Z 118, 154
Székely, Péter 17, 47

Tale of the Eloquent Peasant 11, 12, 13, 14, 15, 18, 42
taxonomographic metafiction. See taxonomography
taxonomography 53, 163, 164, 165, 168, 172, 176, 181, 182, 183
telegraphy 79
Thatcher, Margaret 88

Theory 16, 19, 32, 33, 36, 38, 39, 41, 88, 118, 133, 134, 135, 139, 143, 144, 150, 151, 154, 155, 160, 164, 172, 185, 191, 196, 198
Theses on Feuerbach 185
Thompson, Hunter S. 84
Thornton, Sarah 61
Times Higher Education 50
Tintin and the Secret of Literature 60
Tipping the Velvet 173, 179
Tom Brown at Oxford 49
Toussaint, Jean-Philippe 61
Trauma of Birth, The 195
Trilling, Lionel 120, 121, 123, 124
Tristram Shandy 33
Tudor, Andrew 166
Turn of the Screw, The 171

Ulysses 61, 72, 82
Underwood, Ted 26, 28, 58
Underworld 140
university. See university English
University College London 115
university English 11, 14, 15, 16, 18, 20, 21, 24, 26, 27, 28, 29, 30, 31, 33, 36, 37, 38, 41, 42, 43, 45, 49, 51, 53, 57, 58, 59, 60, 72, 86, 91, 96, 107, 111, 115, 116, 134, 150, 151, 154, 155, 159, 161, 188, 200, 201, 203, 207, 208
   and idealism 43
   and politics 89
   and science 44, 45, 47
   geographical specificity of 50
   history of 115
   object of study 30
   reading practices. See academic readers
university fiction. See campus novel
University of California, Berkeley 148, 149, 194
University of Chicago Press 200
University of London 115
University of Southern California 116

University of Turin 138
Unnamable, The 139
Upstairs at the Party 49
Utopia 90, 100

V. 74, 83, 162
value 13, 16, 20, 21, 22, 24, 25, 28, 33, 36, 51, 57, 59, 63, 84, 86, 91, 97, 105, 107, 115, 132, 188, 200
Varèse, Edgard 83
Visit from the Goon Squad, A 46, 52, 137, 147, 148, 149, 150, 151, 152, 153, 154, 155, 156, 213
Vonnegut, Kurt 124, 127
  Slaughterhouse-Five.
  See Slaughterhouse-Five
von Richthofen, Manfred Albrecht Freiherr 68

Waiting for Godot 51
Walker, Alice 186
Wallace, David Foster 33, 69, 82, 124, 125, 126, 151, 191, 195, 197
  E Unibus Pluram. *See* E Unibus Pluram
  Infinite Jest. *See Infinite Jest*
  Octet. *See* Octet
  Westward the Course of Empire Takes Its Way. *See* Westward the Course of Empire Takes Its Way
Walter Scott Prize for Historical Fiction, the 65
Wark, McKenzie 62
Waterland 80
Waters, Sarah 3, 19, 28, 34, 46, 53, 161, 162, 163, 164, 165, 168, 169, 170, 171, 172, 173, 174, 177, 178, 179, 180, 181, 182, 183, 208
  Affinity. *See Affinity*
  Fingersmith. *See Fingersmith*
  Tipping the Velvet. *See Tipping the Velvet*

Waugh, Patricia 29
  Metafiction: The Theory and Practice of Self-Conscious Fiction.
  See Metafiction: The Theory and Practice of Self-Conscious Fiction
Waverley 65
Weber, Samuel 176
Weisenburger, Steven 187, 189
Western Canon: The Books and School of the Ages, The 84
Westward the Course of Empire Takes Its Way 82
White, Hayden 70, 162, 165
White Noise 77, 190
Whitman, Walt 126
Wittgenstein, Ludwig 74, 83, 160, 166
Womack, Kenneth 17, 46
Woolf, Virginia 31, 60, 73
Wordsworth, William 58
Worstward Ho 73, 139
Wozniak, Steve 84
Wright, Austin M. 49
  Recalcitrance, Faulkner, and the Professors: A Critical Fiction.
  See Recalcitrance, Faulkner, and the Professors: A Critical Fiction
Wright, Richard 117
  Native Son. *See Native Son*
writing back 19, 88, 207, 208

Yale University 58, 85

Zamora, Daniel 183
Zero K 140
Žižek, Slavoj 196

This book need not end here…

At Open Book Publishers, we are changing the nature of the traditional academic book. The title you have just read will not be left on a library shelf, but will be accessed online by hundreds of readers each month across the globe. OBP publishes only the best academic work: each title passes through a rigorous peer-review process. We make all our books free to read online so that students, researchers and members of the public who can't afford a printed edition will have access to the same ideas.

This book and additional content is available at:
http://www.openbookpublishers.com/isbn/9781783742738

Customize

Personalize your copy of this book or design new books using OBP and third-party material. Take chapters or whole books from our published list and make a special edition, a new anthology or an illuminating coursepack. Each customized edition will be produced as a paperback and a downloadable PDF. Find out more at:

http://www.openbookpublishers.com/section/59/1

Donate

If you enjoyed this book, and feel that research like this should be available to all readers, regardless of their income, please think about donating to us. We do not operate for profit and all donations, as with all other revenue we generate, will be used to finance new Open Access publications.

http://www.openbookpublishers.com/section/13/1/support-us

Like Open Book Publishers

Follow @OpenBookPublish

Read more at the Open Book Publishers **BLOG**

You may also be interested in…

The End of the World:
Apocalypse and its Aftermath in Western Culture
By Maria Manuel Lisboa

http://dx.doi.org/10.11647/OBP.0015
http://www.openbookpublishers.com/product/106

The Theatre of Shelley
By Jacqueline Mulhallen

http://dx.doi.org/10.11647/OBP.0011
http://www.openbookpublishers.com/product/27

The Anglo-Scottish Ballad and its Imaginary Contexts
By David Atkinson

http://dx.doi.org/10.11647/OBP.0041
http://www.openbookpublishers.com/product/250

Yeats's Mask - Yeats Annual No. 19
Edited by Margaret Mills Harper and Warwick Gould

http://dx.doi.org/10.11647/OBP.0038
http://www.openbookpublishers.com/product/233